Portraits of Prayer, Vol. 1
Genesis & Exodus

BY

Rev. Roger Theodore Boguski

PUBLISHED BY

Painted Gate Publishing

Acknowledgements

With deep gratitude, we acknowledge the many hands and hearts that contributed to the creation of <u>Portraits of Prayer, Vol. 1: Genesis & Exodus</u>.

First and foremost, heartfelt thanks to author, **Rev. Roger Theodore Boguski**, whose devotion to the Word and prayerful insight form the very foundation of this work. His authorship is a testament to a life steeped in Scripture and service.

Special appreciation goes to **Gayle Leubecker**, Chief Editor, whose careful eye and steady hand helped shape and refine each chapter with clarity and grace.

To **Rebecca Furches**, Executive Secretary, your organizational skill and steadfast support were vital to bringing this project to completion.

We are also grateful to **Joyce Ann Boguski**, Proof Reader, for her keen attention to detail and dedication to excellence, ensuring the text remained both faithful and precise.

Our sincere thanks to **John Hughes**, Book Cover Artist, whose creative vision beautifully captures the heart and spirit of this volume in its visual presentation.

This work draws deeply from the enduring truth of **the King James Version – New Schofield Bible** (1967 edition). Its timeless language and theological clarity remain central to the study and understanding of God's Word.

We gratefully acknowledge *Pleasant View Baptist Church* in Port Deposit, Maryland, and extend our thanks to **Dr. Harold M. Phillips**, Senior Pastor, for his unwavering spiritual leadership and the church's ongoing support of biblical ministry and publishing.

To all who prayed, encouraged, and stood behind this work in visible and invisible ways —thank you. May this book serve as a vessel of devotion, reflection, and renewed prayer for all who journey through the pages of Genesis and Exodus.

The Pierced Hand Publications Team
piercedhandpublications@gmail.com

FOREWORD:

I am so honored to be asked to write a statement about my friend Roger's book, Portraits of Prayer. This book is filled with encouragement as we grow with each entry. Looking into these portraits, we find that prayer is one of the greatest jewels in our possession.

Prayer is one of our greatest assets and one of our greatest resources, yet it is wasted simply because we do not set aside time to meet regularly with God through prayer. This book will, hopefully, bring us into steady relationship through prayer.

When one hears a personal testimony of answered prayers there is always faith growth. Any time God can drag us before Himself in a time of prayer, it is a win, win. A win for us and as we experience God, and a win for God as He experiences us.

When we look at a portrait and wish we could step into it but cannot, we are saddened, but this is a portrait that we can step into as we step into God's presence through prayer.

Maybe, just maybe, there will be portraits painted by prayer in your own life.

May God richly bless you as you bathe in the portraits in this book penned by my friend Roger Boguski.

May God Richly Bless you!

Dr. Harold Michael Phillips

Other books by this author:

Speak Comfortably to Jerusalem

Isaiah 53: The Crown Jewel of the Older Testament

"Portraits of Prayer in Genesis"
"In the Beginning" Prayer #1
Gen. 1:1

Back in the 70's, Dr. Renald Showers at Moody Bible Institute taught an extra class on writing a theology, and I was one of his students. He said all the theology has not yet been written: "prayerology" for example (being one of them). That class has never left my heart or soul, and like a man lost in a desert for many days, I thirst to sip from that well. I am not about to write a "prayerology" from the Bible. In order to do that you must find every verse and reference in the Bible that deals with the subject of prayer, and then catalog and put them in order thematically. I simply would like to go on a prayer journey, an adventure. I'd like to walk on the paths of some of the great biblical prayer warriors of the past, dip my cup into their pools, and sit awhile and sip.

I am not an expert in this field. I was saved in August 1972 and have been serving God full time since August 1976. Webster says an expert is "one with the special skill or knowledge representing mastery of a particular subject." I have learned a lot in 50+ years, but I have so much more to learn, especially from "the worm's eye view" of things concerning prayer.

As we begin our journey to meditate upon the concept of prayer, we must keep in mind what Dr. A.T. Pierson called "the law of first mention." The first mention of a Bible truth usually summarizes any further development of that same truth. Many theologians don't accept "the law of first mention," so they must accept the "science of etymology." According to Webster, that is, "the history of a linguistic form, such as a word, shown by tracing its development since its earliest recorded occurrence in the language where it is found, by tracing its transmission from one language to another, by analyzing it into its component parts, by identifying its cognates in other languages or by tracing it and its cognates to a common ancestral form in an ancestral language."

Webster defines **"etymon"** as "the literal meaning of a word according to its origin and earliest form," and **"logy"** as, "the oral or written expression in doctrine, theory and science." To summarize, it is "the science of the literal and true meaning of a word or phrase according to its origin, history and use in its earliest recorded occurrence in the language where it is found." Or to keep it simple Dr. Pierson called it, "the law of first mention." The book of Genesis therefore, is the only book in which to begin our journey on the road to meditating on the concept of prayer.

Man was described by some as, "a praying animal." In fact, according to one man, "With the creation of man, prayer was a dictate of nature, a constituted instinct, in wrought by the Maker." What is prayer? It is simply the desire, opportunity and privilege of talking to God -- communing with the Creator, whether audibly or inaudibly, in public or in private. Don't make it difficult, He never intended it to be. In Genesis chapter one we find God blessing His creation and man. If blessing something is a prayer (and it is), then God -- not man -- is the first to pray. In chapter two, we find Adam awaking to find Eve, and he expresses what is on his heart, but to whom? Obviously, it must be to *Elohim*, his Creator. After all, that is why God created Adam in the first place, right? Of course right! God created them to fellowship with Him and worship Him in His garden, innocent and bare-naked. However, this fellowship was broken in chapter three, when they looked, took and ate the poison fruit (the poison being disobedience). In chapter four, you find the conversation between God and Cain (defiant and lacking the reverence associated with prayer to a Holy God, yes, but still conversation, still talking to God). We will see on our prayer journey that, sometimes, "prayer to God" can become defiant and almost irreverent (**almost**).

So, as we observe the progression of prayer on this journey -- from Adam, to Cain, to Enos, to Noah, to Abraham, to Moses, to David, to Christ, to you and I -- I trust our understanding and appreciation for this privilege and access to God as a "praying animal" will be broadened. For it is only man, created in His own image after His own likeness, that has been afforded this privilege. Not the animals, nor the angels or demons, but to man and man alone is this power and privilege given. Amen?

*(**Prayer** - "Oh God, help us to understand and appreciate this privilege of access to You. Help us to enter our gardens, our closets, our secret chambers, in the cool of the day, before the sun comes up to scorch us and, having shut the door, may we commune and fellowship with You, bare-naked. LORD, teach us to pray, not how to pray, but, "TO PRAY!" In ha Shem Yeshua!)*

"Now the God of peace, that brought again from the dead our Lord Jesus, that great Shepherd of the sheep, through the blood of the everlasting covenant; Make you perfect in every good work to do his will, working in you that which is well-pleasing in his sight, through Jesus Christ, to whom be glory forever and ever. Amen" Heb. 13: 20-21.

Principles for Prayer:

- Prayer is simply the desire, opportunity, or privilege of talking to God. Don't make this difficult; God didn't!
- Sometimes prayer to God can become defiant and almost irreverent, so be careful in your approach to God!
- Only man has been afforded this privilege, not animals, angels or demons. What a precious privilege mankind has been given by God!

"When we pray according to God's will in faith in the name of Jesus, creative omnipotence springs forward to answer. Why? Because every act of creation in the universe has already been

wrought through Him. So He abides in us and His Word abides in us, and all we have to do is ask to glorify His Father. If He needs to create a new thing, He will in answer to our prayer. So it is worthwhile to pray -- worthwhile for those for whom we pray; worthwhile for us; and best of all worthwhile to God, His Father, Who receives the glory!"

Charles G. Trumbull

"God (*Elohim*) Prays First" #2
Gen. 1:28

"And God (Elohim-plural of El) blessed them..." "Blessed" - (*barak-a* primary root to kneel; by implication to bless God as an act of adoration, and vice versa, man as a benefit). But in this case it was all the living things that moved in the air like birds, etc., and all the living things that moved in the water like fish, etc. However, in Gen. 1:28, God/Elohim blesses (*barak*) man and tells him to, *"Be fruitful, multiply, fill, subdue and have dominion over every living thing that moves on the Earth."* What a beautiful blessing, and what a precious privilege has been granted to us by our Creator. Now if a blessing (*barak*) is a prayer, and to pray (*tefillah*) is a blessing, then God (not man) was the first to pray. Amen? Gen. 1:22, God blessed the birds and the fish; Gen 1:28, God blessed man; Gen. 2:3, God blessed the seventh day and sanctified it, set it apart; Gen. 9:1, God blessed Noah and his sons; Gen. 12:1-3, and God blessed Abraham.

Eph. 1:3 speaks of believers today, the Church, the Bride of Christ, as being blessed with every spiritual blessing in heavenly places in Christ Jesus. Not only has God blessed us but He has also given us the privilege to bless Him, our fellow man and His creation by means of prayer. *"Blessed art thou, Oh Lord, our God, Creator of Heaven and Earth and all that in them is. Hallowed and holy be thy name above every name that has ever been named."*

What more can mortal man want, ask for, or expect than to be "blessed" by the God of creation, the God of the universe? We have been blessed by God! What a shame that, even as we are living in light of this eternal truth, God wishes for us to be blessed more than we desire to be blessed. The half brother of Jesus sums up our dilemma with these words, *"You have not because you ask not!" James 4:2.* I wonder how many more blessings await the child of God who fails to **ASK**! Didn't Jesus Himself, in essence, say, "Ask and you shall receive!" Matt. 7:7-8. But we need to ask with a beggar's humility; seek with a servant's carefulness; and knock with a friend's confidence. Those three words, "**ask, seek, knock**" form the acrostic for the word, **ASK**!

*(**Prayer** - "O, LORD, Bless me, fill me with Your Holy Spirit, draw me to your bosom; quench my thirst for You, O Lord. Fill the void in my life, the emptiness I feel, the vacuum that still exists in the recesses of my soul. I want to bless You, oh LORD, with king David of old. Bless the LORD, oh my soul, and all that is within me, bless His holy name. God, I love You. Fill me now with Your Holy Spirit; and Lord, teach us to pray with all our heart and soul. Amen.")*

The power of the "blessing" instituted by God: **WOW**! He blessed the fish, the birds, the animals and man, and said, "Be fruitful, multiply and fill the Earth." Who thought up birth control? Where did that come in? I bet that pleased God – *not*! To bless God is an act of adoration; to bless man is an act of benevolence. Abraham gave tithes to Melchizedek because he knew he had the power to invoke a blessing on him, Gen. 14:19-20. Eliezer of Damascus invoked a blessing on God in Gen. 24:27. It is never mentioned that Abraham blessed anything or anyone, but his servant did and his son Isaac did. But where did they learn it? God's blessing was put on Abraham in Gen. 12:1-3, then reconfirmed in 13:14-18 after Lot left; then again on Mt. Moriah in 22:15-19; then given to Isaac in 26:24; then to Jacob in 28:13; and to Jacob again in 35:11.

The "blessing of the blessing:" the Orthodox Jews are aware of its power and benefit and invoke its benevolence (especially on the Sabbath) on their children. I am sure the early church did the same, as they incorporated most of their early traditions and customs from Orthodox Judaism. But as time has evolved so have biblical customs, some to our spiritual benefit and some to our spiritual detriment. I for one do not believe the loss of the "blessing" was to our benefit. Just about every one of the Jewish prayers begins with, "Blessed art Thou O, Lord our God, King of the universe…"

How beautiful it would be for the fathers to go around the dinner table every Sunday before or after dinner, lay their hands on each child and pray a blessing over each one individually. Do you think they would remember that, when they grow up? Would you? I was 37 when my father told me he loved me for the one and only time. It was Thanksgiving morning. I was standing in the basement of our home, and my cousin Carol was making him a drink. It's like it happened yesterday, and it was over 40 years ago. It would change our lives forever -- trust me. The power of the blessing! Amen?

"Now the God of hope fill you with all joy and peace in believing, that you may abound in hope, through the power of the Holy Ghost." Rom. 15:13.

Principles for Prayer:

- God is the first to pray by blessing His creation.
- To bless God is an act of adoration.
- To bless man is an act of benevolence.

"Prayer is the final armament. Prayer is the all-inclusive strategy of war. Prayer is the ultimate weapon of God's people. Prayer is to be perservered and prayer is to be watchfully engaged in day and night. Prayer battalions are to be ever on the alert and active. Prayer in the Spirit will obtain the strategy of the Spirit. Prayer in the Spirit is to arm every warrior for God. Prayer demolishes every fortress of hell. Prayer is the all-conquering, invincible weapon of God's Army. Therefore, Jesus, our Victorious Captain,
ever lives to make intercession for us."

Dr. Wesley Duewel

"The Beginning of Prayer" #3
Gen. 2:23

Hebrew, *"B'resheit bara Elohim et shamyim vaet ha aretz"* – *"In the beginning, God created the heavens and the earth."* Gen. 1:1 Genesis is the book of beginnings – the beginning of the universe – the beginning of the Earth – the beginning of mankind and womankind – the beginning of marriage – the beginning of marital problems – the beginning of people, nations, etc. – the beginning of the Jewish people! But one thing we never think of in Genesis is, "**the beginning of prayer**." Why is that? Men and women for centuries have walked and talked with God: Elijah, David, Solomon, Daniel, Hannah, Ruth, Esther, Mary, Dorcas, Peter, James, John, etc. But in the first five chapters of Genesis, you meet a few men who walked and talked with God face-to-face (*paneh*). Men who set the course of spiritual intimacy for ages to come. Men who knew God personally and intimately. But even more important, men who were personally and intimately known by God Himself. There is a big difference between knowing God intimately and personally and being ***known by*** God intimately and personally! Men whom I believe were, "men of prayer!"

Why is it that prayer is the believer's greatest resource and the one least used? His greatest obligation and the one most neglected? The channel to God's grace that for most of us remains clogged? **Why is that?** The only man whom I believe enjoyed perfect, unhindered, sweet communion with his Creator was Adam. I believe Adam walked and talked and had personal, intimate fellowship with God. In fact, Adam was created by God in His own image (*selem*-sculptured image, statue, shadow, phantom) in His own likeness or similitude. Read Gen. 1:26-27 sometime. Why did God create Adam, anyway? To multiply, to subdue the Earth, to dominate the Earth, to till the garden, to name the animals, to have a bunch of children? Yes, all that and much, much more! But, primarily, God created Adam to love Him, to obey Him, and to have perfect, intimate fellowship with Him. Excuse me – intimate intercourse with the Creator of the universe! Or

Spiritual *YADA*! Hos. 6:3, *"Then you will know the LORD when you follow on to know the LORD."*

Webster says, "Intercourse is the exchange of feelings and thoughts, marked by very close association and warm fellowship." Psalm 16:11. Adam walked in the garden (*gan* - an enclosed place with a gate) in the cool of the day, and listened to the voice of God his Creator. Gen. 3:8-9 gives us a hint of this fellowship, this intercourse, this intimacy, this *YADA* between two beings alone on Earth, *"And they heard the voice of the LORD God walking in the garden in the cool of the day: and Adam and his wife hid themselves from the presence of the LORD God among the trees of the garden. And the LORD God called unto Adam, and said unto him, <u>Where art thou</u>?"* Notice God speaks first, and God seeks Adam. The same is true today (John 4:23). Yet it is after the fall, after sin, after Satan's rebellion, and after the creation of hell. But we see from this text four vital principles or elements for an effective or effectual prayer life. You do want an, "<u>effectual fervent prayer life</u>" such as James talks about in James 5:16 don't you? Good!

Before we examine these four vital elements in the garden, back up with me to Gen. 2:23, *"And Adam said..."* Was he talking to the animals, to himself? No, I believe he was talking to **Elohim**, God his Creator. The same One he had been conversing with since he became <u>a living soul</u> in Gen. 1:28ff. God is communing with Adam, giving him His commands; so conversation with God was very natural, very open, very *naked*, to use a phrase. Form, philosophy, posture were unknown at this time, just simply the outpouring of one's heart to the God of Creation. Bare-naked before God, physically and spiritually -- oh, to be like that today! Keep your philosophy, your theology, your pet phrases, your stained glass language. Just stand or kneel before Almighty God, bare-naked, and commune with Him. Innocence, fellowship, communion, obedience, sweet intercourse with the **Sovereign Designer** -- oh, to hear the sound of His voice, walking in your garden, in the cool of the day. That should be our goal in life. After all, that's what He desires from us: communion and fellowship with Him, pure bare-naked worship.

Christ told us in John 4:23-24 that His Father is seeking for those to worship Him in spirit and in truth. The word "seeking" can be translated **desire**. This involves the intellect, emotions and will; my whole person, with God's whole person. John says we are to worship Him in spirit and in truth, no baloney; your whole heart: every fiber, every cell, every membrane. Did you ever look around during a worship service? People are on their cell phones texting, playing games, sleeping, talking, reading a book. If I were God I would ....! This paragraph brings tears to my eyes; does it yours?

So, we should come to God in prayer, not only because He deserves it, but because He desires it as well! To talk with Him and walk with Him because you love Him, need Him and want to please Him. "And Adam said…," to *Elohim*, his Creator, his Master, his Maker, his God. Prayer is simple, naked, sweet, innocent fellowship with our Creator. How do we take something so simple, so beautiful, so natural and make it so difficult! It was never intended to be like that, never! **K.I.S.S.** (Keep It Simple, Sam).

*(**Prayer** - "Oh God, help us to keep prayer simple and beautiful in our lives the way You intended it to be. May we hear Your voice every day walking in our gardens, our secret places, in the cool of the day, in the quiet of the night. Oh LORD, breathe into our nostrils the very breath of life once again, in the form of prayer, the life breath of a child of Yours. Help us to stand before You stripped of ourselves." In Jesus' name.)*

Principles for Prayer:

- God sought for Adam and God spoke first and He still does.
- Form, posture, language is unimportant to God. Just talk to Him.

- You can exchange intimate feelings and thoughts without speaking. Did you know that?

"Why is there so much religious working and so little result in positive conversions to God? So many sermons, and so few souls saved? So much machinery and so little effect? Why? There is not enough '<u>private prayer!</u>' <u>What is needed is more prayer!</u> Pray for three hours and preach for one hour and see what happens!"

J.C. Ryle

"The Lost Art of Prayer" #4
Gen. 3:8-9

In Genesis 3:8-9, Adam gives us three principles or elements for an effective or effectual fervent prayer life, an "E.F.P." The first principle is that they heard the sound, *"...the voice of the LORD God."* They heard (*shema* - to hearken, hear and obey), God's voice. Deuteronomy 6:4 is what the Jewish people call "**The *Shema***," their first prayer in the morning and their last prayer at night; and it's prayed several times during the day, declaring their belief in the one and only true God. *"Hear O Israel: The LORD our God is one LORD."* They hear and do something about it. I love Mal. 3:16, *"Then they that feared the LORD spoke often one to another: and the LORD hearkened, and heard it, and a book of remembrance was written before Him for them, that feared the LORD and that thought upon His name."* Sometimes people ask me, "Don't you ever talk about anything except **Jesus**?" My response is, "Well, sometimes I talk about **Christ**!" What else is there to talk about: the weather, sports, the stock market? Whether the weather be cold or whether the weather be hot, whether the weather be good or whether the weather be not, we'll weather the weather, whatever the weather, whether we like it or not. Amen? Thanks, Vance Havner.

So, talk about something that has *chutzpah*, like Yeshua; He had *chutzpah*! The Hebrew word for voice or sound is (*kole* - to call aloud). He talks and we listen, or at least we should listen. Amen? Now that is a lost art today, especially in prayer, Amen? Listening! We come with our grocery lists, regurgitate them before God, then get up and leave and never give God a chance to speak. How insulting and demeaning is that to the Creator of the universe?

They knew His voice; why? They were accustomed to its sound, that's why! Question: are you accustomed to the sound of His voice? Are you? I Samuel 3:19-21 says, *"And Samuel grew, and the LORD was with him, and did let none of his words fall to the ground. And all Israel from Dan even to*

Beersheba knew that Samuel was established to be a prophet of the LORD. And the LORD appeared again in Shiloh: for the LORD revealed Himself to Samuel in Shiloh by the word of the LORD." And He does the same thing today; He reveals Himself to His people <u>in His Word</u>. You will never be more <u>filled with the Spirit</u> then you are <u>filled with the Word</u>! They knew His voice! Like my children, <u>Adam, Sarah, Rebekah and Roger</u>, I have slipped into chapel and during the service said, "**Amen**!" And they've said, "<u>My dad is here</u>!" Why? They knew my voice! Our dog, Lexi, would get out, and no-body could get her back, I would step on the porch call her one time and she would fly to me. Why? She knew my voice! They were all accustomed to the sound of it; and therein, my friend, lies the key: <u>accustomed to the sound of it</u>!

John 10:4 says, *"And when He puts forth His sheep, He goes before them, and His sheep follow Him, for they know His voice!"* How? They listen to the sound of it; <u>they are used to hearing it</u>. John 10:27-28 says, *"My sheep hear my voice, and I know them, and they follow me: And I give unto them eternal life, and they shall never perish, neither shall any man pluck them out of my hand."* Voice (*phone`*) sound, tone (telephone, phonograph). How do they know His voice? <u>They are in His WORD</u>! Col. 3:16, *"Let the word of Christ dwell in you richly, in all wisdom..."* Eph. 5:18-21 *"And be not drunk with wine, wherein is excess; but be filled with the Spirit;."* Let me say it again: <u>you will never be more filled with the Holy Spirit than you are filled with the Word of God</u>. Let the Word of Christ dwell in you richly and the Spirit of God will be at home in you, also.

What is the first thing you do when your telephone rings after you say, "HELLO?" **<u>You, listen</u>**! The lost art in the ministry of prayer (which needs to be cultivated again) is <u>listening</u>. And the words "<u>listen</u>" and "<u>silent</u>" have exactly the same letters. You can't listen unless you are silent and still. I love Psalm 46:10, *"Be still and know that I am (YADA) God."* The words "I am" are in italics, which means they are not in the Hebrew text. So, be still and *YADA* God; have spiritual intimacy with God! So the first principle of prayer we see in Gen. 3:8-9, is to hear and know His voice. How? Get in His Word, and let His Word get in you! Meditate on it, memorize it, chew on it. Soak it in, peel it back like an onion; taste and see that the LORD is good! Don't just read a verse; ruminate on it until it becomes marrow in your bones and honey in your mouth.

Adam was a man just like us, but he had personal, intimate fellowship with his God before the fall – pure, sweet intercourse with his Sovereign Creator. Interesting: Adam knew the place, (the garden) the time (the cool of the day - early morning), and he knew the voice (the sound) of God. It's no different for us today to communicate with God on an intimate regular basis. We just need a secret place (alone and quiet), a specific time (early morning before the cock crows or late night after every one is down), and we need to hear and know His voice. How precious that is for those of us that have heard it! Chills run up and down your back; your palms get sweaty. His sheep follow Him and know His voice. Amen?

*(**Prayer** - "Oh, LORD, may I know Your voice once again. May I hear it daily, all day long. May I listen for it! LORD may I have that special place just to get alone with you and commune: a secret garden, a pantry of nourishment! And, LORD get me up in the cool of the day, before the cock crows, before the sun burns up the manna and dries up the dew, before the rush of the day destroys the hush of the night. Baruch ha Shem! Blessed be the name of Jesus, in whose name we pray!")*

Principles for Prayer:

- We need to hear the voice of God and be in tune to it.
- You will never be more filled with the Spirit than you are filled with His Word.
- The lost art in the ministry of prayer is listening.

*"Each time, before you intercede, be quiet first, and worship God in His glory. Think of what He can do, and how He delights to hear the prayers of His redeemed people. Think of your place and privilege in Jesus Christ,
and expect great things."*

Andrew Murray

"Prayer's Secret Hiding Place" #5
Gen. 3:23-24

The first prayer principle we learned from Adam in the garden of God was that we must know the voice of God! How? We must become accustomed to the sound of it. How? By immersing ourselves in His Word; being still as a stone; be silent and listen! The second principle is so simple and so obvious, you might not see it. Gen. 3:8, It was in the Garden of Eden. *"And they heard the voice of the LORD God walking in the garden in the cool of the day..."* "In the garden!" The Hebrew word for garden (*gan*) is an "enclosed garden," one with a hedge, a fence or a wall around it and a gate. The word "*gan*" can be translated enclosure. In verse 24 we are told that the LORD posted Cherubim and a flaming sword at the east of the garden of Eden (at the gate) to guard the way to the tree of life. The tabernacle had a gate, the temple had a gate (all facing east), but they knew the place -- a special enclosed place, God's place. How? Listen, they were accustomed to meeting God there! "But, God is everywhere," you say, "He is omnipresent!" Amen! But listen, He meets us **IN** a specific, secret place, at a specific time. Got it? Good: mark it down.

In Matthew 6:6, the Greek word for closet is "storage chamber," a pantry, a storehouse of supplies and nourishment. How beautiful is that? But there is more: the phrase "in secret" in Greek is (*en to krypto*), meaning in **the hidden, unseen, secret place**. We have a definite article in the Greek. Keep it simple, class. The absence of the article qualifies; the presence of the article identifies. So, it is "**THE**" specific, identifiable, definite place. And when you have gone into the secret storage chamber, the closet, the room used to keep nourishment, the pantry, to gather your supplies, what should you do? **SHUT THE DOOR**! Or close the gate! Why? To keep out the snake, the intruder, the adversary, the enemy, who will invade your prayer time: **Satan**! Oh, yes he will! (Adam forgot and left the gate open and Satan slithered in and did his dirty work.) And your heavenly Father is already there, in the secret place, waiting for you, to nourish you and reward you openly!

Churches have missed out on one of the greatest of all blessings by not having a <u>prayer chamber, prayer room, prayer garden, prayer closet</u> where their members could go and seek the face of God before and after the services and <u>pray alone</u> or with <u>someone</u>. An "**Upper-Room Ministry**." WOW! Adam knew the sound of His voice and Adam knew the secret place because he was accustomed to both, but are you? But there is more: a third vital principle to a dynamic prayer life.

Adam had a <u>special time to meet</u> God, "<u>in the cool of the day</u>." How did he know this? Listen, he was accustomed to meeting God at a particular time. David had a particular time, Psalm 5:3 says, *"My voice shalt thou hear in the morning, O LORD; <u>in the morning</u> will I direct my prayer unto thee, and will look up."* When I think of the cool of the day, I think of <u>early morning</u> before the heat of the day, before the cock crows, before the pressures of life crash in on you, before the telephone rings. Yeshua met His Father in the <u>early morning</u> (Mark 1:35). Things are quiet and still in the <u>early morning</u>. Birds sing loudest in the <u>early morning</u>, before the sun burns up the dew. But this phrase in Hebrew is more generally translated as "<u>an evening wind or breeze</u>" off of the Mediterranean Sea. So it does not matter to God whether you are a <u>morning person</u> an <u>evening person</u>, a <u>night person</u>, or a <u>noon person</u>, as long as you are a **praying person**. AMEN?

Before I get to the fourth (and probably the most important) principle of all for an <u>effective fervent prayer life</u>, I was struck by the fact that God went seeking Adam, after Adam sinned. Gen. 3:9 - *"And the LORD God called unto Adam, and said unto him, <u>Where art thou?</u>"* Called (*qara*) - a specific message, to a specific recipient, to elicit a specific response, for a specific purpose - and God spoke first! **Amazing**! God seeks Adam. He goes looking for him and calls out to him, "Adam, where are you?" The word "Adam" in Hebrew simply means a human being, and can be an individual or mankind. And I believe God is still searching, still seeking, still calling out to us, to mankind, to Adams all over the Earth, to worship Him, to have fellowship with Him, to pray to Him (Ezk. 22:30; 2 Chron. 16:9; John 4:23 - God is seeking those to worship Him in spirit and in truth.) What a paradox: God, Who created man, has to search for him to worship Him. God created man for fellowship with Himself! God is calling out to us today, "<u>Where are you</u>?" (The Place; The Time; The Voice!) "<u>Where Are You</u>?" What will we answer today? "<u>Here I am, let's fellowship</u>!" or "I heard Your voice in the garden, and I was afraid because I was naked and ashamed and I hid myself?" Which will it be for you, my friend? Which will it be?

*(**Prayer** - "Oh LORD, may I never hide myself from You, naked or not, sinful though I am. LORD, may I worship You today, in spirit and in truth, naked and unashamed, may I be your gap-man/gap-woman today. May Your eyes not have to go to and fro searching over the whole Earth looking for a man or woman. If You are looking for a place to start a fire, start one here in my heart; and may it never go out, Lord. Never! Thank You for saving me. Thank You for dying for me. Thank You for loving me." "Baruch ha Shem")*

Principles for Prayer:

- God will meet you in a specific place for prayer; Adam had a garden.
- God will meet you at a specific time: morning, noon, evening, night, anytime.
- Just make sure you close the gate or the door and turn off your phone.

"God speaks in terms of wonder. 'Behold, he prayeth!' Can God wonder? Can there be in God elements of surprise and amazement? Can there really be things that are wonderful to God? That is how God speaks in Acts 9:10-43 to Ananias about Paul, 'Behold he prayeth!' It would seem the biggest thing in God's universe is a man who prays! There is only one thing more amazing, 'A man/woman knowing this fact and <u>not</u> praying!' To God prayer is more wonderful than all the wonders of all the heavens: more glorious than all the mysteries of all the earths: and more mighty than all the forces of God's great creation." 'Behold he prayeth!' In a street called straight in a home owned by Judas and his name is Saul of Tarsus! Go find him and heal him."

Samuel Chadwick

"Pray Naked & Unashamed" #6
Gen. 2:23-25

Thus far we have learned some very important principles for prayer from the first man to get alone with God, face-to-face. You must know the voice of God; that means being in His Word (John 10:27). You must know the secret place; that means having a special place to meet God (Matthew 6:6). You must know the right time to meet God; that means having a specific quiet time alone with God (Mark 1:35 – morning; Acts 3:1 – afternoon; Matt. 14:23 – evening; Lk. 6:12 – night). It does not matter to God when, as long as you are a praying person, because He never sleeps or slumbers.

The fourth principle, and probably the most important one, is: you must be naked and unashamed! Now don't get excited; that does not mean doing your quiet time in your birthday suit. In Gen. 3:9, God called Adam and said, "Where are you?" He and Eve were hiding. Why? They were bare-naked and ashamed! But notice who is doing the seeking and who is doing the hiding! Some things never change, Amen? John 4:23 says that the Father SEEKS for those to worship Him... -- (*zeteo*) to look for, seek out, desire, to possess. It is no different today, God is still seeking for worshipers to worship Him in spirit and in truth! Does God show up in your enclosed garden or prayer closet and wait, only to find that you never show up? Does He cry out every day, morning, noon and night, from your prayer closet, your pantry of spiritual nourishment, "Where are you?"

The word in Gen. 3:9, for "voice" or "sound" can be translated "thunder, to yell, call aloud – WHERE ARE YOU?!" Now it gets a little personal, because this word also implies "to call or summon by name!" Note v.9, *"God called unto Adam"*, not Eve. Dads: the family altar is your responsibility not mom's! Notice who speaks first in Gen. 3:9: GOD! He initiates the search and He initiates the conversation. Gen. 3:10 gives us a clue to Adam's problem (and our problem) in this fourth principle. *"And he (Adam) said, I heard Thy voice in the garden and I was afraid, because I was naked; and I hid myself."* He heard God's voice in the enclosed garden, but was afraid! Terrified, Fearful! Why? Could it be sin, disobedience, rebellion, neglect? Good guess! I Sam. 15:23 says, *"For rebellion is as the sin of witchcraft, and stubbornness is as iniquity and idolatry..."* What's wrong, Adam? "I am naked, literally bare-naked!" In Gen. 2:25, *"They were both naked, the man and his wife, and were not ashamed."* But nine verses later they are naked and very ashamed!

Why? What happened in Gen. 3:1-7? The serpent appeared and sin entered the enclosed garden, the secret place, the prayer closet; because Adam left the gate open. He forgot to shut the door! Can you hear the **hissss** of the serpent? God said, "Shut the door" for a very good reason! He (Satan) will do everything and anything in his power to destroy your prayer life and your prayer meetings, and he has done a pretty good job on that one! They are just about gone: family night, Bible study, youth night, small groups, Bible Clubs. Call it anything you want, but don't call it "prayer meeting," because Satan won't like that.

Am I stepping on any toes yet? If this is to convicting, just skip to the next entry and nobody will know except God! I'm writing to myself as well – "Guilty as charged, your Honor!" What's that old saying, "Satan trembles at the weakest Christian on their knees." By the way, how are your garments before God today: spotless, clean, pure white, or filthy? Isa. 64:6 talks about all our righteousnesses as filthy rags. If you read that verse in a Roman Catholic Bible or look up the words "filthy rags" in your Strong'sconcordance, YUCK! It's hard to come before a perfect, holy, pure God in dirty rags, isn't it? It is confession time! Adam was naked and afraid and he hid himself! Are you hiding from God? Have you withdrawn from the LORD lately? Have you left your first love (not *lost*, **left**)? Rev. 2:4. Have you stepped out of the circle? I love that poem by Edwin Markham:

> He drew a circle and shut me out
> Heretic, rebel a thing to flout
> But love and I had a mind to win
> We drew a circle and shut him in

If your love, your passion, your fervor, your relationship, your intimacy, your prayer life is not what it used to be with God, who moved? Who stepped out of the circle, you or God?

Psalm 139 says that God sees every-thing, every-where, every-time! In fact Yeshua/Jesus knows the very thoughts of your mind right now (John 2:24-25 -- He knows all men & He knows what is in all men.) In John 1:48-50, He saw Nathaniel and knew what he was meditating on before he came to Him. God searches our hearts and consciences (Jer. 17:9-10). You can't hide anything, anywhere, anytime from an omniscient, omnipresent God. Nothing! So, why try? Question: are you in your enclosed garden, with the door shut, in the cool of the day? Do you hear His voice walking in your garden? If not, why not? Are you afraid? Are you naked? Are you hiding? Jesus said in John 10:27, *"My sheep hear my voice and I know them..."*

When was the last time you heard His voice? When was it? Can you remember? Have you <u>ever</u> heard it? Have you? Are you thirsty for God? How thirsty? Does your heart pant after God like the deer pants after the water brook, after being chased by a pack of hunting dogs (Psalm 42:1-2)? Jesus said, *"...If any man thirst let him come unto Me and drink... out of his belly [inner most being] shall flow rivers of living water."*(John 7:37-38).

I believe Adam walked with God in the garden, in the cool of the day, before and after the fall and heard His voice calling him. He knew that intimate, personal intercourse with his Creator and had "spiritual *YADA*." He walked before God bare-naked, pure, open, with nothing hidden before the fall. Then he ran from God; he hid from God; and he lied to God. That is the sequence and order of backsliding, run, hide, lie Gen. 3:11-12. But when all else fails, blame the wife! *"The woman whom thou gavest to be with me, she gave me of the tree, and I did eat."* Some things never change. Amen? As someone once said, "The problem was not the apple in the tree, it was the pear on the ground." Question: have you disobeyed God? Have you sinned against Him? Have you left your first love? (Rev. 2:4) Did you buy the lie? Yes, Yes, Yes! God forgive me! Please don't send me out of Your presence, God! Moses prayed that in Exodus 33 after the golden calf. I can't imagine being without God'spresence for five seconds. Adam refused to confess; he refused to admit his sin; he refused to repent; so he was driven out of the enclosed garden and out of God's personal presence (Gen. 3:24). Christian, have you refused to confess, to repent, to admit your sin of prayerlessness? That's the one we are dealing with! How would you rate your prayer life on a scale of 1-10? You can change that right now! With five simple words from Luke 11:1, *"...Lord, teach us to pray..."* Not <u>how</u> to pray, we already know how; we just need to learn **TO PRAY**!

Our basic need is not more theology about prayer (we have filled bookshelves on that), but more **practicology** in prayer! There is only one way to become more proficient in prayer, and that is to take a knee and pray more; like the only real way to learn how to ride a horse is to get on the horse! I just read Luke 11 in my quiet time today, and as He was praying in a certain place at a certain time, one of His disciples said to Him, "Lord teach us to pray." They were used to saying their prayers, reading them out of a book, a "***Siddur***." They wanted to learn to pray like Jesus or John the Baptist, from their heart to the heart of God.

*(**Prayer** - "Father, teach us to pray like Jesus and John prayed from their hearts to Your heart, in sincerity and truth, according to Your will and Your desires. May we always include Your kingdom first and Your will last as we close; and may we be sensitive to the Holy Spirit's leading. In Jesus' name. Amen")*

Principles for Prayer:

- We must come before God naked and unashamed; confession first, petitions last.
- Satan will do anything to destroy your prayer life, prayer time, or prayer meeting. Remember that!
- The sequence of backsliding is run, hide, lie -- in that order.

"Our seasons of <u>fasting</u> and <u>prayer</u> at the Tabernacle have been high days indeed: never has Heaven's gate stood wider. Even if our public work were laid aside to give us space for special <u>prayer</u>, it might be a great gain to our church."

C. H. Spurgeon

"Don't Pray Cain's Way" #7
Gen. 4:6-7

Adam has three sons in Gen. 4: Cain, Abel and Seth; and we need to <u>consider how their lives impact our lives in regards to prayer</u>. Adam knew Eve, and she bore Cain and said, *"I have gotten [acquired-Cain] a man from the LORD."* Cain is a type of the mere man of the earth, whose religion is destitute of any sense of sin or need of atonement. But <u>attainment can never take the place of atonement</u>. Without the recognition of Christ as our substitute and sacrifice there can be no approach to God. This religious type of man is described in 2 Peter 2:2, *"And many shall follow their pernicious ways; by reason of whom the way of truth shall be evil spoken of."* **Seven things** are said about Cain: he worships in self-will, he is angry with God, he refuses to bring a sin offering, he murders his brother, he lies to God, he becomes a wanderer, and he becomes the object of divine anxiety and fear.

This section could be entitled, "The Way of Cain." Previously, we said prayer language can be at times, defiant and irreverent. Prayer is simply talking to God. If that is true, then we have in chapter 4 with Cain what we had in chapter 3 verse 9 with Adam (where God initiated the search and the conversation, "Where are you?") Here He asks Cain a series of questions starting in v.6: "Why are you angry?" "Why has your countenance fallen?" "Where is Abel, your brother?" "What have you done?" Sin separates man from God and it is God, not man, who does the searching for the other at this point. God, more than man, desires reconciliation; and that comes through confession which is prayer! The first prayer a sinner prays is to change his status (Rom. 3:10-11 tells us there is none righteous; there is none that understand, there is none that seek after God). So, it is God who does the seeking initially, as with Cain. A conversation develops between God and Cain as God attempts to restore Cain who is angry with Him; but you have never been angry with God, right? Your countenance has never fallen, has it? You have never felt unaccepted by God, right? We have the same problem Cain had! Admit it!

"Sin lieth at the door!" And God says, "We should rule over it and not vice-versa." Praise God! <u>We serve a God who seeks, searches and saves sinners</u>! Cain answers God, hopefully not the way you answer Him from your prayer chamber. But how about on the street, or at work, or school when you are convicted about your life or habits; or during a crisis, or when circumstances don't go your way? Jude v.11 says, *"<u>Woe to them! for they have gone in the way of Cain...</u>"* The way of Cain is simply will-worship -- doing it my way and expecting God to accept and even bless it -- a fruit offering instead of the firstlings of the flock. There is nothing wrong with fruit, when it's a fruit offering; but God required blood for atonement, not grapes! Cain wanted it his way, like some of our local hamburger jingles, "have it your way," but with God there is only one way: <u>His way</u>!

God desperately tried in His conversation to restore Cain, but to no avail. God is sovereign and supreme, omnipotent and omnificent, but He never forces us to accept Him or His ways. One of the greatest sins of the Christian today is <u>the sin of prayerlessness</u>! God gave us the method; in fact, <u>prayer is His divine plan</u>. God deserves (in fact He desires) our fellowship and our communion with Him. Abel knew that sweetness, and he came God's way. Cain never experienced that sweetness, because he tried to come his own way, through will-worship. Gen. 4:16 says, *"...Cain went out from the presence of the LORD..."* How sad, how tragic!

My friend, it is God Who is seeking you right now to worship Him in spirit and in truth, to worship Him His way, not man's way. Why won't you come? *"The Spirit and the bride say, Come. And let him that heareth say, Come. And let him that is athirst, come..."* (Rev. 22:17). Or will you go out from the presence of the LORD like Cain, into the land of Nod, the land of wandering. Aren't you tired of wandering, tired of drifting, tired of floating down a river like a bubble with no meaning and no place to go but down? In Exodus 33:14 the LORD said to Moses, *"...My presence shall go with thee, and I shall give thee rest."* And Moses said in return, *"If thy presence go not with me, carry us not up hence."* I don't know about you, but I need to know the power of His presence and the presence of His power in my life and ministry, and especially in my prayer life and closet.

(**Prayer** - *"Oh God, Creator of Heaven and Earth, and all that in them is, help us to see it Your way and only Your way. Please LORD, don't stop seeking, searching and speaking to Your creatures. Don't stop drawing Your creation to Yourself. Forgive us our sin of prayerlessness; forgive us for doing it our way. Cleanse us from our will-worship and from going in the way of Cain. Lord, may we know the sweetness that Abel knew in prayer and fellowship with You. In Jesus' name and for His sake, Amen!"*)

Principles for Prayer:

- Without Christ as our substitute and sacrifice there is no approach to God.
- One of the greatest sins in a Christian's life today is the sin of prayerlessness.
- The dynamic for prayer is the power of His presence and the presence of His power

"I can take my telescope and look millions of miles into space, but I can go into my room and in prayer get nearer to God and Heaven than I can when assisted by all the telescopes on earth."

Sir Isaac Newton

"I don't need a telescope, I need a microscope to see Him better."

R.T.B.

"God's Mark is Better" #8
Gen. 4:15

We can't leave Gen. 4 without saying a few words about the mark of Cain. The religious commentators are all over the place on opionions, and nobody has a corner on this market. It seems the deeper they go, the broader the market. Some believe his skin color changed; some believe it was a curse from God. Some believe it was an internal thing; some believe it was banishment. The ancient Rabbis saw it as a horn on Cain's head. Some believe it was a shaking like Parkinson's. Some just don't believe; and some admit they just don't know, and move on. The Hebrew word for mark is (*owth*), and is used 76 times in the Older Testament (75 of those are used as a sign), many as a sign of ownership, with some as a taboo mark for "don't touch!" This mark has been the seed-bed of confusion and debate for centuries. However, the word "owth" [or sign, token, flag, beacon, monument] is used in Exodus 12:13, on the first Passover, when they struck the lintel and the door posts with the three branches of hyssop plunged into the basin of blood. This was a sign of something greater to come! Another sign (token [*owth*]) is the bow God set in the clouds after the universal flood in Gen. 9:13, as a sign of the covenant between God and man that He would never destroy the Earth again by water. Then there is the token (sign [*owth*]) of circumcision that God set up between Himself and the Jewish people, making them His covenant people (*olam*) forever. As you study this word further you see it has a sense of ownership and protection, and it is something that is visible for all to see. It is NOT a sign of God's curse, but of His protection, just like the blood on the door, the bow in the clouds, and circumcision of all the males and a host of others.

The only parallel we have to this marking is found in Ezekiel 9:3-6, with a man dressed in fine linen called the "<u>Ink Horn Man</u>," who went throughout Jerusalem to *"set a mark (tav) upon the foreheads of the men that sigh and that cry for all the abominations that be done in the midst [of the city of Jerusalem]... but come not near any man upon whom* is *the mark."* The mark, or (*tav*) in ancient Paleo-Hebrew, was a symbol of a **cross**, and was the mark of the covenant. Ezekiel was carried to Babylon before they adopted the Aramaic language and alphabet. The cross-references in your Bible to the Ezekiel passage of 9:4-6 are Revelation 7:3; 9:4; & 20:4, which refer to those during the tribulation with the seal of God in their foreheads; and Exodus 12:7; 23 which is the Passover and the blood on the lintel and *mezuzot* or side posts. Then you have the "mark of the beast" in Rev. 13:16-17; 20:4. The 144,000 are sealed during the Tribulation with the Father's name written in their foreheads, Rev. 14:1.

Now back to the mark of Cain. God said to the Jewish people in Egypt, "Strike the lintel with the hyssop dipped in blood; dip it again and strike the two side posts with one swipe." On every door in the land of Goshen you had a '**cross**' in the blood of the lamb. And God said, "When I see the sign, token (*owth*) I will pass over you." In Ezek. 9:4-6, the "Ink Horn Man" put a (*tav*), the ancient Paleo-Hebrew **cross**, on their foreheads and they were not to be touched. Study the book of Numbers. Lay out the twelve tribes and the sanctuary. Get in an imaginary helicopter and look down and you will see that they marched in the form of a cross for 40 years in the desert. Michio Kaku, a Ph.D. Theoretical Physicist said that if you step inside of a perfect cube and look up, you will see a cross. In Revelation 21, the New Jerusalem is a perfect cube; estimates are 1,500 miles x 1,500 miles x 1,500 miles, so when you step inside the lobby and look up you will see one humongous cross! And if you continue your search you will find the cross from Genesis all the way through Revelation. Why? It's God's plan! That's why!

So, what was the mark on Cain'sforehead? A visible mark of ownership and protection, saying, "Don't touch," a walking sermon, a sign of grace, a shaking, if you will. You are entitled to any intelligent opinion you wish to draw on your own. Gather your evidence, form your conclusion, make your proposition. In my humble opinion (and I may be out on a branch all by myself, Dr. Showers), I believe the mark of Cain was an ancient Paleo-Hebrew (*tav*), just like the one the "Ink

Horn Man," put on the men in Ezk. 9:4-6. Every time a person looked at Cain, and every time Cain looked at a piece of glass or into a pool of clear water to wash his face, he saw this symbol. It was a reminder of the One who was to come and die for Him to set him free for the murder of his brother.

And what was this symbol? It was an ancient Paleo-Hebrew **cross**, on which the Lamb of God would die for the sins of the world, including Cain's. But he chose to run, hide and lie, instead of falling on his knees and crying out, "LORD save me!" Three simple words from his heart to the heart of God. When confronted by God for his sin, instead of confessing it, he lied (Gen.4:9). Then he gave God the typical humanitarian excuse, "Am I my brother's keeper?" Will you right now acknowledge your sin, confess it to God, take a knee and pray? Or will you run, hide and lie like Cain and let *Diabalos* mark you for trouble?

The sin we are dealing with on our journey is not murder, it is **prayerlessness**! But it is as deadly as Cain's for a disciple of Christ. Cain'sbrother, Abel, didn't live very long; yet he is listed in the Hall of Faith in Hebrews. In fact, he is the first one you meet as you enter the lobby. *"By faith Abel offered unto God a more excellent sacrifice than Cain, by which he obtained witness that he was righteous, God testifying of his gifts: and by it he being dead yet speaketh"* (Heb. 11:4). What did he offer? The blood of a lamb, a type of Christ; and it started in Gen. 3:21, when God made coats of skins for Adam and Eve. They both knew the way to God, the blood of an innocent lamb (which ultimately leads to Calvary), but only Able did it God's way.

Without the recognition of Christ as our substitute and sacrifice, there can be no approach to God. There has been more persecution on religious grounds than on any other in the whole world. That's why I believe the very mark (*tav*) God put on Cain's forehead was the symbol of the purpose set forth before the foundation of this world, in the council of heaven, rejected by Cain himself: the blood of the Lamb of God! Without the shedding of blood there is no redemption but without the sprinkling of blood there is no salvation. You need both, appropriation and application, the blood was shed at Calvary but if you don't apply it to the lintel and door posts of your heart, you will die, without hope and without Christ and go straight to hell!

*(**Prayer** - "Abba, Father, may we not be marked like Cain for destruction, but like Abel for consecration. It's not enough, O LORD, to **know** the way; We must be **in** the way, like Eliezer, so You can lead us, guide us, teach us, talk to us, touch us, transform us, mold us, instruct us and make us men and women of prayer in these last days." In Jesus' name. Amen!)*

Principles for Prayer:

- I believe the mark of Cain was the ancient Paleo-Hebrew (*tav*) resembling a cross.
- Appropriation and application are needed for salvation; both the shedding and sprinkling of blood are needed.
- Prayer is one of the most common forms of devotion and yet it's the one that is the least understood.

"We are obliged to pray, if we be citizens of God's Kingdom. Prayerlessness is expatriation, or worse, from God's kingdom. The Gospel cannot live, fight, conquer, without prayer. Prayer must be unceasing, instant and ardent!"

E.M. Bounds

"Call for Corporate Prayer" #9
Gen. 4:26

We discussed the "Way of Cain" which was will-worship, and now we turn to his younger brother, Abel (who may have been his twin brother), and here we see, "the way of God." Not much is said in scripture about this first martyr, who apparently left no offspring, but he is mentioned by Christ as an historical figure (Matt. 23:35; Luke 11:51). He was a keeper of sheep, whereas his brother Cain was a farmer (a keeper of carrots). His name in Hebrew (*hebel*) has several meanings: breathe, vapor, vanity, transitory, and can even be translated meadow and morning mist, for brevity of life. We know from the context that the three brothers Cain, Abel and Seth, were guided and taught by their father, Adam, in the proper duty of worshiping Jehovah God. The language implies previous instruction in the mode of worship. "And in the process of time," i.e. "in the end of days," (probably the Sabbath), they brought their offerings. Gen. 4:4. *"And the LORD (YeHoVaH) had respect unto…"* in Hebrew means, "to look at with a keen earnest glance," and has been translated, "to kindle a fire." So, divine approval is shown in a consuming fire, and this is seen throughout scripture.

"By faith Abel offered unto God a more excellent sacrifice than Cain; [Cain offered a bloodless sacrifice to God for sin – unacceptable!] *by which he* [Abel] *obtained witness that he was righteous,* [but to Cain and his offering God had no respect, unacceptable!] *God testifying of his (Abel's) gifts: and by it he being yet dead speaketh."* Heb. 11:4. Abel was the first one in "The Hall of Faith," the first martyr; and his blood is still speaking to God from the ground today. Genesis 4:10 is written in the present tense, as if it is still crying out today. It appears that Abel (not Cain) was going to bear the lineage of the Messiah; and Cain, out of jealousy, killed him, just like Esau was going to do to Jacob.

Abel must have made an altar to present his offering to God. There are three requirements for an altar: <u>sacrifice</u> (the firstling of the flock, and it had to be perfect); <u>worship</u> (attributing worth and praise to *YeHoVaH Elohim* -- *"...the LORD had respect unto Abel and his offering"*); and <u>prayer</u> (communion with the Creator of the universe)! Abel had all three, and he knew that it was the blood that made atonement for his sin, long before Lev. 17:11 was written. *"For the life of the flesh is in the blood: and I have given it to you upon the altar to make an atonement for your souls: for it is the blood that maketh an atonement for the soul."* His father and mother learned that in the garden after they sinned and God had to kill the lambs to atone for their sin and cover their nakedness. The LORD had no respect for Cain and his offering -- why? No blood! And possibly no worship! No sacrifice for sure (you don't sacrifice grapes and apples). To sacrifice means to slaughter, to smite with deadly intent. How do you slaughter fruit? Without blood we cannot enter into the presence of God. Fruit is great, but blood is the requirement. Heb. 10:19 *"Having therefore, brethren, boldness to enter into the holiest by the blood of Jesus..."*

We, too, can enter the holiest, the Holy of Holies, just like faithful Abel, because of the blood of the sacrifice, the blood of the Lamb of God, Jesus! Our sacrifices of prayer and praise (Heb. 13:15) are accepted by His blood. As we enter into the holy place, our prayer chamber, let us be mindful of the shed blood of Jesus Christ, and use it to cleanse us and make us acceptable before a pure and Holy God. Then God will look on us and have respect on us and on our offerings. May we like faithful Abel bring our firstlings, build our altars, pray to *Jehovah Elohim* and worship Him. To be listed in the "Hall of Faith," Abel had to be a man of faith, a man of God, and a man of prayer. Even today his blood still cries out to God. What does that tell you about <u>martyrs</u>? From Abel to Zachariah, to John the Baptist to Jim Elliot to the 200,000+ Christians martyred every year for their faith (500 every day), their blood is crying out to God (and to us) constantly.

Do we even take time to pray for our brothers and sisters who are being arrested, persecuted, tortured, imprisoned and killed for their faith in Christ? Do we? We need to read **Acts 1:8** a little more carefully with a Strong's Concordance. The word "witnesses" is the Greek word for **martyrs**. In fact the name Stephen means crown, "a <u>martyr's crown</u>." When a saint is martyred Jesus stands up to receive them into His presence (Acts 7:55). There have been more martyrs in the last 100 years than in the previous 2,000 years. <u>In fact, the blood of martyrs is the seed-bed of the church</u>.

Alfred Lord Tennyson wrote a poem about Stephen:

> He heeded not reviling tones
> Nor sold his heart to idle moans
> Though cursed and scorned and bruised with stones.
> But looking upward, full of grace
> He prayed—and from a happy place
> God's glory smote him on the face.

And it all started with Abel, who offered a more perfect sacrifice then his brother Cain. Cain killed him and buried him in his garden, and yet his blood still cries out to God from the ground **today!**

We know who was originally intended to carry on the Messianic line: Abel, whom Cain murdered. After that, Eve gave birth to a third son, Seth, in Gen. 4:25, *"...For God [**Elohim**], said she, hath appointed me another seed instead of Abel, whom Cain slew."* Not much is said about *Sheth* or Seth, except that he is the seed of the *Sethite* people and lived 912 years and had a bunch of children in contrast to the Canaanite people. His name means "appointed" or "seat of the body." Eve names him in Gen. 4:25 and Adam names him in Gen. 5:3. He lived 105 years before he begot Enosh, "Mortal" and then lived another 807 years. *"Then began men to call upon the name of the LORD,"* [*YeHoVaH*, the covenant name of God] (Gen. 4:26).

At that point it was 235 years since creation. Could man have waited that long to worship God in prayer, five generations after creation? I don't think so! Adam was created for intimate worship, communion, and fellowship with God. Therefore prayer was a dictate of nature! Prayer was a constituted instinct in-wrought in us by our Maker, or as one man put it, "**Man is a praying animal**." Adam prayed in the Garden in Gen. 3; Abel prayed for his sacrifice in Gen. 4. In fact, Adam was created by God for sweet, intimate communion and fellowship with Him. Therefore prayer had to be a dictate of nature, or as someone put it, "prayer was a constituted instinct in-wrought by the Maker." So fellowship, communion, and prayer had to be going on since day one!

The word "Enosh" simply means "mortal" or man in general whether singular or collectively. The word "men" is not in the Hebrew text, it is added for clarity, so we get all our meaning from the word, "Enosh" meaning, mankind or referring to corporate worship. It is an indication of man recognizing and realizing his frailty and weakness and calling on the LORD, *YeHoVaH* for help. Genesis 4:26 is saying, "Then mankind in general began to call upon the name of *YeHoVaH*." The reference must be to social worship not individual prayer, because the word "call" means "to call out to, to address by name." There is one other possibility for this verse: people were called "**The LORD's people**" to distinguish them from idol worshipers (II Chron. 7:14 -- case in point), though very few scholars hold to this view.

*(**Prayer** - "YeHoVaH God, thank You for corporate worship and prayer. That, not only alone in our closets, but together as a body we can come to You and pour out our hearts and make our requests known. Thank You, that You are the God Who hears the prayers of all mankind, individually and collectively. Thank You for Your word today; it truly was precious and refreshing." In Yeshua's name, Amen!)*

Principles for Prayer:

- Man was created by God for sweet, intimate communion and fellowship.
- Abel was the first martyr; the word in Acts 1:8 for "witnesses" is (*martus*) for martyr.
- Prayer is the highway to the throne of God, and so few Christians ever get on it.

Andrew Murray faithfully prayed for a revival of the Holy Spirit for his congregation every Friday evening for 36 years. In 1860, as revival swept over America, Britain and Africa, Murray broke down. But within a year his prayers were answered and his congregation experienced the outpouring of the Holy Spirit.
Thirty-seven years of praying, fasting, weeping and crying for God's outpouring.

R.T.B.

"Prayer Makes Family History" #10
Gen. 4:26

Abel, Cain's brother, built an altar to present his offerings to God. An altar, as you remember, had three requirements: **sacrifice – worship – prayer**! The **sacrifice** had to be the very best you had -- perfect, spotless, prime, the choicest, and especially the first born of your flock. The **worship** had to be from your heart -- genuine, real, authentic, true praise and adoration, attributing worth and praise to God in song and proclamation. The **prayer** had to be a genuine act of contrition from your heart to God's heart; not just words of repetition, but words of petition, supplication, confession, communion, intercession, and thanksgiving -- *(yada)* intimacy and intercourse on the highest level with your Creator and Friend. Abel had all three in abundance, but he knew it was the blood that made atonement possible! His parents learned that in the Garden (*gan*) after they sinned, and God had to kill the lambs to make atonement for their sin and clothe them (Gen. 3:21). It is interesting: Adam Clarke claims in his commentary that this happened on the first Day of Atonement, and his calendar calculations were one month different than the Jewish one, putting it on **November 1**. Think about the implications of that: their day started the evening before, which would have been **October 31**.

To be listed in the Hall of Faith, Abel had to be a man of faith, a man of God, a man of prayer, and a God pleaser (not a man pleaser)! What are you? Who do you please when you shut your prayer closet door?

To our knowledge Abel never married and he never fathered any children. Eve then gave birth to another son in Gen. 4:25, *"For God (*Elohim*) said she, has appointed me another seed (*zera*) instead of Abel whom Cain slew."*

Eve knew (and we know) who was to carry on the Messianic line, Abel! But Satan had him killed (I John 3:12). God then used Seth to carry on that Messianic line.

So, there's "The Adam's Family." Where do you fit, since we are all distant relatives or descendants? Who are you related to and whose genes are you wearing? Cain was a man of the Earth, religious, but destitute of any sense of sin or need of atonement. What do you bring to the altar: a handful of grapes, a couple of apples? Are your gifts acceptable to Him? Does He have respect for you? Not much is said about Seth (that could be good or bad) other than he had a son, lived 912 years, had a bunch of other kids and sat around a lot on his buttocks (his name means buttocks if that's any help). I think it's a clue. We have a bunch of those in the church today, people who sit on their ... never mind, you get my drift! E-Nosh, introduces the worship of *Yahweh or YeHoVaH* or at least the new pattern for invoking that name in corporate prayer and worship. So he becomes our new worship leader (that's good; I like that) or he gives us a name for our group so we are not listed with the idol worshipers (and that's good too).

Abel did not live long, but he made an impact on the world he lived in and on God. Oswald Chambers died at 42 in Egypt; Eric Liddell died at 43 in a concentration camp; Nate Saint was 33 and speared to death; David Brainerd was 29 and had tuberculosis (his diary moved Jim Elliott, who died at 29 by spears and said, "He is no fool who gives up what he cannot keep to gain what he cannot lose."). William Carey was also moved by Brainerd's diary and said, "Attempt great things for God. Expect great things from God." How does that saying go? "Only one life to live will soon be past, and only what's done for Christ will last."

What will you do with the one life He has given you? Will God have respect unto you and your offering when you stand before Him like Abel, or will you go out from the presence of the LORD, like Cain, because the LORD has "no respect for you or for your offering?"

The choice is yours, I made mine at 27, on December 25th 1972 at 12:00 p.m. at Newark Baptist Church; and I have never, ever regretted it. Never! That was consecration. Salvation came five months earlier on August 27th, 1972 following a morning worship service, when my wife Ann led me to Christ in our living-room, and that moment I will never, ever forget. *Baruch ha Shem!*

"That thou keep this commandment without spot, unrebukeable, until the appearing of our Lord Jesus Christ: Which in his times he shall shew, who is the blessed and only Potentate, the King of kings, and Lord of lords; Who only hath immortality, dwelling in the light which no man can approach unto; whom no man hath seen, nor can see: to whom be honour and power everlasting. Amen" I Tim. 6:14-16.

*(**Prayer** - LORD, may You find us faithful like Abel. May You find us righteous like Abel. And may You have respect unto us and our offerings like You had for Abel's. Father, may we not go in the way of Cain, who worshiped You after his own will; but may we accept redemption by the precious blood of the Lamb. May we worship You Your way, and come to You in prayer through the blood of Your only begotten Son, Jesus the Christ, as a God-pleaser, like Abel.)*

Principles for Prayer:

- Prayer has to be from your heart, genuine acts of contrition, adoration, confession, thanksgiving, supplication;
- Sacrifice has to be from the heart, the very best you have, perfect, spotless, prime, the first born, no blemishes;
- Worship has to be from the heart, genuine, real, authentic, true praise and adoration, accompanied with tears

"The word of God represents all the possibilities of God are at the disposal of true prayer."

A.T. Pierson

*(Do you believe that?
Then why don't we pray like we believe it?)*

R.T.B.

"Enoch Walked with God" #11
Gen. 5:22

We now move away from "the Adams Family" (Cain, Abel, Seth and Enosh and of course Papa who walked face-to-face (*paw-neem*) with God; a deeply spiritual man before the garden incident, who had intimate fellowship with the God of creation, "Spiritual *YADA*"). Imagine just you and God all alone, in a garden, on a planet, in His universe, among His entire creation -- just you and God! Blows your mind, doesn't it? It does mine! But listen, you can have that -- in your closet, pantry, storehouse of nourishment; in the morning, evening, afternoon or at midnight alone with Him. I love that old poem about the garden, I don't know who wrote it:

> "In the garden, was a tree
> Rich with fruit, a token given
> Love's free choice, so soon abused
> Still closer fellowship, refused
> In the garden."

(Read it again)

Adam was created in God's image, after God's likeness, for God's glory, to have intimate fellowship with God. Can I get an Amen there? Sweet, intimate, unbroken fellowship with the entire tri-unity of the God-head! Oh, how we lack that today! The only place I know of today where you can find that intimacy, that fellowship, that intercourse (and it can be found my friend) is on your knees, alone with Him, in your prayer garden or prayer closet. When you pray, you pray to the Father, through the Son, by the Holy Spirit. When you say the word "God," three people say, "What?" So be specific when you address God.

When we looked at Adam in his "prayer garden," we learned four basic prayer principles too often overlooked or, better yet, disobeyed. Take a moment right now and go back and read Gen. 3:8-10. Go ahead, I'll wait... (good less than 20 seconds, and I am a slow reader). What's exciting is that, **first**, God is still seeking people today to have fellowship with Him (John 4:23). So, they knew His voice, why? Because they were accustomed to the sound of it! **Second**, they knew where to meet Him, why? Because they were accustomed to meeting Him there! **Third**, they knew what time to meet Him, why? Because they were accustomed to Him showing up at that time! But the **fourth** principle is a little tougher: they were naked and ashamed. Why? They were NOT accustomed to it! Gen. 2:25 says, *"And they were both naked, the man and his wife, and were not ashamed."* This is the way we should come to God, naked: no secrets, no sins, nothing hidden -- just naked and unashamed. There are no secrets with God anyway; He knows everything, everywhere, every time. He is omniscient! Jer. 17:10 says, *"I the LORD, search the heart, I try the reins [conscience]..."* In John 2:24-25 it says that Jesus knows all men and what is in men.

Now I would like to draw some "prayer principles" from the seventh in the line of descendents from Adam (Gen. 5:18-24); Adam, Seth, Enosh, Kenan, Mahalalel, Jared, Enoch, Methuselah, Lamech, Noah, Shem, Ham Japeth. Why do we skip over names so fast in the Bible? We come to I Chronicles and skip nine chapters, 500 names. Names are important! They tell a lot about people. Like little Jabez right in the middle of those names, I have 155 pages of sermon notes on that character from teaching; and the prayer *of* Jabez is not *about* Jabez.

Or take my name, Rev. Roger Theodore Boguski I. Rev. means a church recognized the call of God in my life, examined my credentials, qualifications, qualities, abilities, gifts, character, commissioned me and sent me out to do the work of the ministry. Roger means warrior, spear man, leader, from the womb to the tomb; marine, police officer, preacher, missionary. Theodore means, God's gift, lover of God, speaker of God, you chose. Boguski is Polish, the ski is a suffix for nobility, and also shows a connection to the name preceding it which is Bog-us or God's gift, again in Polish. Then you have the "I" for first, which means there is a "II." So a name can tell you a lot about a person.

Like the first ten names you have listed in Genesis 5 -- all have meanings in Hebrew and they are all very important. Adam – man; Seth – appointed; Enosh – mortal; Kenan – sorrow; Mahalalel – blessed God; Jared – shall come down; Enoch – teach; Methuselah – death shall bring forth; Lamech – despairing; Noah – comfort or rest. Now let's put all them together from the Hebrew, "Man appointed, mortal, for sorrow, but the blessed God shall come down, teaching that His death, (Whose death? His death!), shall bring the despairing, comfort or rest." That is a summary of the Christian gospel in the Genesis genealogy. It shows that God's plan of redemption was not some knee jerk reaction to sin, but His plan before the creation of the Earth. Thank you, Dr. Chuck Missler.

Enoch (*chanak* – means dedicated) we get the word "Chanukkah" from its root, "The Feast of Dedication" on the 25th of Kislev or December. Proverbs 22:6 says, *"Train up…,"* (*chanak*) teach, dedicate, inaugurate, initiate, swear them in (not swear at them). Enoch is a striking character, one of only two men, the Bible says, "walked with God." (Noah being the other). One of only two men who entered Heaven without passing through the portals of death (Elijah being the other). Other than Jesus, Elijah is the only other man the Bible says, "pleased God!" Six verses, Gen. 5:18-23 and what a biography! In Luke 3:37 he is in Christ's genealogy through Mary; in Hebrews 11:5-6 he is number two in the "Hall of Faith" after Abel; in Jude vv. 14-15 he is the first prophet to predict the second coming (and he did it 1,000 years before the universal flood). But some things seem to stand out in Enoch's life as a man who pleased God; a man whose very breath seemed to be a prayer to God!

"Enoch walked with God…300 years!" "Enoch walked with God: and he was not; for God took him." Amos 3:3 says, *"Can two walk together except they be agreed?"* You can't walk with God without talking with Him, without sweet communion, or fellowship. Elijah also walked with God, II Kings 2:11 and

He (God) took him. Hebrews 11:5-6 says a lot about Enoch, he was a man of faith, *"By faith Enoch...,"* he was a man of prayer, a God pleaser. He believed God and diligently sought Him. Enoch maintained unbroken communion and sweet intercourse with God; he had to, to walk with God. The same is true with Adam, Noah, Abraham, Elijah, etc. God did all the talking. These men were progressive saints. They walked with God; this shows spiritual progress. The Hebrew word for walk means, **"to go on habitually**!" How sweet is that?! So progress in holiness was their habit: sanctification, not salvation. God pleasers in a corrupt time. Enoch fathered Methuselah, who died the year of the flood. Could it be that Enoch's birth initiated God's discipline on the Earth? Enoch walked with God and God took him, probably during his "quiet time!"

That's what we need today: a habitual progress and process in holiness; to go on habitually, to walk and talk with God on a regular basis. As Brother Andrew called it, "practicing the presence of Christ!" These men knew the secret of the inner chamber, and we need to find it again. We need to know the voice, the place, the time. And we need to come before Him bare-naked -- no secrets, no hidden agenda -- just broken and spilled out like an alabaster box. We will come back to Enoch again and again; he has a lot more to share with us about prayer. So, continue to walk with me in, "Portraits of Prayer in Genesis."

(**Prayer** - *"Thank You, LORD for all You are teaching us about this blessed ministry of prayer! "Baruch ha Shem! Please don't stop; we are simply finite creatures and You are infinite. Our cup can only hold so much before it overflows. So, please be patient with us as You mold us into the image of Your Son." In His name we pray. Amen!"*)

Principles for Prayer:

- The only place you can find intimacy with the entire Tri-Unity is in prayer.
- Biblical names are very important; so don't skip over their meanings.

- We need to "practice the presence of Christ" like Brother Andrew suggests, especially in <u>prayer</u>.

"We have lost the eternal youthfulness of Christianity, and have aged into calculating manhood. We seldom, if ever, <u>pray</u> in earnest for the extraordinary, the limitless, the glorious. We seldom <u>pray</u> with real confidence for any good to the realization of which we cannot imagine a way. And yet we suppose ourselves to believe in an infinite Father!"

A.B. Simpson (speaking at a conference in 1910)

"God Took Enoch Home" #12
Gen. 5:24

"Enoch walked **with** God and **for** God!" We are given this fact two times in Gen. 5:22-24. I believe it's repeated for emphasis so we won't miss it. Gen. 5:22 says, *"Enoch walked, (yalak)."* This word means, "to walk about," like the old English movie, "Pride and Prejudice" used to say. It's deeper meaning means, "**to live!**" We will see that a little later. In v.22 the preposition with (*eth*) denotes intimacy and fellowship and appears only in reference to God with Enoch and Noah, the only other man who walked with (*eth*) God (Gen. 6:9). To walk (*yalak*) with (*eth*) God (*Elohim*) is to enjoy uninterrupted, conscious, intimate fellowship with Him. Or to put it another way, "to practice the presence of God!" To walk with God denotes a holy life, a life lived in close, intimate communion with Him -- "**Spiritual Yada!**" (Hosea 6:3) What an epitaph on your tombstone: "_____, walked with God!"

The first thing implied in Enoch's walk with God is "His reconciliation," (II Cor. 5:17-19). Amos 3:3 says, *"Can two walk (yalak) together (yachad – alike, united, in union) except they be agreed (ya'ad-together, appointed, betrothed, engaged: Ex. 21:8-9)"* Answer? **NO!** To walk with God means that you have been conformed to His image, **NOT**, He to yours! So, you have been reconciled to Him! Enoch was 65 when he started walking with God, not 5 or 6, and he walked with Him for **300** years and had about 300 children.

The second thing implied in Enoch's walk with God was his similarity with God's nature. You see, **light has no communion with darkness; NONE!** II Cor. 6:14. No sinner can walk with God, because he has nothing in common with God. In fact, even his mind is at enmity with God. Gen. 6:5 and Isa. 64:6 say we are sinners by nature and sinners by practice. Jer. 17:9 says, *"The heart is deceitful above all things and desperately wicked..."* After all, it is sin that separates us from God, is it not? Isa. 59:1-2, *"Behold the LORD's hand is not shortened, that it cannot save; neither his ear heavy that it* *cannot hear, but your iniquities [sins] have separated between you and your God, and your sins have hid his face from you, that he will not hear."*

The third thing implied in Enoch's walk with God is holy fitness. A holy God does not walk out of His **holiness**. He doesn't step out of His circle; you do, and into His circle again! A Holy God can't walk together with an unholy person (Haggai 2:13). I John 1:6 says, *"If we say that we have fellowship with Him, and walk in darkness, we lie, and do not the truth:"* Walking with God means to cease walking your own way, to abandon the world's way, and follow the divine way. Listen, it's His way or the highway, or should I say, **"Hell's way!"** The fourth thing implied in Enoch's walk is a surrendered will. God does not force His company or His companionship on us. Jesus said, "Take My yoke upon you." He doesn't force it upon anyone. The yoke has two sides, He is under one and you get under the other and you pull together with Him. By the way, Enoch's grandfather was Mahalalel ("Praise to God" or "Blessed God"). A godly grandfather, what a heritage! How many of you still have one? Now how much time do you spend with him talking about spiritual things, discussing the books he has written? Shame on you! How is your walk (*yalak*) today? Are you in agreement with Him? Better yet is He in agreement with you? Together, united, appointed, betrothed, engaged?

Listen, you must be in agreement to walk together, Amen? Amos says you must be betrothed. Christ is the groom and the church is the bride! What a principle for living, what a principle for prayer! How is your walk today? The Hebrew word for walk is (*yalak* – to go on habitually) how sweet is that?! Remember, he is the seventh from Adam, a picture of divine completion, rest after the fall, after the sin nature! But this kind of intimacy and union necessitates communion and talking; and prayer is simply talking to God. Just like a child, they walk first and talk second; and that leads to our next principle.

Enoch talked **with** God and **for** God! In order to walk you must talk! Amen? Are you paying attention or just reading? These are not just words on a page, <u>I'm sharing my heart with you</u>. If you don't have time to really ruminate on what I am giving you right now (like a cow chewing her cud) then stop and come back later when you have time to think about what I'm saying because this is no 5 minute devotion about a walk down the street.

Now where was I? Oh yeah, have you ever taken a walk with someone you really love, I mean **really** love? A lot of communication takes place even through silence. Sometimes your <u>body language</u> speaks louder than your words. Amen? A look, a glance, a gesture, a nod, a squeeze, a touch, a kiss… If you think not, drive on the beltway at rush hour and watch the body language! Some commentators believe Enoch met God in the Garden of Eden. "But angels guarded it," you say. "They guarded the Tree of Life." I don't know if they did meet there, but the Bible says he had intimate fellowship with his Creator for 300 years. Unhindered, unbroken, unsevered, ***spiritual yada*** for 300 years. We cannot even make 40-50 minutes on Sunday mornings for 40-50 years. The Bible tells us that Enoch pleased God! What a sequel to his other epitaph, "Enoch Walked With God!" <u>Put either one on my stone</u>! There is a pair of character qualities to mount in your prayer closet: to walk with God is to please God; to please God is to talk with God. Put that on your refrigerator! Enoch was a God pleaser, not a man-pleaser, like in Jude v.16.

How did he do that? Read Hebrews 11:5. Before his translation, he had this testimony: that he pleased God! How is your testimony today? Are you a God pleaser or a man pleaser? The test is simple, how are your prayer answers? That pretty much will answer your question right there (James 5:16)! How did he please God? Simple, by faith! The word "faith" appears <u>230 times</u> in the Newer Testament, and only <u>twice</u> in the Older Testament (Deut. 32:20; and Hab. 2:4). Ten percent of those mentions appear in Hebrews 11 alone.

Faith is the basic, essential element of prayer. Without it, you cannot please God, and He will not answer prayer. Hebrews 11:6 says, *"But without faith it is impossible to please him [God]..."* The word "impossible is actually the Greek word **adunatos**, so you are absolutely powerless to please God without faith. So without faith it is "impossible" to please God, but might I add that without risk, faith is impossible. Simply put, if there is no element of risk involved, there is no need for faith, because the thing hoped for is a sure thing! You have probably never linked Heb. 11:6 together with Enoch in 11:5 -- I didn't either. So, from now on whenever you think of Hebrews 11:6, think of Enoch who talked **with** God and **for** God, and walked **with** God and **for** God, for 300 years and was not, for God took him! Enoch still has more to share. So, come walk with me one more time....

*(**Prayer** - "Lord there is so much to digest in this portion, it is hard to take it all in at one sitting, so we may have to read it again and again. Please Lord, help us to understand Your biblical principles on prayer and apply them to our lives, in Jesus' name. Or, as Elon Musk's five-year-old son, X, prayed in the night when scared and alone, 'Jesus, please!' Amen!")*

Principles for Prayer:

- To walk (*eth*) with God is to enjoy uninterrupted, conscious intimate fellowship.
- To walk with God means you have been conformed to His image, not He to yours.
- Without faith it is impossible to please God, but without risk, faith is impossible.

"The power of prayer has <u>never</u> been tried to its full capacity in any church. If you really want to see the mighty wonders of <u>divine power and grace</u> wrought in the place of weakness, failure and disappointment, let the whole church answer God's challenge in Jeremiah 33:3."

Hudson Taylor

"Unbroken Communion with God" #13
Gen. 5:24b

What is "faith" anyway? The answer is found in Hebrews 11:1, *"Now faith is the substance of things hoped for, the evidence of things not seen."* **Faith is simply believing God**! Faith is the confident assurance, the confident boasting, of things expected; the conviction, the evidence, the proof of things not seen as of yet! Let me paraphrase Hebrews 11:1-2 from the Amplified Version, *"Now faith is the assurance (title-deed, confirmation) of things [we] hoped for, being the proof of things [we] do not see and the conviction of their reality – faith perceiving as real fact what is not revealed to the senses. For by (faith) and trust and holy fervor born of faith, the men of old had divine testimony borne to them and obtained a good report."* **WOW!** How is that for a definition of faith? A title-deed to property you have never seen as of yet, but it's yours all the same!

Faith is (*hupo* – under) and (*stasis* – to stand) to stand under. This is a present passive participle showing action. A better translation would be "substantiating." Faith is the substance (basis, essence, substructure, foundation) of things hoped for; the evidence (proof, conviction) of things not seen as of yet! Enoch was one of those heroes of faith! You see, faith is not believing God **can** do something. That's just wishful thinking or dreaming. Faith is believing God **will** do it! You say, "I have faith, but I don't believe God will do it." Then you don't have faith! Gen. 1:1 says, *"Breisheit bara Elohim* – In the beginning God." No argument for His existence, no defense for His origin, no apologetic for His presence, no explanation for His purpose. Just a statement of His being! **AMEN!**

Who are we to question God, when we can't even make a rock? God doesn't need defense attorneys; He needs disciples! This may come as a shock to you, but the demons have faith! They believe in the existence of God; they are neither atheists nor agnostics! They believe in the deity of Christ. When they met Him they bore witness to His Son-ship (Mark 3:11-12). They believe in the existence of a place of judgment (Luke

8:31), and they recognize Jesus as the Judge (Mark 5:1-13). They submit to the power of God's Word and tremble at it (James 2:19). I can give you ten arguments for God's existence, but ultimately you must come by faith, because that is how God set it up and that is what pleases Him. Enoch walked with God, hand in hand; and Enoch talked with God, face-to-face. Now there are two prayer principles that can help to revolutionize your "**prayer pantry**," and that leads us to our third principle for prayer from Enoch's life:

Enoch lived **for** God and **with** God! In six verses in Genesis 5 the Holy Spirit gives us a brief but blessed biography of Enoch. What could be said about your life in six verses? The repeated statement about Enoch "walking about with *(eth)* God" implies progress (5:22, 24). One step at a time -- you can't take step two or three until you have taken the first step! **Amen**? (Are you still with me?) You can't become a disciple (miniature Christ) until you become a child of God first! *And spiritual progress is dependent upon unbroken communion!* The Hebrew word for walking, as I said, signifies to go on habitually. In fact, the Hebrew word to "walk about" *(yalak)* means "to live!" So progress in holiness was the habit of this ancient saint. We see the result of Enoch's life with God in his witness for God. Before we can be a witness for God, we must live with God. The order can never be reversed; it is of divine appointment! In other words, if you are not living for God, keep your mouth shut. Too much "witness" for God today is mere wood, hay and stubble. To use a few old phrases, "Put up or shut up!" "Put you money where you mouth is!" James must have run into this. James 2:18 deals with these people, *"...Show me your faith without your works and I will show you my faith by my works."*

Listen to the words of Jude talking about Enoch and remember Enoch lived in the days of Noah; *"And Enoch also, the seventh from Adam, prophesied of these, saying, Behold the Lord cometh with ten thousands of His saints, To execute judgment upon all, and to convict all that are ungodly among them of all their ungodly deeds which they have ungodly committed, and of all their hard speeches which ungodly sinners have spoken against him. These are murmurers, complainers, walking after their own lusts; and their mouth speaketh great swelling words, having men's persons in admiration because of advantage." Jude 14-16.*

How much worse could it get? Read Gen. 6:5-6 and you will get a feeling how God felt. Enoch's son Methuselah died the year of Noah's flood. In fact, the name Methuselah implies that Enoch received a direct revelation from God. There are several translations of his name, but the most popular is, "When he is dead, it shall be sent", i.e. the deluge or the flood!

This prophecy in Jude was made about 1,000 years before the flood, before Abraham on Moriah, before Moses on Sinai, before Christ on Calvary. How did he know all this? He lived in daily communion with God and was in the habit of taking long walks alone with God. One day, God just said, "Come on home!" Gen. 5:24 does not conclude with the three words, "…and he died!" When you live in the innermost presence of God, in His sanctuary, He will reveal to you His inner most secrets.

"And he was not, for God took him." Gen. 5:24; The Hebrew word for "he was not" *(enennu)* means he was translated, carried away. Three times in Heb. 11:5 we have the word "translated." The same word is used for Elijah in II Kings 2:1-11. Jewish tradition states that Enoch was born on *Shavuot* (or Pentecost) and was translated on *Shavuot* (or Pentecost). Early church tradition said that "Enoch and Elijah" were the two witnesses in Rev. 11, and that Enoch was a type of the church. How? The Rapture, the *Harpadzo*, the Great Snatch, the Translation! He did not see death! If we are going to be raptured or translated like Enoch, "How should we then live?" To quote the late Dr. Francis A. Schaeffer, like Enoch!

To walk with God you must be reconciled to God, have a similar nature, holy fitness, and a surrendered will. To talk with God you must be a God pleaser. To be a God pleaser you must have faith, because without it, it is impossible to please God.

No, you are absolutely powerless to please God, but remember, without risk, faith is impossible!

To live for God is "to walk about" to "go on habitually" (*yalak*). Spiritual progress is unbroken communion! Enoch, by faith was pleasing God, walking with Him in daily union and communion, going forward on his knees in prayer and living out God's witness! Enoch, along with his life principles, left us three prayer principles in Hebrews 11:6:

1. Wthout faith we are absolutely powerless to please God!
2. We must believe that He is Who He says He is: GOD! The great I AM! The self-existent, all sufficient, all powerful, *"YHVH!"*
3. That He is a rewarder of them that diligently seek *(ek-zeteo)* Him! Search Him out, investigate Him, scrutinize Him, and don't stop!

Kenneth Wuest says, "Diligent seeking finds its reward!" There is the key, "Don't Stop!" Matthew 7:7-11 tells us to ask, seek, knock and don't stop! Keep asking, seeking and knocking until you get an answer. We give up too soon. Look at the example in Luke 11:5-10: "<u>because of his importunity</u>" "<u>to request or beg for urgently</u>" or "<u>to be overly persistent in a request</u>" or "<u>troublesomely urgent, **shameless**</u>." This is the only time this word is used in the Bible, and it's used in **prayer** for a friend. Or Luke 18:1-8 -- so many examples of persistence in **prayer**! We give up way too soon! In James 5:16 you have Elijah's example, and we will get there. I love that old African proverb on prayer, "<u>When you pray, move your feet!</u>" I wonder if that means, "<u>Put feet on your prayers?</u>"

*(**Prayer** - "Abba, Father, help us to be more like Enoch in our prayer walk. May we be reconciled to You. May we be conformed to the image of your Son. May we step back into Your circle and get back into spiritual shape again with "Holy Fitness." And may Your will be our will. LORD, we believe; help Thou our unbelief! In ha Shem Yeshua's Name, we pray. Amen!")*

Principles for Prayer:

- True Faith is believing that God **will** do it; not that God **can** do it.
- If you live in the inner presence of God, He'll reveal His innermost secrets.
- The only time shamelessness is used in the Bible is in reference to praying for a friend.

"Beware in your prayers, above everything else, of limiting God, not only by unbelief, but by fancying that you know what He can or can't do. Expect unexpected things 'above all that we ask or think.'"

Andrew Murray

"Talking & Walking with God" #14
Gen. 6:9

God saw the wickedness of man and was about to destroy everything that breathed on the face of the Earth, *"But Noah found grace (khane) in the eyes of the LORD."* Gen. 6:8. This is the first occurrence of grace in the Bible, and its root means, "to bend or stoop in kindness to an inferior; to favor or bestow." Judgment is getting what we deserve. Grace is getting what we don't deserve. But there is one better: **mercy**. Mercy is **not** getting what we **do** deserve! Now why did Noah (and only Noah, I might add) find grace in the eyes of the LORD? The answer is in the last four words of Gen. 6:9: *"...Noah walked with God."* As with Enoch, you can't walk with God without talking with Him. Adam, Enoch, Noah, Abram, all walked with God, as did Elijah, David, Daniel, and a host of others. Remember the Hebrew word for walk means, "to go on habitually." A habitual progress in holiness *(halak)* is to walk on continually, and be conversant. If you can imagine two friends walking together on a long journey and never conversing, then you can imagine a man walking with God, like Noah, for 500 years and never **praying**! Noah, like Enoch, walked so close to God that God took him and put him in an ark and shut the door!

Notice, if you will, three things about this prayer warrior in v. 9. **First,** he was a just man (*tsadik*): just, lawful, righteous. **Second,** he was a perfect man (*tameem*): integrity, truth, without blemish, complete, without spot. (Noah was a sinner just like us, but obviously he knew God's way and offered sacrifices like Abel not Cain. But he must have been the only one at this point. Remember, only Noah found "GRACE" in the eyes of the LORD.) A good acrostic for GRACE is, "God Rejects All Carnal Effort" or "God's Riches At Christ's Expense." So, how do we find it today? The same way Noah found it then, except we look back to the "CROSS" (the Lamb of God who takes away the sin of the world) and Noah looked forward to it, (Gen. 3:15) God's plan of redemption. Adam knew it, Abel knew it, Seth knew it, Enosh knew it, Noah knew it, but do you know it? **Third,** he walked with God ("to go on habitually").

Is this not what God requires of every man and woman today? Micah 6:8 says, *"...and what doth the LORD require (seek or ask) of thee..."* Three things: **First**, to do justly; **Second**, to love mercy; **Third**, to walk humbly with your God. To do justly, to love mercy, to walk humbly -- sounds like Noah, Enoch, and Abram. A just man, a perfect man, who walked (*eth*) with God, and found grace in the eyes of the LORD. Noah knew God intimately and habitually, and walked and talked with Him; Noah (above all else) was a man of prayer, a man who had sweet, intimate intercourse with the Creator. And God delivered into his hands the world and the total future population. He built an ark, entered in with his family and **God shut the door (Gen. 7:16)** -- not Noah or his sons! We, too, need to be shut in with the Lord. Matthew 6:6 tells us to go into our prayer chamber, shut the door, and pray to our heavenly Father who is already in there waiting for us. To be alone with God in prayer, having private communion and fellowship, just you and the Tri-Unity of the Godhead. What could be better?

(**Prayer** - *"Oh God, may we habitually walk with You, and may You shut us in alone with You daily. May we do justly, may we love mercy and may we walk humbly before, You, Lord. Help us to be like Noah, Enoch, Abram and especially, Jesus! May we walk and talk with You today and every day. In Your Son's name we pray. Amen!"*)

Principles for Prayer:

- May we, like this prayer warrior, be just, lawful, righteous -- a (*tsadik*).
- May we, like this prayer champion, be complete, without spot or blemish, full of truth and integrity.
- May we, like this prayer guardian, walk with You and go on habitually (*yalak*) to live.

"There is no way Christians, in a private capacity, can do so much to promote the work of God and advance the kingdom of Christ as by <u>prayer</u>."

Jonathan Edwards

"Shut Up with God" #15
Gen. 7:16

"...And the LORD shut him in." (Gen 7:16.) What a precious truth! The invitation was from God (v.1), "Come into the ark," NOT "go into the ark." The invitation is such that God was already in the ark and was inviting Noah and his family to join Him inside for the voyage. And the LORD shut him in! We too need to be shut in with the LORD! How can a man like Noah, who walked with God, be shut up with Him and not pray? Impossible! Oh, the sweet communion the two of them must have had -- the fellowship on the ship alone with God. The world's clamor, noise, pull, filth and sin, shut out by God! Imagine, if you can, the sweetness of being shut up alone with the Creator of everything for a year. Just you and Him, alone on a ship together! Oh that's right, he had those animals and his three sons and their wives and his wife, but I'm sure they all got along *hunky-dory* or is it *dunky-hory*. Anyway, back to Noah. The word "shut" (*sawgar*) means "to be shut up," but figuratively it means "to surrender, to give over, to enclose, to shut in oneself, to shut out something or to be shut up together with." I am jealous; how about you? Manure and all!

Oh, to be shut up alone with God in prayer! What ecstasy, what joy, what fellowship! Isn't that what Elisha did with the Shunammite's son in II Kings 4:33? *"He went in...shut the door...and prayed unto the LORD."* And he was brought back to life! What a precious promise of prayer came to Jeremiah when he was "shut up" in the court of the prison in Jer. 33:1 and because of that we have the promise of verses 2 and 3, *"Call unto me, and I will answer thee, and shew thee great and mighty things, which thou knowest not!"* Our part is to call; His part is to answer! Our highest form of service is the ministry of prayer, the ministry of intercession, the ministry of the interior for our fellow man! Jeremiah was shut up alone with Jehovah, *Yahweh*, the *YHWH*, the LORD who made it, the LORD who formed it, the LORD who established it, the LORD is His name. He is the One that gave us that promise. Go ahead, call on His name, I dare you (I double dare you), and see what great and mighty things He will do. "Shut up with the LORD!" What greater joy could there be this side of heaven? None I know of! **Shut up with the Lord!**

In Acts 9:40 Peter went to Dorcas in an upper-room (maybe the upper-room), put everyone out, shut the door, knelt down and prayed. And Dorcas was brought back from the dead! "Shut up alone with God!" I challenge you to take a Bible, a canteen and a blanket; find a cabin, shut the door and wait on God, alone! Our own Lord and Savior Jesus Christ many times was shut up, or shut out alone with His heavenly Father: the Mount of Temptation; the Garden of Gethsemane; the Cross of Calvary; the Garden Tomb. In fact in Matt. 6:6 Jesus Himself gave us instruction concerning prayer. Listen to His words, *"But thou, when thou prayest, enter into thy room (closet, secret chamber, storage pantry) and when thou hast shut thy door, pray to thy Father who is already in the secret place..."*

The word for "closet" (*tamion*) means a chamber on the ground floor of a home generally used for storage or privacy, a secret chamber. And when you have entered your secret chamber, shut the door and pray to your heavenly Father who is already in the secret place waiting for you, to reward you openly. Noah was a just man and a perfect man who walked humbly with his God and was shut in with his God on a ship for a year. I'm sure he prayed much with Him and had continual, habitual communion with his Creator. How's yours?

*(**Prayer** - "Oh LORD God, Creator of Heaven and Earth, help us to find a secret place, a private place, a storage chamber to fill our hearts and minds with your power and presence." And after entering into it may we shut the door and lock it from the inside shutting You, Lord in alone with us. And may we enter into that sweet, sweet communion with You. In the sweet and holy name of Your Son, Jesus Christ we pray, Amen!")*

Principles for Prayer:

- Our highest form of service is the ministry of intercession, the ministry of the interior.

- Just like Noah, the LORD is inviting you into your closet, Matt. 6:6. He's already in there waiting.
- Just like Jer. 33 tells us, our part is to call/pray; His part is to answer – and He will!

"The Gospel commands the sinner to come and the Christian to go!"
D.L. Moody

"Where's Your Family Altar?" #16
Gen. 8:20

"And Noah built an altar unto the LORD..." Gen. 8:20. The first thing this man who walked with God did when he got off the ark was to build a family altar and worship the God of creation. What's the first thing you do after a long trip in the car: get out, empty the trunk, run for the bathroom, open the house, check the mail, or bow your head and offer a prayer of thanksgiving for traveling mercies to the God of Heaven and Earth? Noah has been shut up with God for over a year in the ark, unable to offer sacrifices. I'm sure he had plenty of prayer time during those 360 days, but he could not sacrifice to his Creator. What a growth period that must have been for him, Amen? Not only do we need to pray, talk to God, we need to worship and sacrifice and walk with God. That's just what this man of God did the minute he stepped off the ark, *"Noah built an altar unto the LORD..."* There are three things that characterize an altar: worship, sacrifice and prayer.

Those three elements are what constitute an altar. What has happened to our family altars? As I said, we get home from a trip, we unpack the ark, get a drink, and call mom. What we should do is pause and praise and thank God (Heb. 13:15), and offer a **"sacrifice of praise"** and thanksgiving to God, the fruit of our lips giving thanks to His name.

A sacrifice calls for death. In the Older Testament it was an animal that died, but in the Newer Testament it is the personal ego that must be slain. We must sacrifice our judgment, opinion, and evaluation of what is right and good and praise God for all things, including the good, the bad and the ugly. And this **"sacrifice of praise"** is incomplete until it is expressed. Noah was in constant communion with God, unbroken fellowship, so it was only natural for him to build an altar and worship God before anything else. Oh, to have a heart after God like that again, to have that fervor and love for God like we did when we first met Him. Can you remember what you were like when you first got saved? Embarrassing, wasn't it? You couldn't stop talking about Jesus, or handing out tracts, and every time the doors were open at church you were there.

Notice Gen. 8:21, *"And the LORD smelled a sweet savour…"* a sweet soothing aroma. It was the smell of wickedness, it was the stench of sin, (Ch. 6) that caused God to be sorry He made man on the Earth. It was the aroma of their evil deeds and thoughts that grieved God's heart. But here from this man of God, He smells a soothing aroma, ahhhh! Is your prayer life a soothing aroma to God? Do your sacrifices, your worship, your altars have a soothing aroma? Meditate on those words for a moment, *"<u>The LORD smelled a soothing aroma.</u>"* Is that really what He smells when you pray, when the angel ignites the incense in your bowl of prayer before the Almighty (Rev. 5:8 & 8:3)?

Do your sacrifices, worship, and altars have a soothing aroma to the Creator, or are they a stinking, pungent stench in His nostrils, an (*odzo*) the odor of a decaying corpse? Our prayers are a picture of the evening incense wafting its way before the nostrils of Almighty God. (Psalm 141:2 -- Read it, meditate on it, chew on it. Write it on the back of your hand in ink.) Better yet, how is your bowl today, empty or full? Oh, how we need to spend time at our altars worshiping, praising, sacrificing, praying, **not because we feel like it or we get thrills**, but because He deserves it and He demands it. And it **can** and it **will** make a difference!

"Something happens when I pray that does not happen when I don't, and it works with mathematical precision!" I don't know who said that first but it works for me. Look at Gen. 6:6-7. Read it and tremble, my friend. God was going to destroy man and beast from off the face of the Earth. He was grieved that He created them, **GREIVED!** But Gen. 7:21 says, *"And the LORD smelled a sweet savor (a soothing aroma) and the LORD said in his heart, I will not again curse the ground any more for man's sake."* Hallelujah! I can't help but think of II Chron. 7:14 in this context. Think of America, think of my church – your church, think of my family – your family, think of <u>my pitiful prayer life and your prayer life</u>.

*(**Prayer** - "Oh God, hear us, help us, heal us, teach us, show us, lead us, walk with us, talk with us, so we might talk with You and keep our bowls full. Help us to build family altars again, to offer sacrifices of praise and thanksgiving continually. Let us learn that one man – one woman can make a difference – all the difference in the world with You beside and inside of us. In Jesus' name I pray Father. Amen!")*

Principles for Prayer:

- Not only do we need to pray, talk to God, we need to sacrifice, worship, and walk with God.
- When was the last time you offered a sacrifice of praise to God, the fruit of your lips?
- Our prayers should emit a sweet smelling aroma, not the odor of a decaying corpse.

"I know of nothing that has so impressed me with a sense of importance of praying at all seasons, being much and constantly in prayer, as the thought that it is the principle occupation at this time of our risen Lord and Savior Jesus Christ right now."

Charles Alexander

"God Bless You?" #17
Gen. 9:1

Excuse me, did someone sneeze? Oh, that's not a tag-line, it is actually a prayer and a very powerful, valuable one at that! *"So God blessed (barak) Noah and his sons, and said unto them, Be fruitful and multiply, and replenish the Earth."* Gen. 9:1. In Gen. 1 remember God blessed the animals and man, and in Gen. 2, God blessed the Sabbath, but in Gen. 7 & 8 God destroyed everything that had breath on the face of the Earth, except for what was in the ark.

So, now God re-institutes His blessing (*barak* – to speak or invoke words of divine favor). As I said earlier, a blessing is a prayer and a prayer is a blessing. So, here again God prays for His creation and gives them a sign of the covenant He established with them, *"the bow in the cloud:"* the rainbow." Gen. 9:13.

What a comfort to know we have been blessed by God! In Eph. 1:3 we are reminded that we have been blessed with every spiritual blessing in *"heavenly places in Christ."* We have also been given that same beautiful privilege of blessing others as well. In fact, Noah later (in Gen. 9:25-27) curses Canaan (or Ham) and blesses the LORD, Shem and Japheth. It almost makes you want to cry out with the Psalmist in Psalm 103, *"Bless the LORD, Oh my soul, and all that is within me, bless His holy name."*

Bless the LORD, O my soul! What a privilege to bless not only man but God, not only the creation but the Creator as well. You see this principle, this privilege, given to man by God throughout the rest of the Bible, right through the book of Revelation. In fact the last verse in the Bible is a blessing, *"The grace of our Lord Jesus Christ be with you all. Amen!"* Rev. 22:21.

You can see this beautiful truth and concept continually if you study prayer for yourself throughout the scriptures. The awesome power of prayer; to be able to ask the omnipotent Creator to bless someone and He does, is mind blowing. Why do we use this privilege, this power so little? Why? Noah did it, Abram did it, Melchizedek did it, Eliezer (Abram's servant) did it, Laban did it, etc. This was a common experience in the scriptures. Why have we lost sight of this privilege? May God help us to see what we have lost or are neglecting, and cause us to not only be a blessing but to pray and ask God for a blessing on those we come in contact with.

However, the church is asleep in the midst of this crucial hour. While Christ is in the "Garden of *the Olive Press*" sweating great drops of blood (*hematohidrosis*) His disciples are asleep, Luke 22:45. Why? What is the reason or the chief cause of the church's prayerlessness at this critical time? Many reasons could be suggested I suppose, but the chief one is, lack of faith in the integrity of God's Word. **IF** we were really convinced that what He said in His Word was true, I believe we would pray more. Like John 14:14, *"If ye shall ask anything in my name, I will do it."* Matt. 7:7, *"Ask, and it shall be given you; seek and ye shall find; knock and it shall be opened unto you."* Jer. 33:3, *"Call unto me, and I will answer thee and show thee great and mighty things which thou knowest not."*

If we really believed the promises in God's Word, prayer would be the main business of the Church today, not programs, not missions, not economics, not culture, not busyness. "Unbelief" is another main cause of **prayerlessness**. And this unbelief is so deep-rooted in our hearts and minds today we are not even conscious of it, but it is exposed by the feeble, anemic prayer life of the Church and Christians today. *"What, could ye not watch with Me one hour?"* (Matt. 26:40). Oh how it would change the world we live in if we all showed up for prayer meeting, to pray! That's why He asked them to watch, Matt. 26:41, *"Watch and pray..."* The spirit is willing but the flesh -- oh that flesh is so weak! That is why He says we need to pray, my friend! The flesh is so weak!

(**Prayer** - *"Blessed art Thou, Oh LORD our God, Creator of Heaven and Earth. Truly You and You alone are worthy and deserving of all* our praise, all our worship, and all our blessings. Oh Lord, truly bless our families, our churches, the nation of Israel, our nation, and our ministries. Bless those, Oh LORD, that we come in contact with today and every day, and bless Your chosen Jewish people and the Bride of Christ and make us a blessing today." In Jesus' precious Name. Amen!)

Principles for Prayer:

- What a privilege to bless not only the creation but the Creator as well.
- Lack of faith in the integrity of His Word is a chief cause of prayerlessness.
- Prayer is undoubtedly man's greatest obligation and yet it's the one most neglected.

D.L. Moody was the founder and director of Moody Bible Institute in Chicago, IL, and he was a far greater prayer warrior than an evangelist or preacher. The man who followed him was R.A. Torrey, and the man who followed Torrey was Charles Alexander (a hymn writer, but a far greater prayer warrior). I attended MBI from 1976 – 1979 and could still feel their prayers as I walked the halls.

R.T.B.

"Personal Piety for Prayer" #18
Gen. 6-9

As we said previously, Keil points out that there are three elements of Noah's story in Gen. 6-9: his piety, his preservation and his proclamation. However, we need to concentrate on the first element, "Noah's personal piety of godliness," for an **effective prayer life**. This first principle is found in Gen. 6; *"Noah found grace in the eyes of the LORD."* This is the first time in the Bible the word "grace" is used. Notice its context: Gen. 6:5-8, where it grieved God that He made man and anticipated his total annihilation. Once again we have the "law of first mention."

Noah found *(masa)* favor in another's eyes, namely God's. The idea is to gain acceptance or win approbation. Noah found grace *(khan)* in the eyes of the LORD -- grace, favor, mercy, pity, acceptance; unmerited, unwarranted, undeserved favor! Moses found grace in the eyes of the LORD in Exodus 33:13, right after the golden calf, before he was put into the cleft of a rock.

Listen, justice is getting what we deserve. You are doing 90 in a 50 and a trooper gives you a ticket; that's justice. Grace is getting what we don't deserve. You are doing 90 in a 50. The trooper pulls you over and gives you a warning; that's grace. Mercy is not getting what we do deserve, you are doing 90 in a 50. The trooper pulls you over. His captain is standing next to him. He writes you a ticket for $200.00, reaches in his wallet, takes out $200.00, hands it to you to pay the ticket and tells you to slow down. Now that's mercy!

That's what Jesus did for us. He reached in His wallet and paid our fine, let us nail Him to a cross for our violations and said, **"Forgiven!"** The first principle from Noah's life for our prayer life is finding grace in the eyes of the LORD! Question: have you found it? If not, you can't pray for things or people or events -- only salvation! If you have not found grace in the eyes of the LORD the only prayer you can utter from your heart to God's heart is, "**LORD, save me**!"

Eph. 2:8 says, *"For by grace are ye saved through faith..."* Eph. 1:7 says, *"In whom we have redemption through his blood, the forgiveness of sins, according to the riches of his grace."* This grace, this gift of God, provides us with a transition into the following tragedy, namely, "The Flood!" By the way, Dads, listen up! Only Noah found grace in the eyes of the LORD. His family rode in on his boat tails! So the first principle for prayer from Noah was his piety, his godliness. He found grace in the eyes of the LORD in the midst of a wicked, wicked, wicked world!

The second principle is: "Noah was a just man." The word for "just" *(tsa-dek)* means righteous, just, lawful in conduct and character. The root of this word is to be straight, not deviating from the standard. Noah was the *"heir of righteousness by faith."* Heb. 11:7. Psalm 145:17 says, *"The LORD is righteous (Tsadek) in all his ways, and holy in all his works."* This word describes three aspects of our personal relationships: 1 – Ethical (ourselves); 2 – Legal (others); 3 – Theocratic (God).

In the supreme sense, the righteous man is one who serves God (Mal. 3:18). Noah was righteous in his moral relation and service to God. Whom do we serve? In Ezek. 14:14 & 20, Noah, Daniel, and Job are declared to be righteous *(tsadek)*. Question: if you were put on trial for being a just man or woman, would they have enough evidence to convict you? A just man gives freely without regard for gain, Psalm 37:21. Do you need a tax receipt for every gift you give to the Lord's work? Listen, righteous conduct can only be secured by plowing up fallow, dormant, inactive ground, sowing in righteousness and reaping in mercy. That is making a new foundation for righteousness, for *(tsadek)* Hos. 10:12.

Where are you today? Are you "JUST" ethically, legally, and theocratically? Or do you need some prayer in those areas today? Noah found grace *(khan)* and Noah was just *(tsadek)* -- two very important principles for our prayer lives.

However, there is a third principle that is missing in politics, religion, the home, marriage, our military, Wall Street and Main Street today. Gen. 6:9 says *"Noah was perfect (tameem – complete) ..."* The root *(tam)* refers to integrity. Some might say,"I have found grace." Others will say, "I guess I am just." But this third thing: **integrity** -- what's that?

Webster (in 2005) said, "Integrity is a firm adherence to a code, especially of moral values; incorruptibility; an unimpaired condition; soundness; the quality or state of being complete or undivided." Listen to Webster in 1828, "Wholeness, entireness, unbroken state; the entire, unimpaired state of anything, particularly of the mind; moral soundness or purity; in-corruptness; uprightness; honesty; integrity comprehends whole moral character but has a special reference to uprightness in mutual dealings for others." In 1828 Buckminster wrote, "The moral grandeur of independent integrity is the sublimest thing in nature, before which the pomp of eastern magnificence and the splendor of conquest are odious as well as perishable."

Where is that kind of integrity today? What has happened to it? Amos 5:10 says, *"They hate him that rebuketh in the gate, and they abhor him that speaketh uprightly (tameem – with integrity)."* That was Noah for 120 years! Brown, Driver, Briggs said of this word, "What is complete, entirely in accord with truth and fact." II Peter 1:5 says we are to add to our faith "virtue" *(aretay* -- moral excellence and purity in feeling and action. In this chapter, Peter lists seven things to add to your faith, but the first is *(tameem)* integrity/virtue, moral purity in action and feeling. What has happened to our leadership and society?

What did Noah do for 120 years besides build a huge boat? Preach righteousness to a sin cursed world. Peter calls him a, *"preacher of righteousness"* in II Peter 2:5. Note, if you will, in Gen. 6:9 there is no conjunction connecting "just and perfect" so it would be better written, "Noah was a, righteous-perfect man" *(Tsadek-Tameen).* This compound indicates a phrase or double expression covering a state of perfection as nearly as man can accomplish it. Let me say this: divine approval on God's part does not imply perfection on man's part. It merely implies that those things that God sought in man were present in Noah. God simply desired for man to believe Him and His promise of salvation through the seed of a woman, and Noah did!

Noah found grace in the eyes of the LORD. Noah was a just man *(tsadek)*. Noah was perfect *(tameem)* complete. Noah walked with *(eth)* God. Noah talked with God (you can't walk with God for 450 years and not talk with Him). However, there are many ways to communicate; <u>speech is only one of them, and the least of all</u>. In fact, you never find Noah speaking one time in Gen. 6-9 until Ham's sin in Gen. 9:25, but his walk was so close he didn't need words. How is yours?

A lot of things impress me with Noah:

1. The fact that he preached for 120 years and no one got saved (would you still support him?)
2. His obedience to God in light of his huge task (Gen. 6:22 says, *"Thus did Noah; according to all that God commanded him, so did he."*)
3. His righteousness, his integrity, his walk with God, his persistence!

But the thing that impresses me the most is, after spending a year on that boat with all those animals and complaining kids, the first thing he does when he gets off the ark Gen. 8:20 is <u>build an altar and worship God and pray with his family</u>. That blows my mind! He doesn't call his mother, get a beer, kiss the ground, unload the trunk, or hit the men's room. He builds an altar and prays! What is the first thing you do after a long journey? What's the first thing you should do? **PRAY!** The altar speaks of three things: <u>prayer, sacrifice & worship</u>. And listen: the altar **preceded** the rainbow (Gen. 9:13).

Noah's Principles for Prayer

- Are you just? Do you ethically, legally and theocratically believe God? That will impact our prayer life.
- Peter says, "add to your faith virtue." (2 Peter 1:5). Noah did that in Gen 6:9 – a righteous perfect man.

*(**Prayer** - "Father, help us to remember You at the end of our journeys, not just at the beginnings. We pray for "traveling mercies," never realizing how many dangers, perils and hazards You spared us from. We have learned much from Noah today. May we find grace in Your eyes and mercy at Your throne. Thank You for sending Jesus to pay for our ticket in full." In His name we pray. Amen!)*

Principles for Prayer:

- Noah found **grace** and Noah was **just**: two very important principles for our prayer lives.
- Divine approval on God's part does not imply perfection on man's part.
- Integrity in prayer means "what is complete, entirely in accord with truth and fact."

"The great battles, the battles that decide our destiny and the destiny of generations yet unborn are not fought on public platforms, but in the lonely hours of the night and in moments of agony on our knees in our prayer closets alone."

Samuel L. Brengle

"Building Your Family Altar" #19
Gen. 12:7

We have talked about Adam the garden tiller, Enoch the God pleaser, and Noah the ship builder. Now we turn our attention to Abraham the altar builder. God created man *(adom)* in His own image, after His own likeness; and Adam walked and talked with God bare-naked in the garden, Gen. 2:25. That is until he ate the forbidden fruit; until he disobeyed God's commandment; until he rebelled against God; until he lied to God and hid from Him; until he refused to confess his sin and blamed his wife! But Adam taught us three things in the garden *(gan)*, "the enclosed place," about prayer before the fall (Gen. 3:8-10):

1. He knew the place, why? He was accustomed to it!
2. He knew the voice, why? He was accustomed to it!
3. He knew the time, why? He was accustomed to it!

Adam and Eve were cast from the garden and gave birth to Cain and Abel. Cain slew Abel and was marked. Then Adam and Eve bore Seth and he fathered Enosh, which means "mortal." In Gen. 4:26 we have the first mention of prayer in the Bible, and it began with Enosh. *"...then began men (mortal man) to call upon the name of the LORD."* (**YHVH** – the GOD of redemption) Very Important!

Then came Enoch, the seventh from Adam, who walked and talked with *(eth)* God for 300 years; and he was not, for God took him. Gen. 5:21-24, (A pre-rapture rapture, the Hebrew word is "translated"). From Enoch we learned three things about prayer in Heb. 11:6-7, along with his life, three life principles: 1) he walked with God; 2) he talked with God; and 3) he lived **with** and **for** God!

Without faith *(pistis* – noun) we are absolutely powerless to please God. We must believe *(pisteuo* – verb) that God is Who He says He is; and we must believe that He is a rewarder of them that diligently *(ek-zeteo)* seek Him. The keys to Enoch are faith, believe, trust, and confidence, etc. Enoch was a God pleaser, not a man pleaser; and that is the key to "E.F.P.," an, "**Effectual Fervent Prayer" life**.

Then we talked about *No-akh* the ship builder, a man who *(eth)* "with God walked" for 450 years; and we learned three more principles for prayer for this godly man:

1. "*No-akh* found grace *(khan)* in the eyes of the LORD"
2. *No-akh* was a just man *(tsa-deek)* righteous, lawful in conduct and character. In fact, he was the heir of righteousness by faith (Heb. 11:7)
3. **No-akh** was perfect *(ta-meem)* -- a man of impeccable integrity and a preacher of righteousness (II Peter 2:5)

Three things you and I must have, to have "E.F.P." with God:

1. **Grace**, unmerited, undeserved, unwarranted favor;
2. **Righteousness**, ethically, judicially and theocratically;
3. **Integrity**, moral purity of mind, body and spirit (II Pet. 1:5) add to you faith "virtue."

As Micah 6:8 puts it, *"**Do justly** ...**love mercy**, and ...**walk humbly** with thy God."* Adam, Enoch, and Noah were men of faith, men of prayer, men who literally walked and talked, face-to-face *(paw-neem)* with their Creator God. (Not to mention Enosh – mortal man, who began to call on the name of the LORD.)

Now we come to Abram or Abraham, the father of a multitude, the founder of the Hebrew nation, the first Jew, the friend of God, and the father of the patriarchs. There are many types of Christ in the scriptures, but Abraham is the only type of God the Father. I don't know how you remember this Bible character, but let me offer you one suggestion: **Abraham the altar builder!** Everywhere he went, God had an altar! Matthew Henry said of this friend of God, "Wherever he had a tent, God had an altar, and an altar sanctified by prayer." I like that! Gen. 12:7 says, *"And the LORD appeared unto Abram, and said, Unto thy seed will I give this land: and there builded he an* *altar unto the LORD, who appeared unto him."* The Hebrew word for altar is *(miz-bay-akh)* a slaughter place, from the root *(zaw-bakh)* to slaughter, to kill, to sacrifice; *(miz-bay-akh)* is simply the place to do it. This is typical of the fact that the only way to God is through the sprinkled blood of a sacrifice, picturing the blood of His Redeemer, *Yeshua/Jesus.*

But why build or establish an altar? Remember *No-akh* built an altar in Gen. 8:20 when he got off the ark with his family and offered burnt offerings to God. But you say, "The book of Leviticus was not written yet to tell him how to do it and besides, was he a priest?" Was Job, or Isaac, or Jacob? How about Abel in Gen 4:4? He brought the fat of the firstlings of his flock to God on an altar *(miz-bay-akh)*. How did Abel know how to do all this? Ready for this great biblical secret? <u>His father Adam taught him</u>!

The "altar" *(miz-bay-akh)* indicates that from the earliest times "sacrifice" *(saw-bakh)* accompanied prayer and worship; it's a trilogy! Here is Abram (exalted father) building or establishing an altar in Shechem by the plain *(el-own)* oak or tree of Moreh. I don't believe this was his first one, do you? He didn't need instructions, like Noah with his ark. The very next verse he moves to Bethel and the first thing he does is build an altar for <u>prayer, worship and sacrifice</u>, (Gen. 12:8). Bethel on the west, "the house of God" and Ai or Hai on the east, "ruin or heap, translated bald or hard."

Question: <u>Are you between God and a hard place right now</u>, between Bethel and Ai? Then you need to build an altar for prayer, sacrifice and worship! Abram built or established an altar "to the Lord." Why? To call upon the name of the LORD (v. 8.)! Let me spell it out for you in case you are having difficulty with this. Why did Abram build an altar? For **P-R-A-Y-E-R**! Who is with him when he builds his altar in Shechem? Sarai, Lot and Abram's household servants. Let's sum it up in one word: his **FAMILY**! Who is with him when he builds an altar between Bethel and Ai? One word: his, **FAMILY**! Who was with *No-akh* when he built an altar in Gen. 8:20? His wife, his sons (Shem, Ham and Japtheth), and their wives -- his **FAMILY**! Are you getting the same picture I am getting? Just about every time an altar is built to God in this book, it is for corporate **FAMILY WORSHIP**! Question: how is your **FAMILY ALTAR?** Do you even have one anymore? Mine is missing quite a few stones. Always keep one thing in mind: an altar is a place for three things: **Prayer** – **Sacrifice** – **Worship**! It is not a place for an indepth Bible study, a game of life or monopoly, or a family play-time. It's a time for **Prayer** – **Sacrifice** – **Worship**, and those three things cost -- COST! Got it? Good! Now build one!

(Prayer - "Father, we have been negligent, derelict, in our family altars, please forgive us and help us to rebuild them stone by stone! Only You can ignite that fire once again. And may it ever be burning on the altars of our hearts and may it never, ever go out again. We bow before You in shame and disgrace with no right to call You Abba, Father, but for the blood of Your Son Yeshua/Jesus, Who died on a cross to give us access into your throne room. Oh, God, hear the anguish of my heart, catch the tears from my eyes. I know You must feel the pain in my soul, so restore unto me the joy of Thy salvation and hold me in Your hand." In Jesus' name! Amen!)

Principles for Prayer:

- Without faith we are absolutely powerless to please God and pray to Him.
- The key to Effectual Fervent Prayer is to be a God pleaser, not a man pleaser.
- Matthew Henry said of Abraham, "Wherever he had a tent, God had an altar sanctified by prayer."

"The devil is not afraid of machinery; he is only afraid of God, and machinery without prayer is machinery without God! There is only one limit to what prayer can do, and that is what God can do!"
So prayer is omnipotent!

R.A. Torrey

"Failure under Fire" #20
Gen. 12:10-20

Abram slips in Gen. 12:10-20. He fails under fire and forsakes the place of the LORD's blessings. Why do we do that? Especially those in ministry? Famine strikes and down to Egypt *(Miz-rai-im)* he goes. He tells a half lie (which is a whole lie), that Sarai is his sister. They both have the same father (Gen. 20:12), but she is still his wife, and she is 60+ years old and beautiful. ☺ So they pick up Hagar as a handmaid (possibly one of Pharaoh's daughters -- bad news). Egypt sounds more like "misery-im" than *Mizraim*." Why is it when we fall, we forsake God, His Word, His people, His place of blessing, and **prayer**? Why? Conviction, sin, guilt! But you know what is great? The return trip! Amen? Because God is always right where we left Him! He never moves. (Rev. 2:4 says, "**You** left your first love;" He didn't! **You** stepped out of the circle. He didn't!

Now watch this: in Gen. 13:1-4, Abram, his wife, Lot, and all that he has return right back to the place where his tent had been at the beginning; to the place where he made the altar, between Bethel and Ai. And who is with him? **His family!** *"And there Abram called on the name of the LORD."* Listen, *failure isn't fatal; quitting is!* Back to Bethel! Back to the house of God! Back to Prayer! Back to the God he left! Back to the family altar! Back to the Bible! By the way, Abram never built an altar in *Mizraim* – Egypt, never! I wonder why. God was still waiting; He never left Bethel! Abram did. He came full circle and so must we, Amen? (Rev. 2:4; Matt. 6:6.) He left his first love. What was the first thing Abram did when he got back to Bethel? He prayed! He called upon the name of the LORD! Sounds like Enosh in Gen. 4:26.

Prayer is simply an address or petition to God by word or thought, simply talking to God; don't make it difficult. God never intended it to be. **Sacrifice** is simply the act of offering something precious to God, whether it is time, talents or treasures; and again don't make it difficult or expensive. It's the thought that counts (just don't make it an after thought). **Worship** is simply to honor, reverence, or venerate a divine being. It's a human response to divine revelation. Why is it at church we sing, have announcements, sing, take the offering, sing, then preach (divine revelation), give an invitation and go eat chicken? Shouldn't we preach first, receive the divine revelation, and then spend the rest of the time worshiping God in response to His divine revelation? Just a thought!

Who is with Abram back at Bethel, back at the altar he built? **"His family!"** Implant that thought in your heart and mind. The altar is for Family – Prayer, Worship, Sacrifice. By the way, where is Shechem? The West Bank! Bethel? The West Bank! Ai? The West Bank! Hebron? The West Bank! They are all in what the Bible calls the mountains of Israel in Ezk. 36:1;4; 6;8, which Jehovah promised to Abraham, Isaac, Jacob and their descendants.

Now we move into Gen. 13:14-18, and it would do you well to read that passage a couple of times. Verse 15 says, *"For all the land which thou seest, to thee will I give it, and to thy seed forever."* Who is talking? **Jehovah**! Who is He talking to? **Abram**! How long is this promise for? **Forever**! *(olam)*. Can God break a covenant promise? **NO**!

The first thing Abram does when he moves into a new neighborhood is to build an altar for family worship! Abram builds this altar between *Mamre* (Hebrew for strength and fatness) and *Hebron* (Hebrew for communion, association, to unite or bind together). How beautiful is that? The family altar is a place to grow strong and fat in the LORD, and to unite or bind yourselves together and commune with the LORD. "The family that prays together," (WHAT?) "stays together." What is the first thing you do when you move into a new neighborhood? Join the YMCA? Have a party? Find a Wal-Mart? The first thing Noah did when he disembarked from the ark was to build an altar for family worship. By the way, who is with Abram in Hebron? His family (less his nephew Lot), right! Genesis 13 is a picture of "The Spiritual Man" (Abraham) vs. "The Carnal Man" (Lot).

In Gen. 14, Lot takes his possessions, servants and cattle and goes to Sodom, which was like the *"garden of the LORD,"* Gen. 13:10 (the Garden of Eden). There is no mention of Lot having a wife before he went into Sodom, only after he came out; so it is very possible he married a Sodomite, which would explain a lot about Lot. Maybe that is why Mrs. Lot longed to go back, and Mr. Lot lost two of his daughters to that wicked, sinful lifestyle. Genesis 19:26 says that Mrs. Lot looked back. The word "looked" *(na-bat)* means to gaze upon, to consider, to long for. However, in Luke 17:32 the context seems to infer that she didn't just glance back; she turned back to return to the city. Then Abram had to take 318 of his men to rescue Lot from four kings at Hobah and Damascus. The key, I believe, is in Gen. 14:13; 15:2; and his name is Eliezer (El-ezer) "God's helper," who becomes Abram's most trusted servant.

Abram meets Melchizedek, king of Salem, and pays him tithes of all, 720 years before the law. How did he know? Adam, Abel, Enoch, Noah, etc., did it. If **10%** bothers you give **12%** or **14%**, but you will never out give God, never! Why did Abram give tithes to Melchizedek? Because he knew he had the power to bless him, that's why! *Melek* means king, *Tsadek* means righteousness -- the "King of Righteousness." The ancient Rabbis believe this was Shem, Noah's son. You will find Melchizedek three times in the Scriptures: Gen. 14:18 (historically); Psalm 110:4 (prophetically); and Hebrews 5:6 (doctrinally). [Have fun – great study!]

I love Psalm 110. *Yeshua/Jesus* used it to silence the mouths of the Scribes and Pharisees when they questioned His deity. But v.7 says, *"He shall drink of the brook (mud-puddle) in the way..."* He came to this stinking Earth and drank out of our mud-puddle! Can you fathom that?

Lot never built an altar in Sodom, Never! He lost two daughters to the world, two to incest, two sons-in-law to hell, and a wife to lust and covetousness. She didn't glance back; she lusted, longed after and turned back. Abram also never built one in Egypt, and look at the trouble he is about to face. How is your altar? Have you bought some bricks, some mortar and a trowel? Have you started to build it yet? Don't wait for trouble to start; because it will come, as sure as sparks fly upward, and the cement won't have time to dry. So start now, right now -- today!

*(**Prayer** - "Abba, Father, it is hard for us to comprehend why You allowed Your Son to come to this Earth and drink from our mud-puddle, when we all deserve to drown in it. But when we see your unfathomable grace in the life of Abram, who ran and lied, but came back to the "House of God," to the altar he built, and You were patiently waiting with open arms to receive him and restore him, our faith is rekindled. Father, open Your arms, draw us to Your bosom, hold us ever so close, that we may smell the fragrance of Your robes." In Jesus' name! Amen!)*

Principles for Prayer:

- Why is it that when we fall or backslide, we forsake our prayer-life? Why, God, why?
- Prayer is simply an address or petition to God by word, note or thought!
- Remember: don't wait for trouble to build your altar; the cement won't have time to dry!

> *"If we are going to have fellowship with our Lord and Savior Jesus Christ in His present work in Heaven, we have to spend much time in prayer. We must give ourselves to earnest, persistent, sleepless, overcoming prayer"*
>
> *Charles Alexander*

"Look Up & Say Amen!" #21
Gen. 15:6

In Genesis 15, Abram had a vision, but we don't like to talk about those in fundamental circles today. So, let's call it a **"D.M.I."** a "dynamic mental impression." Gen. 15:2, I believe, is a prayer, *"And Abram said, "Lord GOD (Adonai Yehovah). what wilt Thou give me, seeing I go childless, and the steward (heir) of my house is this Eliezer of Damascus* (a Gentile)*?"* In Gen. 15:6, we have the affirmation of his faith in the LORD, *"And he believed in the LORD; and He counted it to him for righteousness."* The word for "believed" in Hebrew is *(Aw-mane) - t*o verify, confirm, or agree with heartily. How we need the Amen of faith today, especially in prayer. Martin Luther said, **"And make your Amen strong!"** The object of Abram's faith was God Himself. Abraham was called "the friend of God," (II Chron. 20:7; Isa. 41:8; James 2:23, *"And the scripture was fulfilled which saith, Abraham believed God, and it was imputed unto him for righteousness: and he was called the Friend of God"*).

It would be important for you to read Gen. 15:7-21, where GOD cuts a covenant with Abraham, and not the other way around. This covenant is permanent and unconditional; Abraham is asleep. He simply prepares the animals by killing most of them and splitting them apart, three of the five (v. 9 *"Take me an heifer of three years old, and a she-goat of three years old, and a ram of three years old, and a turtle dove, and a young pigeon."*). Five animals representing the five offerings of Leviticus -- and a pillar of smoke and a pillar of fire passed between them (v.17). And v.18 *"In the same day the LORD made a covenant with Abram."* An unconditional, eternal covenant for the land from the river of Egypt, the *"Wadi-el Arish,* to the Euphrates, not the Nile River. A river just south of *Kadesh-barnea* in the Gaza strip. This is just a reconfirmation of Gen. 13:14-15. What a chapter! You have prayer in v. 2, sacrifice in v. 10, and worship in vv. 17-18" at the altar by Mamre (fatness) in Hebron (communion). **Prayer – Sacrifice – Worship** -- all at an altar Abraham built. In chapter

16, Sarai's scheme with Hagar fails. In chapter 17, Abram's name is changed to Abraham, "father of a multitude" and Sarai's name is changed to Sarah, "princess, or noble woman." In chapter 18, three men show up to dine with Abraham and reveal the LORD's plans for Sodom's destruction (two angels and the LORD Himself). In chapter 19, Sodom and Gomorrah are destroyed and Lot and his two daughters are rescued. In chapter 20, Abraham has another lapse in Gerar, and lies about Sarah once again (and this time she is 90 and still very beautiful). Abraham has to **pray** for Abimelech or God won't heal him and his people. God is limited many times by our prayers, or man's blessings are dependent upon our prayers (we will come back to this). Abimelech is innocent, but God is just!

In Gen. 21, after Abraham's lapse in Gerar, lots of things happen. Isaac is born, Hagar is cast out, and Abraham settles in Beer-Sheba. Now it does not specifically mention the word "altar" here, but I believe it is specifically implied! **First** – a covenant is cut, implying the sacrifice of animals! **Second** – Abraham plants a grove and calls upon the name of the LORD, "*El Olam*" the "Everlasting God" implying prayer! **Third** – Jacob, Abraham's grandson, offers a sacrifice in Beer-sheba (the well of seven oaths) on his way to Egypt to meet Joseph after 22 years, implying worship in Gen. 46:1! I believe Abraham built the altar after Abimelech and Phicol left. He built it for prayer, sacrifice and worship! Why? Because he was going to live there with his family for many days (v. 34). In fact, I believe all the rest of his days. His first concern was God, then his family, but especially his family worshiping his God. Who is with him? Sarah, Isaac, Eliezer and his servants -- his **family!**

Abraham's last altar is in Gen. 22 on Mt. Moriah (*Ra-ah* means to see and *Yah* means Jehovah). We will deal with this later, but here he offers his greatest sacrifice, his only *(ya-chid)* beloved son, Isaac. Question: how is your family altar coming? Do you have one yet? What are you waiting for, a special invitation? God invites us to build or establish a family altar, just like our prayer closet or quiet time, and He is waiting for an R.S.V.P. (which is an acrostic for the French phrase, **répondez s'il vous plaît**. However, God's R.S.V.P. for your family altar stands for, "**R**-ead, **S**-hare, **V**-enerate (worship), **P**-ray." Listen, a family altar may keep your children from being sucked into this world's system, or your spouse from falling into immorality, sin, pornography, or covetousness. Or it may prevent you from losing your focus, your purpose or calling in life. From the moment Abraham entered the Promised Land, God had an altar, and an altar sanctified by prayer, sacrifice and worship: Shechem, Bethel, Ai, Hebron, Beer-sheba, Moriah, etc. A time and place to bring those you love the most, your family, for prayer, sacrifice and worship. Don't make it difficult or long: "K.I.S.S." – "Keep It Simple, Sam." And "RSVP" (Read, Share, Venerate, Pray) -- and do it every day!

(***Prayer*** - *"Almighty God, Creator of the heavens and the Earth. Abraham looked up and saw Your splendor and said, "Amen!" because the heavens declare Your glory and the firmament shows Your handiwork. And You counted it to him for righteousness. Abba, as we gaze upon and accept the "Cross of Calvary," may we see Your glory fulfilled in Jesus, The Christ, and receive His righteousness for our righteousness."* In ha Shem Yeshua we pray! Amen!)

Principles for Prayer:

- How we need the Amen of faith today in prayer. As Martin Luther said, "Make it strong!"
- Man's blessings are dependent on prayers, and God is limited by them many times.
- A Gentile has been used many times in history to rescue God's chosen people. Eliezer is one example.

"When the fog settles on a ship, the top-mast is clear. Then a sailor goes aloft to see what the helmsman can't. So, prayer sends the soul aloft, to give us a chance to see which way to steer."

C. H. Spurgeon

"Shaalu Shalom Yerushalayim" #22
(Pray for Jerusalem's Peace)
Gen. 12:1-3

Genesis 12:1: *"Now the LORD had said unto Abram..."* There is no indication here that Abraham was in prayer: However, Abraham must have been a man of prayer, and a man of God before he left Haran. Terah, Abraham's father, was originally on his way to Canaan with his family from Ur of the Chaldeans when he stopped in Haran, dwelt there and died. He had to die for Abraham to become the patriarch of the family and finish leading his family into Canaan. But was God directing Terah with his family first? Could he have gotten the call before Abraham? We will never know, but who taught Abraham about the one and only true God, how to address that God and please Him, worship Him and serve Him? The LORD appears to Abraham (or Abram) after Terah dies in Haran, when Abram is 75 years old. Genesis 12:4: *"So, Abram departed, as the LORD had spoken unto him; and Lot went with him..."* How or why Abram received and responded to God's covenant invitation is not revealed, but we do know that he had to recognize God's call! He was 75 when he got his call, and Moses was 80 when he got his; and we think we are too old to serve God. I was 75 when I thought I would retire. What a joke! I'm busier now than I ever was. You want to make God laugh? Tell Him your plans!

Abraham is listed with the heroes of the faith in Hebrews 11; he is a God pleaser (Heb. 11:6), like Enoch -- a man of faith, a man of God, and a man of prayer. The LORD gave Abraham a seven-part promise in Gen. 12:2-3, *"And I will make of thee a great nation, and I will bless thee, and make thy name great; and thou shalt be a blessing: And I will bless them that bless thee, and curse him that curseth thee: and in thee shall all the families of the Earth be blessed."* What a precious promise from the LORD, the God of redemption, to Abraham, the father of the Jewish Nation. And remember we said earlier that a blessing was a <u>prayer</u>; and here God promises <u>His prayers, His blessings,</u> on Abraham and his seed.

How do we please God like Enoch, Noah, Abraham, Isaac, Jacob, Moses, Joshua, David, etc? Hebrews 11:6 - by the exercise of our faith! I Cor. 1:21 says that preaching the gospel brings salvation. Isa. 53:10 tells us that it pleased the LORD to bruise His Son. The atonement for our sins pleases God. Isa. 55:10-11 says that His Word going forth pleases Him because it produces life. Preach, teach, **pray**, give, go, serve; but we must leave room for God to work. We must give Him "elbow room," (like Abraham did) to break in and do His work in our lives. Seek the kingdom first. It is our Father's good pleasure to give us the kingdom Luke 12:32, but we must be careful where our heart is, because that is where our treasure is. We must pray, "LORD, help me to keep my priorities straight, to focus on You, to seek Your kingdom, **to pray**, '<u>Thy kingdom come, Thy will be done, in Heaven, as it is in Earth</u>!' And in my heart and life as well!"

Psalm 69:30-31 says that praise, thanksgiving and a song pleases the LORD more than an ox and a bull. Proverbs 16:7 says that when a man's ways please the LORD, he even makes his enemies be at peace with him. We must pray, according to Psalm 19:14, "Father, help me; show me the way I should walk and talk, so the meditation of my heart and the words of my mouth will be acceptable and well pleasing to You."

In Genesis chapters 1-11, we have the history of the human race, about 2,000+ years; and beginning in Gen. 12:5 we have His-story of how the Jewish race began for about the next 400+ years. Meditate on this principle for a moment, "I will bless (<u>pray for</u>) those who bless (<u>pray for</u>) you." God is referring to the great nation He would make out of the loins of Abraham, Isaac and Jacob: Israel, the Jewish people! If we bless them [*(ba-rak)* to kneel, by implication to bless God as an act of adoration or man as a benefit], then God promises to bless us. But if we curse them [*(kaw-lal)* to be or make light of, or to bring into contempt, to despise, to lightly esteem], then God promises to curse [*(aw-rar)* execrate, to bitterly curse, to denounce] us. According to Webster, this word means to detest utterly, to abhor, to abominate, to call down evil upon. Therefore, God says if we only **lightly** esteem the Jewish people, He will utterly and completely detest and hate us. The implications of this principle are earth- shattering, and make me tremble.

Do you pray for and bless the Jewish people, Israel, God's chosen people continually? You do want to be blessed, don't you? You do want to prosper, don't you? Psalm 122:6 says, *"Pray for the peace of Jerusalem: they shall prosper that love thee."* Abraham, as we shall see in v. 7, is a man of prayer; but the question is: are you? And do you pray for God's chosen people habitually? James 2:23 says that Abraham, was called a friend of God. Isa. 41:8 says, *"...the seed [descendants] of Abraham my friend."* The word used for "friend" here is *(ahav)*, the Hebrew word for lover. The same word is used in II Chron. 20:7 when referring to God giving the land of Israel to, *"the seed of Abraham Thy friend (*ahav *– Thy lover) for ever?"* So the two times in the Older Testament when God is referring to His friend, Abraham, He uses the word "ahav – love/lover - to have affection for, to be loved." So how can we be a friend of God's if we are not a friend of Israel's? Impossible. Unthinkable. Improbable. Inconceivable!

(**Prayer** - *"Abba, teach us to pray, to bless those around us, to befriend Your chosen people. Help us to pray continually for the Jewish people, and for the peace of Jerusalem! May we be like faithful Abraham: faithful in worship, faithful in love, faithful in sacrifice, faithful in prayer, faithful to your chosen people, and faithful to the Bride of Jesus Christ." In ha Shem Yeshua, we pray. Amen!*)

Principles for Prayer:

- Pray, give, go, teach, serve, but leave God "elbow room" to work in lives.
- God said in Gen. 12 that He would bless those who bless Israel. Can God lie?
- He also said He will call evil down on those who lightly esteem the "Jewish people."

"I shall count the days not by what I have of new instances of usefulness, but by the times I have been enabled to pray in faith, and to take hold of God."

Andrew Bonar

"Returning Home for Communion"
#23
Gen. 13:4

As I said earlier, I hesitate moving on too quickly away from this "friend of God's" without drawing all the principles for living we possible can from his prayer garden for ours. So, let's see if we can learn anything else from this great patriarch of Israel.

After Abraham built his altars in Shechem and between Bethel and Ai, Gen. 12:9 says he, *"...journeyed, going on still toward the south."* The word, "south or Negev" means dry, and he ends up in Egypt. Another word for Egypt, as we have seen, is *Mizraim* and sounds a lot like our word "misery." Egypt represents the world! Why is it that we so often leave Bethel, leave the house of God, for *Mizraim?* There are no altars in Egypt; only compromise, only half truths, only lies! Finally, Abraham is forced out of Egypt by Pharaoh himself (he did not go willingly), and he returns to Bethel, "The House of God," and to the altar he built for his family at first. There is an old saying, "What goes around, comes around." Many times we have to return to the place where we left God, or left off serving God, or left off growing for God. Jacob's grandson will do exactly the same thing in Gen. 28 and 35. When we run from God He will always try to bring us back, and usually succeeds, usually! If our big, fat ego doesn't get in His way. (Ego stands for "Edging God Out")

There is no mention of prayer, altars, sacrifice or worship of God from when Abraham left Bethel until he returns. It is impossible to build and maintain a godly influence, testimony and altar in a pagan land with idols and demons, inhabited by pagans. If you disagree, talk to Daniel and his friends. Gen. 13:4 says, *"...and there Abram called on the name of the LORD."* In Bethel -- oh what a sweet reunion that must have been. We should be so thankful that God never gives up on us. NEVER! He is constantly trying to conform us to the image of

His Son, drawing us back to Himself, back to our Bethel, back to our altar, to our place of **prayer**, **sacrifice** and **worship**, back to the **cross**. Abraham needed wisdom at this time to separate from Lot, and he gets it at Bethel, at the altar, not in *Mizraim*. We all need to part friendships in this way. But in order to do that we all need to have our own personal altars and Bethels, where we can meet God alone, face-to-face, and offer our prayers, sacrifices and worship (and we need to bring our families to that altar with us).

It was God who drew Abraham back to Bethel from *Mizraim*, and it was God who made Pharoah throw Abraham out of Egypt, but it was Abraham v.4 who had to call on the name of the LORD at the altar for confession, restoration, repentance, reunion, and fellowship. Oh, my friend, have you been to, or are you in *Mizraim* right now? Return to the first place. Return to your first love. Return to the LORD God before it's too late. Abraham called (*kara* - to call out to, call upon, to cry unto) and he identified with, which means to encounter. Abraham not only called but **cried** unto the LORD, *Yehovah*, the self-existent and eternal God. He encountered the LORD in prayer! Oh, how we need to continually come back and cry unto the LORD. Why? Because, David wrote in Psalm 65:2, *"O thou that hearest prayer, unto thee shall all flesh come."*

God is waiting at Bethel, at the house of God, at the altar, at the slaughter place, for all of us to come and to call upon Him, and to encounter Him. Oh, won't you come back to Him today? Right now it's not too late. As long as you have breath, it is never too late. "Oh God, Thank You for waiting. Thank You for drawing us back. Thank You for forcing us back. Forgive us, cleanse us, revive us; restore us to our first love!"

"...And there built he an altar unto the LORD...," Gen. 12:7. Nine simple words, and you can almost glance over them in a very nonchalant way without even so much as a thought. Yet in them lies the secret and the power of Abraham's relationship and friendship with God. Abraham obeyed God's call in Gen. 12:4, left it all and entered Canaan, the "Promised Land." He stopped in Shechem, where God appeared to him

and promised him the land, *"...And there builded he an altar unto the LORD...,"* v.7. From this point on anywhere, he went he must have an altar, and an altar sanctified by <u>prayer, sacrifice and worship</u>.

Did you ever notice in the **"Older Testament,"** when it comes to prayer, God speaks to men more then men speak to God. There is a principle for living there we need to note: we talk too much when we pray. Listening, is a lost art in prayer! The words, "silent" and "listen" have exactly the same letters, but you can not listen if you are not silent. How much time do you devote to listening to God during your prayer time? Psalm 46:10 says, *"Be still and know (*yada*) that I am God..."* "Be still," God says, "and listen to Me." Abraham said nothing, when God said, "<u>Sacrifice Isaac</u>!" We need to cultivate listening in our prayer life. Prayer is a two-way street, not a turnpike; we need to slow down and listen.

A key to remember in our text is that Abraham was a family man, and where ever he went, he took his family and his possessions. Also, he made sure God was in the midst of that family; and he did that by building an altar to the LORD. Oh my friend, that is what is needed in our homes today: family altars -- a place to <u>sacrifice, pray and worship</u> together. A place to meet God as a family. We need to teach our children to call on the name of the LORD and to listen to His voice and know the sound of it. Abraham did more than just build altars, he built **<u>family altars</u>**. Amen?

*(**Prayer** - "Oh LORD, please help us to establish and consistently maintain a family altar, a place of prayer, sacrifice and worship. A place where we can not only call on Your name, Father, but seek Your face and wait on You and be silent and listen to the sound of Your voice as well." In Yeshua/Jesus' name we pray. Amen!)*

Principles for Prayer:

- It was God who drew Abraham back to Bethel, and God had Pharaoh throw him out of Egypt, to restore him.

- In the O.T. God spoke more to men than they spoke to Him. Why? They listened more, and we don't know how!
- Prayer is a two-way street, not a turnpike, or an expressway. You speak/God listens, God speaks/you listen! Got it?

"Prayer is not a little habit pinned on to us while we were tied to our mother's apron strings. It is the most serious work of our most serious years."

E. M. Bounds

"Prayer between Fatness & Communion" #24 Gen. 13:18

"Then Abraham removed his tent, and came and dwelt (by the oaks) in the plain of Mamre [fatness], which is in Hebron [communion], and built there an altar unto the LORD." Gen. 13:18. Abraham moves again after the LORD tells him in v.17 to, *"Arise, walk through the land in the length of it and in the breadth of it; for I will give it unto you."* Oh, the promises of God and the fellowship Abraham must have had with his Creator. He pitched his tent in Mamre, which means lusty, vigor, fatness, by the oaks or the terebinth trees. Webster says, "They are of the sumac or cashew family and yield turpentine."

He stays there for awhile, and buys the cave and field of Machpelah in Mamre (where he and Sarah are buried as well as Isaac and Rebekah and Jacob and Leah). He was in Mamre when Lot was captured and when the three heavenly visitors came to him on their way to Sodom. Mamre was in Hebron (which means, seat of association, or to join, to league, couple together, or to have fellowship with). So here by the trees of "fatness – Mamre," which was in "communion – Hebron," Abraham chose to pitch his tent, bury his family and then build his family altar; what a **Kodak moment**!

He finally settles down (for awhile anyway), and unpacks his camel. When he does, he builds a family altar in a place of fatness, where he can have sweet fellowship and build a friendship with God. Our altars should be just that, a place of fatness; a place where we can grow fat on the "Word of God;" a place where we can grow and mature (and our families with us). It should also be a place of fellowship, communion and togetherness with our families, but most of all with God. That's what God desires more than anything else, even more than sacrifice. That sweet intercourse, that sweet union with Him, that intimate communion (*yada*) and fellowship through **prayer** -- "talking to God," a place of friendship!

Do you want to be a friend of God's? Do you want to have that fellowship and experience that Abraham had? Then today build that family altar in your Mamre, in Hebron, your fatness in communion, and take your family there and all your possessions and pitch your tent. Remember, everywhere Abraham had a tent (except Mizraim), God had an altar; an altar sanctified by **prayer**!

The three essential prerequisites to having an altar are <u>the place, the time and the voice</u>. The three essential elements of an altar are <u>sacrifice, worship and prayer</u>. The three lasting benefits or results of a family altar are <u>fatness, fellowship and friendship</u>. Got it? Now go build it, you will be glad you did!

Oh LORD, may we find our Mamre in Hebron, our fatness in communion, and grow fat in our fellowship with You. Oh LORD, may we pitch our tents and build our altars with our families so that we may build our friendships together with You. LORD, help us to find our Mamre, our Hebron and help us to find it soon, today LORD. In Jesus' name, Amen!"

"And Melchizedek *king of Salem brought forth bread and wine: and he was the priest of the most high God."* Gen. 14:18. *Melchizedek* is referred to as a type of Christ (Heb. 7:1ff), he has no beginning and no ending, (Heb. 7:3). There is no Levitical priesthood at this time, and ancient Hebrew scholars believe this person could have been *Shem*, Noah's son. According to the genealogical records Noah was alive while Abraham walked on the Earth, and Shem was alive after Abraham died, so it is feasible. Anyway, he brought out bread and wine, the basic elements of the Earth; bread being the staff of life and wine the fruit of the vine, the same elements used by *Yeshua* to establish communion and the same elements found on the Passover table and on every Jewish *Sabbath* table as well. They were basic to life, ***"L"Chaim!"***

Gen. 14:19 says that *Melchizedek* blessed Abraham, *"And he blessed him and said, Blessed be Abram of the most high God, possessor of heaven and earth:"* which is very normal, and something we need to do. Blessing man is simply invoking

God's riches or grace on man, or to put it simply, praying for mankind – "intercession." He blesses Abram and back in Gen. 12:1-3 God said, Those that bless you I will bless." so here *Melchizedek* not only blesses man, but the Jewish nation to be, as well. But then he blesses God, *"And blessed be the most high God..."* (v 20). Blessing God is unusual but it is biblical (Psalms 103, 104, 134, etc.). Blessings are prayers, prayers to God for men, and prayers to God for God. How often (or better yet, how seldom) do we invoke or pray for blessings on mankind, let alone God? When was the last time you blessed God like His servant David, "Bless the LORD, O my soul, and all that is within me bless His holy name." "Behold, bless the LORD."

How do we pray for God? Well, praise is prayer, and that exalts God. Thanksgiving is prayer and that honors God. Confession is prayer and that glorifys God. We can pray against the deeds of the wicked, and that helps God (Ps. 141:5); but most of all **Ps. 72:15** says, *"...prayer also shall be made for Him continually; and daily shall He be praised."* To pray for God, to bless God, is a startling thought! It almost seems profane, but it is not; it is very beautiful, very holy, very biblical, and the most holy of all prayers.

Think of the "Lord's Prayer" in Matthew 6. Why did Christ teach us to pray for His Father first? "Hallowed [holy and sacred] be Thy name, Thy kingdom come, Thy will be done..." Wasn't our need for daily bread greater? NO! God's heart was famished, and starving without fellowship, without communion, without our daily love and devotion. Oh my friend, to bless God, to pray for God, for His will, His works, His glory, is greater! *"Not unto us, O LORD, not unto us, but unto thy name give glory,"* (Psalm 115:1) is the highest form of prayer known to man. Again, how often (or how seldom) do we pray or ask for blessings on mankind, let alone God?

To pray for God the Father and the Son -- what a radical thought, yes, but radically beautiful. Prayer; communion; blessings; tithes; victory; fellowship, WOW! What a gathering we have here in Gen. 14, all the elements of a glorious worship service. (Are you still walking with me?)

*(**Prayer** - "Oh LORD, teach us not only to pray for man but for You LORD. Not only to bless man, but to bless You LORD. "Hallowed be Thy name. Thy kingdom come, Thy will be done." Teach us to be bridge-builders, believer priests (I Peter 2:9), like Melchizedek. For ha Shem Yeshua's sake. Amen!)*

Principles for Prayer:

- Oh, the promises and fellowship you can experience at your altar with God, but are you?
- Blessing man is simply invoking God's riches and grace on them.
- To pray for God or to bless God is a radical, startling thought, is it not?

"Prayer is reaching out after the unseen, but fasting is letting go of all that is seen and temporal, to show God we are ready to sacrifice anything for the Kingdom of God."

Andrew Murray

WOW!

"Prayer on Mt. Moriah" #25
Gen. 22:9

"...And Abraham built an altar there." v.9, on *Mt. Moriah,* to offer his son, Isaac, as a burnt offering. Remember, whenever you have an altar you have <u>worship, sacrifice and prayer</u>. I'm sure Abraham was in prayer the night God told him to go out of the land of the Philistines and into the "<u>Land of Promise</u>" to offer up Isaac. Prayers are often absent when we should naturally expect them. In fact the absence of prayer many times makes it even more conspicuous. For instance, <u>Joseph never prayed; at least it is never recorded in Scripture</u>. There is no mention in our text about Abraham praying or struggling with his decision. In chapter 21:11-12, he had to throw out Ishmael and it, *"was very grievous in Abraham's sight,"* and then here 22:9, he had to slay his son, Isaac. To think he didn't struggle and pray much about these decisions is very naïve, but it's not recorded for us anyway. <u>It's probably too personal</u>.

God calls him by name, "Abraham," and he immediately answers, "Here I am." He knew the voice of God. How? He was accustomed to the sound of it. He spoke to Him often. Do we know the voice of God (John 10:27)? Remember, there were no chapter or verse divisions in the original scrolls, so twenty words before this command you have Abraham calling, "on the name on the LORD, the Everlasting God, *El Olam*." I'm sure he prayed all night long. I'm sure he prayed during his three day journey. I'm sure he prayed as they ascended Mt. Moriah. I'm sure he prayed as they built the altar together. And I'm sure he prayed as he bound his son, laid him on that altar, and lifted that knife to slay him. All this time there seems to be silence in heaven, until v.11. And then, **"Abraham, Abraham!"** And he said, **"Here I am!"** Abraham was going all the way, we too often are guilty of going only so far, half way and stopping short. Abraham lifts his eyes and sees the ram caught in a thicket. The ram was there the whole time, just like Gen. 21:19 with Hagar -- the pool of water was always there, **but God had to open their eyes to see it!**

The key is prayer -- earnest, effectual, fervent, desperate, destitute, prayer -- that's what opens our eyes to God's blessings and provisions. He calls the place *Jehovah-Jireh*, "the LORD will provide;" and He will for us today as well, if we will just pray and ask Him to open our eyes in the midst of our calamity. Gen. 22:1 was a test from God, *"And it came to pass after these things, that God did [test] (nasa) Abraham..."* In Hebrew this word means to try, prove, assay, test, or put to the proof. The idea behind this word is that of testing or proving the quality of someone or something, often through adversity and hardship. Is God testing you right now? Are you climbing your *Mt. Moriah,* or are you still on your three day journey? Are you wandering in the wilderness, hot, dry, thirsty, and tired? Are you doubting God, His direction, His will, His Word, right now? Then pray! I mean **PRAY**! Really **PRAY**! Earnestly, fervently, desperately **PRAY**! And He will open your eyes to see that pool of water or that ram of provision.

Abraham held back nothing from God, and God held back nothing from Abraham. Prayer opens our eyes to God's provision in our wilderness experience. What a paradox. As we close our eyes to pray, God opens our eyes to see: our inner eyes, our spiritual eyes. Following this experience Abraham, packs his camel and moves back to Hebron, where he buries Sarah in the cave of Machpelah and lives another 38 years. John Bunyan said, "Pray often, for prayer is a shield to the soul, a sacrifice to God and a scourge to Satan." A shield, a sacrifice, and a scourge!

We could have entitled this section, "The God Seer" instead of "Mt. Moriah," or "Jehovah-Jireh; The Lord Provides ahead of time, *or The Lord Sees to it ahead of time."* Moriah is made up of two Hebrew words, *(Ra-ah – to see)* and *(Yah- Jehovah or Yehovah)* or "to see Jehovah." In John 8:56 *Yeshua*/Jesus said, *"Your father Abraham rejoiced to see my day: and he saw it, and was glad."* So who is the, Angel of Jehovah in Gen. 22:11? Many times He is just called, Jehovah if not *Yehoshuah.* As revealed by Rabbi Kaduri on You-tube at 108 years old, before dying.

Mt. Moriah appears only two times in the Scriptures: here in Gen. 22:2 as the *"Land of Moriah,"* but *Yehovah* points out a mountain in the land of Moriah or, "Mt. Moriah." The other reference is in II Chron. 3:1, where Solomon builds *Yehovah* a house in Jerusalem on Mt. Moriah on the threshing floor of Ornan the Jebusite in Jerusalem, where David built an altar to stop a plague. **Read** I Chron. 21:1-30., especially v. 24, *"Nay, but I will verily buy it for the full price: for I will not take that which is thine for the LORD, nor offer burnt offerings without cost!"* What a beautiful lesson! Tie this in with Malachi 3, when you build your altar and sanctify it with <u>prayer, sacrifice and worship</u> it should, <u>COST</u> you! Time, Talents, Treasures -- if it costs you nothing, it is worth nothing! He gave you everything: His best, His beloved, His only begotten Son, and we bring Him our lame, blind, sick, leftover, junk. Shame on us! Moriah was also in the vicinity where (still later) *Yeshua*/Jesus offered Himself without spot on an old rugged cross. (What a coincidence!) Unless you are spiritually blind you should begin to see many biblical types beginning to surface in this chapter. You could write books on Genesis 22, but we are looking for principles for <u>prayer</u> in the life of Abraham, and specifically on Mt. Moriah.

*(**Prayer** - "Oh God, as we give ourselves to prayer -- earnest, fervent, prayer -- open our eyes to Your blessings and provisions that surround us. May we trust and believe You and Your Word, and be counted as a "Friend of God." May we pass Your test today and every day. Thank You for these precious truths. In Your holy name we pray, Amen!")*

Principles for Prayer:

- When you pray, if you hold back nothing from God, He will hold back nothing from you!
- Like Abraham with Ishmael's banishment and Isaac's sacrifice, his prayers were too deep to utter!
- Only effectual, fervent prayer opens our eyes to God's blessings and provision.

"If I am concerned that my flock be men and women of prayer, then as their pastor, I must lead the way. Apathy in me will produce apathy in them."

J. D. Drysdale

"A Crisis Strengthens Prayer" #26
Gen. 22:9

Abraham's spiritual life was marked by one crisis after another, and each one drew him nearer to God and increased his prayer life. Do yours? In Gen. 12:1-3, God called him to leave his home, his country, his kindred, and his family (which he loved); and his father died in Haran making him the family patriarch. So what does he do? He builds an altar in Bethel (Gen. 12:8), "the house of God." In Gen. 13:1-8, God calls him to separate from Lot his nephew, his kinsman and fellow believer, whom he loved. So, then what does he do? He builds another altar in Hebron, near Mamre, "Communion & Fatness" (Gen. 13:18). In Gen. 21:10-11, God calls him to lay aside his plans for Ishmael, his 14 year old son whom he dearly loved, and send him away. So what does he do? He builds another altar in Beer-sheba, "the well of seven oaths" (Gen. 21:33). In Gen. 22:1-14, God calls him to surrender his only beloved son, Isaac, the son of promise, the son of his old age, whom he and Sarah loved. So what does he do? He builds an altar on Mt. Moriah, "Jehovah-Jireh," (Gen. 22:9) to sacrifice him!

What do you do when God calls you to give up something or someone you love very much? Cry, throw a fit, get depressed, step out of the circle, take drugs, get drunk, quit, what? What should you do? Build an altar and pray, sacrifice and worship." Job 1:21, *"The LORD gave and the LORD hath taken away; blessed be the name of the LORD."* What was Job's wife's name; anybody know? How about Lot's wife? Hmm! We know from Gen. 17:17-19 that God promised Sarah (age 90) and Abraham (age 100) a son named Isaac, "laughter." So, Sarah is 90 when she gives birth to Isaac and 127 in Gen 23:1, when Abraham returns from offering Isaac on Mt. Moriah. Do the math: how old is Isaac when Abraham binds him and puts him on the altar? Thirty-seven! What seemed impossible in their old age happened. Sarah gave birth at 90 and nursed Isaac (Gen. 21:7), and this would be the key to Abraham's future. Thirty-seven years pass in Genesis 21. *Isaac* would have sons, and those sons would have sons, and from one of their offspring would come the Messiah, One by Whom all the nations of the world would be blessed, **Jesus, the Christ** (Gal. 3:16).

Can you imagine the shock to Abraham and Sarah when God told him to take his only beloved son, the son of promise, and sacrifice him on Mt. Moriah as a burnt offering to God (Gen. 22:2)? She is now 127 and he is 137 years old. A "burnt offering" was a total sacrificial offering; all of it was offered by fire. **All of it!** Listen, a burnt offering was of man's voluntary free will, and it was acceptable by God for atonement. That is what God was asking His "FRIEND" to do! Only a friend, can ask a friend to sacrifice! Amen? And Abraham was a true friend of God! John 15:15 says, *"Henceforth, I call you not servants; for the servant knoweth not what his lord doeth: but I have called you friends..."* We sing it: "What a friend we have in Jesus, all our sins and grief's to bear..." We mouth it, we pray it, but do we believe it? Better yet do we live it?

Gen. 22:2 says, *"Take now thy son, thine only son Isaac, whom thou lovest..."* This is the first time in the Bible we have the word "love." It is the Hebrew word (*ahab* or *ahav*) and means to love, lover, lovest. In Hebrew the ***aleph*** means ox or strength, and the ***bet*** means house; and when put together they spell ***"AB"*** or father or "the strong one of the house." When you put the Hebrew **"hey"** in the middle to get (*ahav*-love, lover) it means, "the heart of the Father." Isa. 41:8 says, *"But thou, Israel, art my servant, Jacob whom I have chosen, the seed of Abraham my friend."* Abraham, My friend (*ahav-lover*), My lover, whom I lovest. Our word friend comes from the old English word freond – to love, attached to another by affection. We use this word too loosely. Jesus **is** a true friend -- someone who loves me and is attached to me by affection. Why? Because He died for me, to set me free from the prison and poison of sin.

God tested His friend's loyalty, sincerity, love and faith. God did not **tempt** Abraham; He **tested** him. To tempt is to appeal to the worst in a man, desiring him to yield to the wrong. To test is to appeal to the best in a man, hoping that he will endure the trial and benefit by it. Satan tempts to bring about evil; God tests to bring about good. James 1:13 says, *"Let no man say when he is tempted: I am tempted of God, for God cannot be tempted with evil, neither tempteth He any man."*

God did not bring Abraham to this test to determine whether or not Abraham would obey Him. NO! God is omniscient; He knows every thing. He knew in advance that Abraham would obey! He knew it! Then why did He allow it? For the same reason He allows you and me to go through the waters, fires, trials and tribulations of life. <u>There is a principle for prayer here</u>. The purpose of this experience <u>was not to enlighten the LORD</u>; it was to <u>enrich Abraham's prayer life</u>! Got it? Write it down!

God knows how it is going to come out in the end (He wrote the Book), but you and I need the experience in order to be assured and better prepared for the rough places in life. Listen, there is nothing happening in your life right now that God is not fully aware of or not totally in control of. **NOTHING!** You got that? Nothing! You are a King's kid! He knows every hair on your head (He counts them), so I'm sure He is aware of your mortgage, your job, your marriage, your cancer, your operation, your decision, your bills, your big toe, whatever! Is He your Friend, your "Freond," not just an acquaintance? Hos. 6:3

*(**Prayer** - "Father, we desire more than life itself to be Your friend, but we are so unworthy to claim that title, even though we are Your children by adoption through the shed blood of Your only begotten Son. Though we cry out* Abba Father, *many times we feel like orphans and not Your heirs. Forgive our sins, cleanse our souls, renew a right spirit within us that we may seek Your face; humble our hearts and heal our land." In the name of Your Son* Yeshua/Jesus *we pray. Amen!)*

Principles for Prayer:

- Listen, only a true friend can ask a true friend to sacrifice something!

- Listen, there is nothing happening in your life right now that God is not aware of and in total control of!
- The Chinese word for **crisis** is made up of two words: danger & opportunity. How is yours spelled?

"Prayer is not our message. It is the method of God for the message. Everything is done by prayer. Then I discovered that Charles Finney's revivals were based on prayer, that the Spirit of prayer is the Spirit of Revival."

Armin Gesswein

"Godly Abandonment Involves Prayer"
#27
Gen. 22:8

*"And it came to pass after these things, that God did [test] **(nasa)** Abraham, and said unto him, Abraham: and he said, Behold, here I am."* Gen. 22:1. There is an immediate and ready response from Abraham, "Behold! Here, I am!" (***hin-ne*** – a particle of interjection in Hebrew) Or an idiom, "Behold, me!" or "Here I am!" The word "here" is in italics added for clarification by the translators. Any time you have the word "behold" in your Bible, you need to put an **RXR** (for a railroad crossing sign) in your Bible margin. When you come to a railroad crossing sign there are three words around it, "Stop, Look, Listen." So, when we come to this word in our Bibles we need to **"stop;"** then we need to **"look"** all around and notice the context; then we need to **"listen"** to what the Holy Spirit is trying to teach us. This is very important! Abraham says, "Behold, *here* I am!" three times in this chapter. Here in v.1 to God; in v.7 to Isaac; and in v.11 to the Angel of Jehovah.

Then God gives Abraham a command that would shake any saint's foundation, no matter how strong he or she was! *"...Take now thy son, thine only son Isaac, whom thou lovest, and get thee into the land of Moriah; and offer him there for a burnt offering upon one of the mountains which I will tell thee of."* v.2. I don't know about you, but I can't fathom that! Bible critics for ages have asked how God could demand a human sacrifice, like Jephthah's daughter in Judges 11, but they miss the point. God did not let Abraham make a human sacrifice, nor did He intend to. Now Jephthah's vow was rash and stupid. Listen, what God wanted was a living sacrifice not a dead one (Rom. 12:1-2). He wanted Abraham, not Isaac. Isaac's day was coming (oh yes, the twins, Jacob and Esau), but this was Abraham's day and Abraham's test.

Listen, the **real** test of **real** faith, is in its willingness and readiness to abandon all, and devote all to God. **"ALL!"** And that, my friend, is a principle for prayer. Go and offer up thy god (little g-o-d) -- son; daughter; car; boat; finances; butts; beer; wine -- whatever! What is your little g-o-d? God wants you to take it up to Mt. Moriah and sacrifice it to Him as a whole burnt offering, all of it, today, right now! Security, home, retirement, job, hobby, or lack there of. Are you listening, are you paying attention, or just skim reading? **The real test of real faith is in its willingness and readiness to abandon all and devote all to God!** (BIG, G-O-D!) Because without faith -- real faith, true faith, genuine faith -- you are absolutely powerless (***adunatos***) to please GOD, so why even pray?

God did not tell Abraham the reason for His command, neither does He always explain the reason behind the things He tells you and me to do. Amen? That's why we need to keep singing that old hymn, "Trust and Obey." Abraham's response to God's instructions is seen in Gen. 22:3-10. Notice v.3, Abraham didn't hesitate or call a committee meeting or throw out a fleece three our four times, read his horoscope, or check his tarot cards. He woke up early, saddled his ass, took his son and went. Sometimes we deliberate too long; sometimes we just need to step out of the darn boat. It was his business to obey. It was God's business to work out the details. Amen? And it is no different in your life and mine today! They arrive on the third day (v.4). Interesting -- Christ arose on the third day, never after the third day, always on the third day (check it out). The parallels between this event and Jesus going to Calvary are amazing, too similar to be coincidental.

I love v.5; Abraham says to his young men, *"...Abide ye here with the ass; and I and the lad will go yonder and **worship** and come again to you."* (**Prayer – Worship – Sacrifice**) Watch this, "and come again to you" in Hebrew "and we will come back to you." If he is going to kill Isaac, how is he coming back with him? Abraham believed God would resurrect Isaac from the dead. Heb. 11:17-19, *"Accounting that God was able to raise him up, even from the dead; from whence also he received him in a figure."* This was a profound expression of Abraham's faith. Abraham believed God! **PERIOD!** YES,

LORD! That's faith! If you are saved, there are two words you can never say in the same sentence, *"No, LORD!"* Because if He is in fact your LORD, you can never tell Him, "No!" NEVER!

By the way, look at Gen. 22:19, *"So Abraham returned unto his young men, and they rose up and went together to Beer-sheba;"* You don't see it in the English, but in the Hebrew, Isaac is not with Abraham. Abraham says, "Let's you and I return to Beer-sheba," and they did. The ancient Rabbi's claim five verses later Sarah saw Abraham and the two servants returning from Mt. Moriah without Isaac the son of her old age and had a heart attack and died at the age of 127 (speculation). Isaac stays on Mt. Moriah with the Angel of Jehovah, and you don't see him again until he takes a wife (Rebekah) in Gen. 24:63-67 (a picture of Christ and the church but I will go off tangent and chase a rabbit, so I will stay on track -- you chase the rabbit!).

In Gen. 22:6 Abraham takes the fire and the knife and lays the wood for the sacrifice on Isaac's shoulder and they begin their ascent up Mt. Moriah. You can almost feel Abraham's heart pounding in his chest and then in v.7 his son asks the inevitable question, *"Behold, the fire and the wood: but where is the lamb (sey - small sheep or goat) for a burnt offering?"* I don't think Abraham told him, do you? Would you if the tables were turned? So this is a complete surprise to Isaac, and v.8 is probably one of the most prophetic verses in the Bible, if not the most prophetic. *"And Abraham said, "My son, God will provide Himself a lamb for a burnt offering: so they went both of them together."* We'll look at that more closely next time!

(**Prayer** - *"Father, as we come into Your presence and lay our all on the altar of sacrifice, we beseech You in the name of Your blessed Son, Yeshua, to lean down Your ear and hear. We are unworthy to enter Your throne room, but we come through the blood of Calvary. We know that without faith we are absolutely powerless to please You, so we pray with Your disciples, "Lord, give more faith to us; increase our faith; strengthen our faith; build our faith." In Jesus' name and for His sake. Amen!)*

Principles for Prayer:

- What God wanted on Mt. Moriah was a living sacrifice, not a dead one; this was Abraham's test!
- The **real** test of **real** faith is in its willingness and readiness to abandon all and devote all to God. ALL!
- If you are truly saved, there are two words you can never say in the same sentence, "No, Lord!"

"The great use of a life is to spend it for something that outlasts it."

William James

"Paper Clip Moving Prayer" #28
Gen. 22:13

As I said, Gen.22:8 is one of the most prophetic (if not the most prophetic) verse in all of the Bible: *"...My son, God will provide Himself a lamb for a burnt offering..."* In English you don't see the profound impact of this verse and the peace that came over Isaac, because of his father's answer, that allowed him to continue walking up Mt. Moriah with his father.

I was studying the Torah in a synagogue with several Jewish people. The teacher was Dr. Rabbi Peter Grumbacher. Hebrew was his mother tongue, and he even went to Israel for two years to refine it. When we came to this verse, I asked him, "Can this verse be translated, 'My son, God will provide Himself *AS* a lamb for a burnt offering?'" (Emphasis mine.) He asked me why it would be translated like that, and I told him I heard it could be.

So, he looked at it for awhile and finally looked up and said, "Yes, the word 'himself' is a reflexive pronoun, and can or should be translated, 'God will provide Himself **as** a lamb for a burnt offering.'" I almost jumped off my seat, and he said, "What difference would it make?" It would be a good idea to add that little two letter word in the margin of your Bible.

Now you can see John 1:29 in a much clearer light, when John the Baptist stood in the Jordan River and declared, *"Behold, the Lamb of God which taketh away, the sin of the world."* Notice the definite articles: "**the** Lamb, **the** sin, **the** world." The absence of the definite article qualifies, but the presence of the definite article identifies. Then again in John 1:36, John the Baptist states it again to two of his disciples, *"Behold, the Lamb of God!"*

In Gen. 22:9, Abraham builds an altar and Isaac, his son, allows him to bind him and lay him on that altar. Isaac is **not** 12 years old, as many believe. Do the math. He is 37, and his father is 137. He could have easily overpowered him, but he willingly laid down his life, trusting his father's will and word. In v.10 Abraham lifts his hand with a knife in it to slay his son, whom he loves. Listen, I don't care if he is 7, 17, 27, 37, or 107; he had such trust and confidence in his father and in his father's will that he allowed him to bind him and put him on that altar. In fact, he helped him build it, and he carried the wood up the mountain. How many of us would allow our father to tie us up and light a fire under us? Yet, some of us could use a little fire under us at times! Amen? Don't be too quick to judge your kids, Dad, and put them on the altar. How many of your kids would let you put them on the altar? Do your children have that kind of trust in you, in your life and your walk, your words, your will, your wisdom and your love for them? Would they carry the wood up the mountain and help you build an altar and let you bind them (*Akeda*)? How is your family altar? I am speaking to myself here as well. I would have given anything to have heard my father pray one time, just one time! Yet Abraham knelt on the floor three times a day and prayed for his meal before he ate.

There are two very important principles here regarding **prayer**. Remember, without FAITH we are absolutely powerless to please God! The **first principle** is this: the test of true faith is in its willingness and readiness to abandon all and devote all to God. "Take now thy son." **YES LORD!** The **second principle** is this: the fruit of true faith is in its willing obedience to the explicit commands of God. (To obey is better than sacrifice…) Listen, the **test** of FAITH is total surrender; but the **fruit** of FAITH is total obedience. Remember Heb. 11:6, *"…without faith,* [total surrender] *it is impossible to please him* [God]… [you] *must believe* [total obedience] *that He is, and that…"* Listen, trust and faith are nouns. Obey and believe are verbs, action words, and they have the dynamic, propelling power of verbs! The test: **trust Him implicitly**! The fruit: **obey Him explicitly**!

Now we come to the LORD's provision for Abraham, Gen. 22:11-19. *"And the angel of the LORD [YHWH Jehovah] called unto him out of heaven, and said, Abraham, Abraham: and he said, Here am I."* Seven times in Scripture you have this repetition of names: Abraham, Jacob, Moses, Samuel, Martha, Peter, and Paul. It's an interesting study. But why the urgency in the Angel of the LORD's voice? The knife is coming down! Abraham turns and there is a ram (*ah-yil,* not a lamb, *sey*) caught in the thicket by his horns; and he becomes the offering for Isaac. Abraham calls the place, "*Jehovah-Jireh*" (the LORD will provide ahead of time) or *Yehovah-Yireh. Jireh* has the same Hebrew root as Moriah (*ra-ah* to see); the LORD will see to it; the LORD will take care of it. I love the end of v.14, <u>*"In the mount of the LORD it shall be seen."*</u>

The ram was already there; why didn't they see it? Maybe their eyes were on the fog and not on God. Maybe the weight of the test was so heavy they could not see. Maybe the Angel of the LORD put it there at the last second. <u>Maybe we just don't know</u>. Many times God's blessing, God's answer, God's way of escape is right in front of us (or behind us) and we can't see it. In v.<u>5 they are worshiping</u>; in v.<u>9 they are sacrificing</u>; and I am sure in v.<u>10 they are both praying</u> as he prepares to slay Isaac.

Here is the **third prayer principle**: <u>prayer opens our eyes so we can see God's provision or His answer</u>. That is why Satan does not want you or your Church to get serious about **prayer**. Listen, after you have prayed, "<u>turn around</u>" v.13 and see if your ram or answer is caught in the thicket by its horns. <u>The test of faith: total surrender! The fruit of faith: total obedience! The yield of faith: total provision! The result of faith: answered prayer!</u> It's that simple! Got it? Good!

(**Prayer** - *"Father, iIncrease our faith as we approach the coming day when the trumpet will sound, the clouds will part, and Your Son will return, and our faith wavers. You said to Peter, "Oh thou of little faith," after he walked on water. How small is ours when we can't stand on a puddle? Lord, give more faith to us. You said if our faith was like a mustard seed, we could say to a mountain, "Move," and it would move. Yet we can't even move a paper clip. LORD, please increase our faith. In Your Son's holy name we pray. Amen!"*)

Principles for Prayer:

- Prayer opens our eyes so we can see God's provision and His answers.
- The test of faith is total surrender, but the fruit of faith is total obedience!
- Prayer – the test: trust Him implicitly. The fruit: obey Him explicitly!

"Our Lord in His teaching always made prayer, not preparation for work, but the work!"

Oswald Chambers

"Running into God's Angel" #29
Gen. 16:7

"You are the God Who sees!" Gen. 16:1-16. Hagar knew about the God of Abraham, but she also had a pagan background pulling her back to Egypt, *Mizraim*. Ishmael, I believe, knew and believed in the God of his father, Abraham. He hunted with him, built altars with him, offered sacrifices with him, prayed with him and lived with him for 14 years before his first flight. His father's love for him was strong, but his biological mother's influence over him was stronger, and he finally took an Egyptian wife. As you look through Genesis, you find some very interesting characters. From many we have learned some tremendous principles for prayer, and I hope you are applying some of them to your prayer life.

From Adam, the garden tiller, we learned that he knew the place, the voice, the time, and that and he came bare-naked. From Enoch, the God pleaser" we learned faith, believing, and persistence, and that without faith it's impossible to please God, but without risk faith is impossible. From Noah, the ship builder, we learned grace, righteousness and integrity (ethically, judicially and theocratically) were tantamount to our prayer life. Abraham, the family altar builder, gave us prayer, sacrifice and worship. Then Mt. Moriah explained the prayer of faith in a new and living way. The test of true faith was total surrender – "I Surrender All." The fruit of true faith was total obedience – "Trust and Obey." The result of true faith was total provision – *Jehovah-Jireh*. The lesson seen on Mt. Moriah was that prayer spoken on faith-based initiative opens our spiritual eyes to see God's provision. However, Abraham was not the first one to show us this; Ishmael was 16.

Now we come to a woman, an Egyptian woman, a pagan woman, the possession or property of Abraham's wife Sarah, Hagar, the handmaid! The name Hagar is of Semitic origin, not Egyptian. Maybe she was given this name after she ran (in fact the three letter Hebrew root *[hey, gimmel, resh]* means "**to flee**," and is also found in the Arabic name for Mohammed's famous flight, *"The Hegira"*). Her name, which means flight, is found three times in the Bible: 1) Gen. 16:1-16, pregnant and running from God; 2) Gen. 21:9-21, "pathetic and running into God;" 3) Gal. 4:21-31, prophetic and running for God (you can preach that!). Genesis 16 is a short chapter with only 16 verses, and it breaks down into three equal parts: Sarah's stupidity, vv.1-5; Hagar's haste, vv. 6-10; and Ishmael's influence, vv. 12-16. That will preach also.

Sarah is about 75, barren, and childless, and Abraham is about 85. They have been married almost 60 years, and she is getting a little desperate and beginning to distrust God and His promises to her husband. She gave him *Hagar*, her handmaid whom she picked up in Egypt, as a wife until she bore a child. This was legal in that time and culture, and still practiced today in some cultures. The ancient Rabbis teach that *Hagar* comes back as *Keturah* in Gen. 25 (after Sarah dies), and bears Abraham six more sons. Anyway, Abraham consents to Sarah's wish and has relations with *Hagar* (**dummy**), and she conceives! Sounds like Gen. 3:12, "Want a bite?" Remember I Tim. 2:14-15 says that Adam was not deceived, only Eve. Adam knew what he was doing. So did Abraham, and Israel's trouble starts here, with the expansion of the Arab nations. Joktan, the son of Eber, was the founder of Arabia, Mohammed, and that whole lineage.

Sarah wants sons for two reasons: **One** – because of social pressure in the Far East. Many sons equaled honor, influence and strength. (Every father wants a son, but needs a daughter.) **Two** – It is every Jewish mother's dream to bear Israel's Messiah (Gen. 3:15; Ezra 9:2; Isa. 7:14; Mal. 2:15). The problem is, she has to be and remain a **virgin** until she delivers the child (Isa. 7:14), and the moment she conceives (in fact has sexual relations), she is no longer a **virgin**. Abraham was told three times that he would have a son; and the last time he was told that his heir would be his son. *Hagar* is only his wife until she conceives. This is still a practice today in some far eastern countries. They are surrogate mothers, and *Hagar's* child would legally be Sarah's. Legend also says that *Hagar* was one of Pharaoh's daughter's, making Ishmael half Egyptian and half Jewish. <u>Oh, how the plot thickens</u>.

Hagar conceives in v.4, and immediately Sarah is despised in her eyes (or lightly esteemed or of little account). So Sarah immediately passes the buck back to Abraham in v.5, *"My wrong be upon thee...the LORD judge between me and thee."* You got a problem? Blame your spouse! It worked for Adam in the garden, "The woman You gave me..." So, Sarah thought she would give it a shot here. However, Abraham read the same book and hands it, "Right back at you," in v.6 *"Behold,* (there's our railroad sign) (***hin-ne***) t*hy maid is in thy hand, do to her as it pleaseth thee."* Now be careful here. In Hebrew, the phrase "as it pleaseth thee" (*ayin tov*), an idiom for "a good eye, a generous eye," not a "stingy eye" (*ayin ra'ah*). Be kind, be generous, and be benevolent to Hagar. Now look at Matt. 6:19-23 in light of this principle. The context is about your treasures in Heaven in regards to giving. The evil eye in Matt. 6:23 is a stingy eye or person. The healthy eye or good eye is a generous person. But what does Sarah do? She beats Hagar, afflicts her, oppresses her, and bruises her. Hagar is treated badly by a child of Jehovah; not good! So what did Hagar do? She fled, ran for her life! Remember, Hagar means flight, and she was on the first flight to, Shur (the wilderness of Shur, that is).

Hagar runs from her situation right into the, "Angel of the LORD." The "Messenger of Jehovah" a Theophany or Christophany, a visible manifestation of the invisible God. Sounds like Heb. 1:3. (By the way, this never happens in the Newer Testament; never!) The Angel of the LORD is none other than Jesus the Christ, appearing to mankind in a physical form, vv. 7, 9, 10, 11 -- four times in one chapter, **WOW!** The first time is here Gen. 16:7 to Hagar; second time at Mt. Moriah Gen. 22:11 to Abraham; and the third time in Ex. 3:2 to Moses in the burning bush. Now we are looking for <u>prayer principles</u>. *"And the angel of the LORD found her* [Hagar] *by a fountain of water in the wilderness, by the fountain in the way to* Shur.*"* Meditate on that verse until our next chapter, *"And the angel of the LORD **found her** by the fountain."*

*(**Prayer** - "Father, help us, as we meditate upon these words, to draw from your fountain; water that will refresh our sin-parched, thirsty souls. Renew a right spirit within us. O, God, establish our ways, set our feet upon a rock and guide us in the way everlasting." In ha Shem Yeshua's name. Amen!)*

Principles for Prayer:

- The Angel of the Lord comes searching for us <u>to pray and to seek God's face</u>.
- You can't run from an <u>omnipresent God</u> because, every direction you run, He is there!
- Abraham's prayer life influenced Ishmael's life, **for life**; it had to. The Angel heard the **lad's** cry, not Hagar's!

"Men cannot represent God who do not get answers to prayer from Him."
E. M. Bounds

"Prayer on the Edge" #30

Gen. 16:7

In Gen. 16:7, we find that the Angel of the LORD finds Hagar, although God knew where Hagar was all the time, Amen? He wasn't really looking for her, He knew where she was. The word "found" (*mat-sa*) means to appear, exist, come forth, meet, or be present. He just made His presence noticeable, that's all. He is omnipresent! He was there when she was born, purchased, conceived and ran. He found her by the fountain of water, in the wilderness, running for home and running from her problems. *Hmmmm?* Question: are you running from your problems, and in a real sense running from God? Or are you just wandering in the wilderness today? Did He really find her, or did Hagar finally find God? The God of Abraham, her master? Obvious, my dear Watson, isn't it?

Where was Hagar when the Angel of the LORD revealed His presence? *"By a fountain of water in the wilderness?"* Or, *"By the fountain in the way to Shur?"* v.7. The word "Shur" means "wall." and was on the very edge of Canaan before entering Egypt. In other words, she was on **the very edge of no return**! One more step! She was **that** close! Moses entered Shur after crossing the Red Sea in Exodus 15:22. Saul and David fought the *"Ge-Shur-ites"* and Amalakites there. The Angel of the LORD found Hagar by the living water, a gurgling, babbling, bubbling spring. This word "fountain" (*ayin*) is used as a symbol of the LORD's power to refresh. A flow of water from an opening in the hillside, in the desert. *Ahhhh,* how refreshing!

God, my friend, searches for you, but not until you are lost! He feeds your starving soul, but not until you are hungry! He quenches your ardent thirst, but not until you are parched! God will make His presence known to you only when you realize and recognize your desperate, destitute condition and need! When you stick up your hand and call out, "Help me!" The Angel of the LORD found Hagar, in the wilderness, right next to the living water, running from God's perfect will. What a picture of believers today! Question: Did He find you today? In the wilderness or in your closet? In the desert or in your garden? By the coffee machine or by your fountain of living water? Did you hear His voice this morning before the cock crowed, or did the alarm clock wake you?

Don't you just love God's probing questions when you are in flight? v.8 "Hey Hagar, where are you coming from? Better yet, where are you going? You are on the edge, My child, and about to step over the line and fall off the cliff!" Listen, God is not only omnipresent, He is also omniscient. He knows everything about everyone. Then why did He ask? Hmmm? Confession (*achan*) is good for the soul, it gives glory to God (Joshua 7:19), and it is part of the restoration process. Remember, we confess our sins to God, and our faults to the brethren. (Remember that.)

Hey, Hagar, where are you going?"

"To be honest, I am running away from my problems! I'm being beaten, afflicted, dealt with harshly. You understand, God, you are omniscient. You would not want that right?"

"**WRONG!** I want you to return and submit (*anah*), Hagar. (This is the same word for affliction under Sarah's hands.)

Oi Gevault! Sometimes life, the Christian life, is just hard for no apparent reason at all. This is the same word you find in Isaiah 53:4 with our LORD on the cross. "Surely He has borne our griefs, and carried our sorrows, yet we did esteem Him stricken, smitten of God and afflicted (*anah*)." Listen, compared to Christ on that cross, your problem is **diddly**! Return and submit? This is insane! No, it is God's perfect will in this case. He found her (v.7); He restored her (v.8); He returned her (v.9). **WHY?**

So He could bless her (v.10)! Obedience brings blessing; disobedience brings confusion, chaos, and curses (Lev. 26 and Deut. 27). *"I will multiply (rabah) thy seed exceedingly (rabah), that it shall not be numbered for multitude (rab),"* (v.10). Sounds a lot like Eph. 3:20, *"Now unto him that is able to do exceedingly (rabah) abundantly (rabah) above (rab) all that we ask or think..."* He gave her a promise (v.10), His pledge, *"I will multiply thy seed."*

The seed or semen comes from the male. God not only knows where we are and why we are there, but He knows who we are and what we can and will become. He had to do this because of His promise to Abraham in Gen. 15:5 to make Abraham's seed like the stars of heaven. Not Sarah's, not Hagar's, Abraham's! Can you number the Arabs today, plus the Jews? Can you? Try it! Over one billion! Counting as fast as you can, 24 hours a day, it would take you 18 years to count to one billion. Take time out to sleep, eat, and for personal hygiene, and now it's up to 30 years, and they are at 1.25 billion. Question: does God keep His word? All the time!

He found her in the wilderness! He restored her to fellowship! He returned her to His purpose and will! He blessed her with divine blessings! **WOW!** God said it! That settles it! I believe it! Now watch this principle for **prayer** in v.11, *"The angel of The LORD"* speaks for the **third time**, *"Behold, thou art with child, and shalt bear a son, and shalt call his name Ishmael; because the LORD hath heard thy affliction."*

"You shall call his name 'Ishmael' [or *'**Ye-Shama-El**,'* which means 'God shall hear']." Why? *"Because the LORD hath heard [shama] thy affliction."* "*Shama*" means to hear, to listen, and to obey. Deut. 6:4 is referred to, for Jewish people, as *"The Shema,"* and is prayed daily. "*Shema*" means to hearken, to hear, **and then to do something about it**. Did the LORD hear Hagar's cries of affliction? He says He did! Does He hear yours? Psalm 65:2 says He does! Listen, God not only hears, but He cares, I Peter 5:7, *"Casting all your care upon Him, for He careth for you."* So, why pray? Because God hears and because God cares! And his name shall be called "Ishmael – God shall hear." I like that! Because *"El-Shama* means "God heard."

(**Prayer** - *"Father, no matter how hard, how bad, how difficult, how terrible, things may seem, may we stand at the foot of the cross and look up and remember all that your Son went through for us, <u>and never forget</u> that **You never forget**. Compared to His **anah**, our **anah** is nothing! Please forgive us for even bringing it to mind and burdening You with such trivia. We love You. Thank You for finding us by the well of Shur, before we took that final step. In ha Shem Yeshua, we pray. Amen!"*)

Principles for Prayer:

- Confession is good for the soul, gives glory to God, is part of the restoration process, and is the heart of <u>prayer</u>!
- Remember, we confess our sins to God and our faults to mankind, not the other way around!
- God knows where we are, who we are, why we are there, and what we will become. So talk to Him; He knows!

"This ministry of intercession is a glorious and mighty ministry and we can all have a part in it. But we must, if we maintain this spirit of constant prayer, take time, and take plenty of it, when we have shut ourselves up in <u>the secret place with God for nothing but prayer</u>. The key to unlock the door to God's throne room and His heart is prayer, <u>much prayer</u>."

Charles Alexander

"A Cry is Prayer Language" #31
Gen. 16:11-12

Ishmael's international influence begins (Gen. 16:11-12). The first "**son-a-gram**," Hagar knew she was pregnant, but not with what! Hagar is told he will be a "wild man," in Hebrew, "a wild (*pere* – wild ass of a man – *adom*)." Untrainable, unattainable, untouchable, and untamable! *"His hand will be against every man, and every man's hand against him."* It's no different today; fight, fight, fight! The only thing that unites Arabs is a common enemy, like the Jewish people! The Sunnis fight the Sunnis, and the Shiites fight the Shiites, and the Sunnis fight the Shiites. And they both fight their own clans and tribes and the Goi"im, and especially the Jews and the "Great Satan – America." *"...He shall dwell in the presence of all his brethren;"* pitch his tent among them but remain independent. Listen, trying to conquer a bunch of nomadic Arabs in tents is like trying to count the stars in the sky.

We will pick up on Ishmael next time in Gen. 21. Suffice it to say he was the progenitor of the Arabs (the traditional enemies of the Jewish people), and the child of Abraham and Sarah's lapse into unbelief. Moreover, **Islam** (founded by **Mohammed**, who descended from **Ishmael**), is perhaps closest to <u>**Christianity**</u> and the hardest to penetrate with the **Gospel** of Christ, because <u>**it is a way of life**</u>.

Hagar names the well or fountain where the Angel of the Lord found her "*Beer-La-Hai-Roi*" (Gen. 16:13-16), "The Well of the One Who Lives and Sees Me" in my affliction, in my distress, in my predicament, and in my present situation. You see <u>Hagar's extremity became Jehovah's opportunity</u>! Does yours become His? Not only has He seen me, but (v.13), *"Have I also here looked after* [seen] *Him, that seeth me?"* Sounds like Jacob on the river of Peniel in Gen. 32.

Where did Hagar learn to **pray**? In Egypt or at Abraham's family altars? She named the well, "The Well of the One Who Lives and Sees Me!" Amen? He is interested in me, personally!

WOW! If He heard the cries of an Egyptian handmaid, I'm sure He will hear the cries of an adopted child of His. It has been said, "**Prayer knows no language but a cry**." Hagar offered a heart felt cry in the hour of her deep need. Hagar's need was **prayer**, and God met her in the wilderness by a well or spring of living water. Isn't that Christ's invitation to us in John 7:37? *"...If any man thirst let him come unto me, and drink..."* It's not a question of God's ability to quench; it is a question of our desire to be quenched. Are you thirsty? Are you really, really thirsty? How thirsty? Willing to kneel and dip both hands in the water and drink till you are satisfied? Then kneel and repeat after me, "Our Father, Who art in heaven, hallowed (holy and sacred) be Thy name, Thy kingdom come, Thy will be done in Earth....."

The most difficult journey has a beautiful, refreshing climax when the goal is God. Harsh treatment gave birth to a beautiful principle in vv.13-14, "the God who lives and sees me." In our affliction, in our deepest need, even when we can only cry in our soul and not pray audibly, God hears the affliction. Only God can hear affliction. We can feel it, sense it, see it; but only God can hear it. Meditate on that principle!

What is your real need, your real heart felt need at this very moment? I believe it is the prayer God will hear and the one He will answer. Are we fleeing from our affliction, our harsh circumstances, and our trials or testing? I hope you stop by the well long enough to take a drink, to imbibe, to hear His voice, to listen to His instruction. He hears those cries of your heart, even if they are not uttered. After all, He lives inside of you. Your body is His temple, if you have been born-again into His family and adopted as His child! Don't worry: the Holy Spirit will make groanings for you which cannot even be uttered.

Gen. 16:15, "Hagar *bare Abram a son: and Abram called his son's name, which* Hagar *bare, Ishmael. And Abram was four score and six years old..."* This is very important, Abraham is 86 when Ishmael is born, because he is 100 when Isaac is born and 103 when Isaac is weaned, making Ishmael 17-18 in Gen, 21 when he and Hagar depart for the second time (not 4 or 5 years old as many believe). He was the "apple of Abraham's eye" for 14 years, and a thorn in Sarah's flesh for three more years. I am sure he got to know the God of his father, Abraham, in a very special, personal, intimate way. Hunting, herding, building altars, sacrificing, worshiping, praying, etc. But that's for another chapter.

What can we learn about <u>prayer</u> from Hagar, the Egyptian? When we cry out in the midst of our affliction, <u>God hears</u> and <u>God sees</u> and <u>God cares</u>; and that's a comfort. God knows where we are at all times: in the desert, by the well, on the road to Egypt, or on the very edge of going over. Confession and repentance are the keys to restoration and God's blessings. <u>Return is the way of victory</u>, not retreat; and you can't run from your problems. Divine blessings are the result and fruit of our human obedience. Why Pray? Ishmael – God hears. Why call on God? Ishmael – God hears. Why go to church? Ishmael – God hears. Why go to prayer meeting? Ishmael – God hears. What a beautiful name, <u>Ishmael – God Hears</u>.

<u>Hagar saw the God who sees us and cares; have you</u>? Where do you see Him, by the fountain of living water in John 7:37 or in the living Word of God? Hagar learned a lot in trying to run from her problems, from her master's God, from her situation and affliction. But three things seem to stand out: **One** – <u>she learned that God shall hear, and even named her son, "God shall hear;"</u> **Two** – <u>she also learned that the God who hears her is also the God who lives and sees her in every situation</u>, and named the well "*Beer-La-Hai-Roi*;" **Three** – <u>she learned that the God who hears is also the God who cares</u>. What did you learn from Hagar today regarding your prayer life?

(**Prayer** - *"Oh LORD, may the real needs and cries of our hearts be lifted up to You this day. May You hear our afflictions. Only You know exactly what we need and what our families need. You are **El Roi**, the God-Who-Lives-And-Sees-Us. Oh LORD, quench our thirst! In Yeshua/Jesus' name. Amen!"*)

Principles for Prayer:

- In prayer, our extremities become God's opportunities.
- Cry out in your affliction. God will hear, God will see, and God really cares. That is such a comfort!
- Prayer's most effective language is a cry, a groan, a moan, a sigh; don't worry, the Holy Spirit will translate.

"Prayer is releasing the energies of God. For prayer is asking God to do what we cannot do."

Charles Trumbull

"God Hears and Answers" #32
Gen. 16:15

The word or name "Ishmael" or *"Yi-Shama-El"* means "God shall hear and answer!" <u>His very name implies prayer</u>. In fact, Ishmael's name is a monument of God's goodness in answering prayer. Now, we could call him, "<u>Ishmael the bow-hunter</u>," as Gen. 21:20 states, *"...he grew, and dwelt in the wilderness, and became an archer."* However, the Hebrew word for Archer is *"Qash-shat,"* which is the intensive form of *"Qe-shet"* for "bow." *"Qe-shet"* is the weapon and *"Qash-shat"* is the wielder of that weapon; the bow-man, the archer; the shooter. Now you cannot see it in the English, but in the Hebrew there are two words for "archer," 1) *"rabah,"* (to become great), and 2) *"Qash-shat"* (bow-man or archer). So Ishmael was not just a bow-man, but a great archer – maybe the greatest archer that ever lived. Because the intensive Hebrew word for "archer" (*Qash-shat*) is used only one time in the Bible, right here; and has the word *"Rabah"* (great or to become great) attached to it. He kind of reminds me of Legolas, the master archer in "Lord of The Rings."

So we have Ishmael, the first born of Abram, whose name means, "God shall hear," who becomes the greatest archer that ever lived. Nobody else in the Bible has this title, nobody! He becomes the, "Annie Oakley" of the Older Testament, and he dwells in the wilderness of Paran, "The Place of Caravans." His mother, Hagar, gets him a wife from Egypt, and he has 12 sons which become Arab chieftains (much like Isaac who has 12 sons which become tribal princes of Israel).

By the way, Ishmael is not the founder of the Arab nations; Joktan the son of Eber was. Ishmael just joined them and adopted their lifestyle. Historians tell us a pure Arab race came from Joktan to Mohammed, and a mixed Arab race came from Ishmael, but I am getting ahead of myself.

Hagar, whose name means "flight," runs away from Sarai (her mistress) in Gen. 16. The Angel of The LORD finds her by the well in the wilderness of Shur, which she names, "*Beer-La-Hai-Roi*," ("The well of Him who hears and sees me"). He promises her a son named Ishmael, "God shall hear." Why? Because, Gen. 16:11 says that the LORD heard her affliction (*anah*) -- same word we find in Isa. 53:4 of our LORD's suffering. We learned from Hagar that God hears, God cares, and God sees us in our affliction, in our distress and in our dire needs (when we are between a rock and a hard place), but we want to look at her son's life and draw some principles for prayer from "**God Shall Hear**" to apply to our lives.

First let's look at the great archer's early life. Hagar returns to Sarai and submits. Her son is born, whom Abram (at the age of 86) names Ishmael (Gen 16:15-16). In Gen. 17:1, Abram is 99 years old when the LORD appears to him. Fourteen years pass between those two verses. The LORD talks to him and says, *"I am the Almighty God [El Shaddai*, the All-Sufficient God],*"* and Abram falls on his face. A good position to be in when God speaks is on your face, prostrate! God then changes his name from "Abram" (Exalted Father) to "Abraham" (Father of Many Nations).

Now, there are 27 verses in Gen. 17 and 21 that deal with prayer, and prayer is a two-way street. God talks, you listen; you talk, God listens. It's that simple. Most Christians miss this point! Abraham is lying on his face before God as God is talking for **20 verses**, and Ishmael (who is 13 years old now) is probably lying on the ground prostrate right next to his exalted father. He is the apple of his father's eye, the son of his old age, who had become a great archer. God affirms His land covenant with Abraham, and gives him circumcision as a sign between Him and the children of Israel. Sarai's name is changed to Sarah, "Princess – Exalted Woman, or Noble Woman," and God tells Abraham that He will give him a son by Sarah.

Abraham falls on the ground again, laughs, and asks if a child can be born to a man 100 years old and a woman who is 90 (Gen. 17:17). Paul affirms this condition in Rom. 4:18-22. He said Abraham's body was dead and so was Sarah's womb. But

I want you to note the gravity and the urgency of Abraham's words in Gen. 17:18. This is not a question, but a statement, *"And Abraham said unto God, Oh, that [Lu- I wish; if only] Ishmael might live before thee!"* Before Thy face or before Thy presence! Note the exclamation point in your Bible! He is begging and pleading for Ishmael. Oh, how he loved the son of his old age; who doesn't? Did he doubt God? NO! Rom. 4:20 says he didn't! He loved Ishmael, and Ishmael loved him back. How much? Enough to let his father circumcise him at the age of 13 (v.25) with a sharp stone (ouch!). Now that is love, sharp or not! They shared this moment, this covenant together, father and son! Wow! Ouch!

Question: do you think Ishmael believed in and loved the God of his father Abraham? Do you? *El Shaddai* promised to bless Ishmael, to make him fruitful, and to multiply him exceedingly (Gen. 17:20) at the age of 13, his *Bar-Mitzvah*, if you will! Ishmael is with Abraham in Gen 18 when the LORD and the two angels appear to his family and Abraham intercedes for Sodom. Listen, God reveals His plans to us so we will intercede/pray. Has He revealed His will to you? Then pray! (Isa. 45:11.) If not, then listen! I would say Ishmael is standing right next to his father in Gen. 19:28, as they watch the smoke ascending from the plains of Sodom while Lot and his two daughters escape. That's why Abraham prayed! God is somewhat bound by our prayers. Look at Lot's life and Abimelech's life; if Abraham doesn't pray, Abimelech dies. God reveals His plans to us so we will intercede/pray! Ishmael was also with him in Gerar when his father lied about his 90 year old step-mother Sarah.

He is crushed at the birth of Isaac in Gen. 21. He lost his total inheritance at the age of 14, and was humbled when Isaac was weaned (when Ishmael was 17, and he mocked or laughed [*tsaw-khak*]). The same word is used in Gen. 17:17 and 18:12, where Abraham and Sarah laughed at the news of a child being born to them. This is the root word for "*Yitzak*" Isaac!

Question: Was Ishmael a God fearing, God honoring young man? I believe he was. Not only would he have learned to pray, worship, and sacrifice with his father, but I'm sure he helped build those altars and gather those stones. A key passage for me in Ishmael's upbringing is Gen. 18:17-19, where the LORD asks Abraham if He should hide anything from him. (**Read it. I'll wait. What did you think?**)

What lessons have we learned so far from Ishmael's early life that can help us in our spiritual walk or journey, or in our prayer life (besides prayer being a two-way street; and God revealing His will to us so we can intercede)? Listen, Ishmael loved his father. He obeyed his father. He honored his father. He trusted his father. He served his father. He worshiped his father. Now apply that spiritually to your "Heavenly Father" and watch what happens.

(**Prayer** - *"Father, please teach us to listen twice as much as we talk in our prayer time and maybe, just maybe, we might accomplish a whole lot more. Thank You for what we have learned from, "God Shall Hear." Yet we have so much more to learn, so teach us."* In ha Shem Yeshua! Amen!)

Principles for Prayer:

- Prayer is a two-way street; we need to listen twice as much as we talk in prayer.
- God reveals His will and plans to man so he can intercede and pray for them.
- Ishmael loved, honored, obeyed, trusted and worshiped his father. Do that with God and He'll answer your prayers!

"If you are going to win the Province of North Hunan you must go forth on your knees. The closet must give to prayer vitality, and vitality springs from Calvary in action in the believer's life."

Dr. Hudson Taylor (to Dr. Goforth)

"Prayer Opens Our Eyes" #33
Gen. 21:19

Now we need to look at the great archer's later life and draw some <u>principles for prayer</u> from it. In Gen. 21, Isaac is born. Isaac is weaned at age three; Sarah sees Ishmael laughing and casts out the bondwoman and her son. She never accepted Ishmael as her own, **never!** Note Abraham's response in Gen. 21:11: *"And the thing was very [meh-ode] exceedingly grievous [yara –* to tremble or quiver] *in Abraham's sight because of his son."* He loved Ishmael very much, and I believe he had an attachment to his mother, Hagar, as well. Have you ever been grieved to the point of trembling and quivering? Not mad -- grieved? I have, and it is very unsettling. He is all shook up, but in v.12 God says, *"Let it not be grievous in thy sight because of the lad, and because of thy bondwoman..."* Basically, God is telling him, "It will be all right. He is your seed, and I will make it right."

After assurance from God, Abraham sends them off early in the morning with a skin of water and a loaf of bread into the wilderness of Beer-Sheba. From riches to rags, from prince to a pauper, from caviar to bread crumbs. Do you think Ishmael was upset? Wouldn't you be upset? And on top of all that, they are lost in this desert wilderness (Gen. 21:14). The word "wandered" is (*ta-ra*) which means, "to err or to go astray, to be deceived, to stagger." His father is gone, his water is gone, his bread is gone, the road is gone, and his inheritance is gone. His brother got it all, and he is sitting under a bush in the hot desert sun about to die. **BUT** his God, *El Shaddai,* is not gone! Remember, He is the one in v.12 that told Abraham to send them away. His mother, Hagar, is a bow-shot away, and for the great archer, that is a long way off. She lifts up her voice and weeps or wails, (*Bek-ah -* to cry, shed tears, wail, weep bitterly, or mournfully).

What did Ishmael, "God Shall Hear," learn from his father, Abraham, to do in a situation like this, when he was "between a rock and a hard place," like Ur, Haran, Canaan, Egypt,

Damascus, Bethel, Moriah, or Gerar? **PRAY!** Verse 17 tells us, *"And God heard the voice of the lad..."* (*na-ar* – covers ages from weaning to marriage). Not Hagar's wailing; God heard **Ishmael's** praying! The angel of God calls out from heaven, *"What aileth thee, Hagar?"* What is your problem? He saw her, in her affliction (*anah*) but He heard the lad, Ishmael in his prayer. Then He says to Hagar, *"Fear not!"* Why? v.17, a second time, *"For God hath heard the voice of the lad where he is."* **Right there**! Not only did He hear him; He knew right where he was!

Now here is your principle for prayer in v.19, and it is a BIG ONE! *"And God opened her eyes, and she saw a well of water; and she went and filled the bottle with water, and gave the lad drink."* Listen, the well of water was there the whole time, they just could not see it. Abraham gave her a bottle, but God gave her a well! Amen? Listen, prayer opens our eyes so that we can see God's provision. Let me repeat that: **prayer opens our eyes so that we can see God's provision!** What does v.19 say? *"And God opened her eyes, and she saw..."* When did He open her eyes? After Ishmael prayed -- not after she wept -- after the lad prayed! Then you move into vv. 20-21 and it says that God was with the lad and he grew and dwelt in the wilderness of Paran and became a great archer. However, his mother took him a wife from Egypt. You can take the woman out of Egypt, but you can't take Egypt out of the woman. Amen?

This is not the end of Ishmael. He comes back with Isaac in Gen. 25:9 to bury his father, Abraham, with Sarah in the cave of Machpelah. Then in Gen. 25:17-18 we have a strange ending, and I will take it literally. He is 137 years old, *"and he gave up the ghost and died (mooth); and was gathered unto his people."* (Paradise). But v.18 says, *"...and he died (naw-fal) in the presence of all his brethren."* This other word speaks of a violent death, to fall in battle, to be attacked and killed. Some authors see it as dividing up the land, I don't! Yeshua/Jesus said to Peter, "If you live by the sword, you will die by the sword." In fact, if you change the vowel points *(napal)* becomes *(nepel)*, which is a miscarriage, or an untimely birth or an abortion. Remember, in Gen. 16:12 God said this man would be a "wild man," and his hand would be against every man and every man's hand would be against him.

However, Ishmael leaves us one giant principle for prayer: **prayer opens our spiritual eyes to see God's provision.** <u>Why pray? Because we are blind! Prayer gives sight to our eyes, direction to our hearts, taste to our mouths, smell to our nostrils, sound to our ears, touch to our finger tips, and life to our cold dead souls. Prayer is to our spiritual lives what breathing is to our physical lives. If you stop breathing, you will die physically; and if you stop praying, you will also die spiritually.</u> That is an incontrovertible fact. God's will, God's plan, God's provision, God's way of escape is no mystery; but it is only seen through the eyes of prayer. In this case it was a lad. How humbling! Imagine hearing God say, "What ails you, mom or dad? I have heard the voice of your son or daughter. Go fill your water bottle!" <u>Prayer doesn't conform God to our desires; it conforms us to His desires.</u> It's a shame we have to wander in the wilderness dying of thirst when the spring of living water is just a prayer away. We need to teach our children very early to pray. Not just how to pray, or what to pray, or when, or where, but why we pray at all. "<u>Shhhhhh, Ishmael, God shall hear</u>!" That's why! (Psalm 65:2.)

(**Prayer** - *"Oh God, help us to be an example to our children. Help us to be men and women of prayer, so that we might teach our children and grandchildren to pray. LORD, teach us to pray, so that we might teach others to pray."* In *Yeshua's name we pray. Amen!*)

Principles for Prayer:

- <u>If you stop breathing, you will die physically; if stop praying, you will die spiritually</u>.
- Man gave Hagar a bottle of water; God gave her a well of water. Prayer showed her where to fill it!
- It's a shame we wander in the desert dying of thirst when water is just a prayer away!

"I want to have fellowship with Him, and to that end I have asked the Father that whatever else He makes me, to make me above all else an intercessor, to make me a man who spends much time in prayer with Jesus."

Charles Alexander

"Planting Tamarisk Salt Trees" #34
Gen. 21:33

Ishmael is not the only one to learn this very valuable prayer principle. Many other giants of the faith experienced this same eye opening <u>prayer principle</u>, but have you? That's the real question! But before we camp out with some of these giants of the faith briefly, let's pitch our tent by a tamarisk tree with Abraham and get out our canvas and brushes. After Sodom's destruction, Abraham moves his family from Mamre to Beer-Sheba (actually south between Kadesh and Shur; later it is named Beer-Sheba) (Gen. 21:31). This is after Abimelech and Abraham make an oath, and Abraham gives Abimelech seven ewe lambs. Beer-Sheba means, "well of oath, or well of seven" (*be-ayr* and *sheh-bah*). The first word is a pit or well, and the second word is the primary, cardinal number: seven.

In Gen. 26:23, Isaac goes to Beer-Sheba to live and builds an altar. Jacob (in Gen. 28:10) leaves Beer-Sheba for Uncle Laban's (for a wife) and stops in Beer-Sheba with his family on his way back to Egypt for a 400 year lay over. In Gen. 45:1-5, Jacob offers sacrifices, probably on the altar his father Isaac built. There is no mention that Abraham built an altar in Beer-Sheba. However, it was true that everywhere Abraham had a tent, God had an altar! In Gen. 21:12, God speaks to Abraham as he struggles with the decision to send Hagar and Ishmael away. His fellowship and communion with God were pure and unhindered. He was a true "friend of God," something we all desire, or should desire, and possess.

Gen. 21:33, *"And Abraham planted a grove in Beer-Sheba, and called there on the name of the LORD, the everlasting God."* Abraham plants a tamarisk tree." Webster says, "The oriental tamarisk, is native to Arabia, Persia and the East Indies and is encrusted with salt, which is used by the natives and is sometimes called, the <u>tamarisk salt tree</u>." Your Bible may say, *"And Abraham planted a grove..."* (*ay-shel*) tamarisk tree (Strong's #815). He can't build an altar. He is not in the Promised Land, so he plants a tree instead and calls on the name of the LORD, the *"everlasting God,"* (*El Olam*). Very important: he could only build altars in the Promised Land; in other lands he would plant a tree to worship God. *El Olam* expresses the eternality of God, and the eternal duration of the Being of God -- the perpetual, eternal, continual, always-there, and without-end God! Psalm 90:2. This name doesn't just mean that He is everlasting but He is also, God over everlasting things. Like His everlasting covenant to Noah (Gen. 9:16) & Abraham (Gen. 17:13) and His everlasting possessions and promises (Gen.17:8 & 48:4). That's the God Abraham is calling upon: the God everlasting; the God eternal; the God Who always was, Who always is and Who always will be. The great, "I AM!" (Ex. 3:14) (*Ehyeh Asher Ehyeh*)! That's his God! The God of Adam, Noah, Abraham, Ishmael, Isaac, Jacob, Joseph, Moses, Joshua, David, Paul, Peter, Roger ... and your God!

Why did He plant a tree, a living thing? Maybe he recognized God is the God of the living! An altar requires a sacrifice, and a sacrifice is dead. We, like Abraham, need to call on the name of the LORD, the everlasting God, "*El Olam.*" The God who always was and always will be, from everlasting to everlasting. The One Who gives to us everlasting life (or we choose everlasting Hell). After leaving Mamre (fatness) and Hebron (communion) to journey south in the Negev-dryness (after his lie to Abimelech; after he had to send his son and Hagar away; after his battles with Abimelech's men; and after his wandering and journeying in the desert), Abraham realizes he had to plant a tree and call on the everlasting God Who knows all and is always there. He is omnipresent, omniscient, omnipotent and omnificent. He's here, He knows, He can do it, and if need be, He can create something new from nothing! You also have a tree, planted on a hill, which brings everlasting life. It's called "Calvary!"

How about those other spiritual giants whose eyes were opened by a simple prayer. In Gen. 22:9-14 we have Abraham, the friend of God, and Isaac on Mt. Moriah. Abraham is about to slay Isaac when the "Angel of Jehovah" calls out from heaven, "Abraham, Abraham!" In v.13. Abraham lifts his eyes and looks and behold, right behind him is a ram caught by his horns in a thicket. Where did it come from? When did it arrive? Was it there the whole time and they just didn't see it, like Hagar and the well? Jehovah-Jireh, "The LORD will see to it ahead of time," on Mt. Moriah. (*Ra-ah* to see & *Yah-Jehovah*). To see Jehovah! Yeshua/Jesus said in John 8:56-58 that, *"...Abraham rejoiced to see my day: and he saw it..."* If this wasn't it, then when was it? An altar serves three purposes: **sacrifice, worship and prayer,** and we saw with Ishmael that prayer opens our spiritual eyes so that we can see God's provision. In Ex. 3:1ff Moses is on the back side of the Midian desert, alone. Yes, he has a few sheep but I believe he's searching for God's direction (praying, meditating alone), and he comes upon Horeb, the mountain of God and a burning bush. And the Angel of the LORD appears to him in that burning bush and says, *"Draw not nigh hither* [near here]*: put off thy shoes, from off thy feet, for the place whereon thou standest is holy ground."* Then he receives his assignment. "Go tell Pharaoh to let My people go!" His first response is, "Who am I?" What changed his mind, what opened his eyes, what changed a stuttering, stammering, sheep herder into a fearless, courageous, valiant leader? One word: **Prayer!**

In Josh. 5:13-15, Joshua is about to conquer the Promised Land. The people are circumcised, celebrating Passover, and eating the grain of the land, because the manna had ceased. Joshua is meditating, **praying** for direction alone when the Angel of Jehovah appears with His sword drawn. He tells Joshua the same thing He told Moses, "Take off your shoes; you are standing on holy ground." Once again, **prayer** and meditation opens Joshua's eyes so he can see the LORD's provision. In II Kings 6:17 Elisha is surrounded by the Syrian army and his servant is scared. Elisha **prays** for God to open his servant's eyes, so he can see that they that are with Elisha are more than they that are with the Syrian army, and He does. Once again, **prayer** opened his eyes to see God's provision.

In I Chron. 21, David numbers the people and God sends a plague and kills 70,000 men due to David's pride. The Angel of the LORD is about to strike Jerusalem, with his sword drawn, when David sees him. Why? **Prayer!** In verse 16, he and the elders are dressed in sackcloth, fasting and mourning for God's mercy. Again, **prayer** opened their eyes to see God's provision and hand. In Dan. 9, Daniel is **praying** for 21 days when the angel Gabriel comes to him at 3:00 p.m., the time of the evening offering (v.21). Only Daniel saw the vision: why? The length of **prayer**, the depth of **prayer**, the fact that he was **fasting** (v.3) for three weeks and they were not? I don't know, but I do know this: that God opened his eyes so he could see the angel like Ishmael, Abraham, Moses, Joshua, and David. **Prayer opens our eyes!** In Luke 24, the two disciples on the road to Emmaus who walked and talked with Yeshua/Jesus did not recognize Him because their eyes were **holden**. It was after Christ took bread and blessed it and broke it that their eyes were opened. After He **prayed!** (Lk.24:31). **Prayer opens our spiritual eyes so we can see God.** Their physical eyes saw a man!

So what did we learn from Ishmael, "God Shall Hear?" **1)** He loved his father. He obeyed his father. He honored his father. He trusted his father. He served his father. He worshiped his father. There are many types in the Bible, but the only type of, God the Father is Abraham, Ishmael's father. So as "God Shall Hear" honored, obeyed, trusted, loved, and worshiped his earthly father, so should we do likewise with our heavenly Father. And **2)** we learned that prayer (an address, entreaty or petition to God whether verbal or mental, in word or in thought) opens our spiritual eyes so we can see God's provision or answer to our request. If you can't see clearly, pray, and God will open your eyes (whether it's to a well, a ram, a burning bush, a talking donkey, a flaming chariot, or an angel with a sword drawn). Listen, if He can open the eyes of Balaam's donkey, He can open your eyes. Don't make prayer difficult! It is simply talking to God like you talk to a friend, it's a two-way street. You talk and He listens, then He talks and you listen (and don't forget that part). Listening is a lost art in prayer; let's find it and bring it back.

(**Prayer** - *"Father, please help us to apply these prayer principles to our lives, so we can be more effective in our prayer closets and in the* war against evil in our day. It feels like we are losing the battle every day -- not winning it. We need help, Father, and we need it now, before it is too late. In Jesus' name we pray. Amen!")

Principles for Prayer:

- What changed Moses from a stuttering coward into a startling leader? One word: **prayer**!
- **Prayer** removes Satan's scales from our eyes so we can see what God's plans are and what He wants us to do.
- If you can't see clearly, ask God to open your eyes. If He did it for Balaam's donkey, He can do it for you!

"The word of God represents that all the possibilities of God are at the disposal of true prayer. Help is at hand, and often comes before the prayer is complete, because God hears the unspoken sigh and groan."

A.T. Pierson

"Paint Pigments for Prayer" #35
Gen. 15:1

We need to take out our palettes and mix some other pigments to get the right shades of color for the portraits of prayer we desire for our canvas. So, with brushes in hand, we back up a bit to Gen. 15:1, where, *"The word of the LORD came unto Abraham..."* <u>Prayer is simply talking to God</u>! In fact, <u>conversation with God is called prayer</u>! What a beautiful, intimate relationship God and Abraham shared, to simply converse back and forth! Isn't that what God desires for every one of us? A simple, plain, naked relationship; to share our burdens, our cares, our needs, our desires, our wants and our lives with Him? We need to talk to God, He hears, He cares, He listens, He heals, He provides, He protects, etc.

What a beautiful chapter to meditate on: Gen. 15. Verse six says, *"And he believed in the LORD, and He counted it to him for righteousness."* Do we believe God, you and I? I mean do we **really** believe Him, against all odds, all circumstances, and all situations? Even to the point of offering your only son whom you love with all your heart on a rock, in a barren land (Gen. 22)? Abraham believed, Abraham obeyed, and Abraham was blessed! **Remember, God's delays are not God's denials!** The word for "believe" here is amended, he said, "<u>Amen, to God</u>." Have you?

The lesson here in prayer is that what God has promised He will do in His own time frame, **but He will do it!** <u>What we need is the Amen of faith in our prayers</u>. God cuts a covenant with Abraham, and a pillar of fire and a pillar of a cloud pass between the animal parts. Was God showing Abraham how He was going to lead His people out of Egypt after 400 years? I don't know! Abraham was open and honest with God and talked with Him; he hid nothing from God, **nothing!** Do you hide anything from God? Some secret sin that does so easily beset you (Heb. 12:1)? We all have them! He stood like Adam, bare-naked before his Creator and talked, face-to-face. That is the only way to come!

We too, need to be open and honest with God in our prayer gardens. He knows everything, anyway. We can't hide anything, right? Of course! Abraham just walked and talked with God and shared everything. We call it prayer, communion, worship; <u>God calls it fellowship</u>! We need to talk to God, to be open, to be honest; He hears, He cares, He listens. So tell Him what's bugging you (after all, He created the bugs too)! "Oh LORD, may we be honest and open in our prayers, our conversations with You! Thank You, for hearing, for caring, for listening and for loving us." Did you get to splash a little color on your canvas today? Good!

Gen. 17:3 says, *"And Abraham fell on his face."* Abraham is 99 years old and the LORD appears before him and says (v. 1), *"I Am the Almighty God, (El Shaddai) walk before me, and be thou perfect* [blameless]." Then Abraham fell on his face and God talked with him. <u>Prayer is a two-way street</u>; we talk to God and He listens; God talks to us and we listen, or do we? We need to develop the lost art of listening in our prayer closets. Abraham fell on his face! Good position – humble; not kneeling, NO! Prostrate! Face in the dirt! He couldn't get low enough before, *El Shaddai*! What a chapter, Gen. 17; Abram becomes Abraham; Sarai, becomes Sarah; circumcision is instituted, 700 years before the law; they are promised a son; Abraham is 100 and Sarah is 90; and God's covenant is re-established, **WOW!**

Notice: God does all the talking from v.1-17, then Abraham gets a word in edge-wise in v.18 (**seven words**), and then *El Shaddai* takes over again. Then when God is finished talking with Abraham in v.22, *"God went up."* <u>This was a face-to-face encounter with God</u>. When was the last time God talked face-to-face with you? Then when was the last time you took God at His word literally? Abraham believed God and **"IT"** was imputed unto him for righteousness! Believed! Amended! He said, AMEN! To God! God said it and that settled it! Amen, God! When we pray, we need to be like Abraham and fall on our faces before *El Shaddai* and be still and **"LISTEN"** to God. And when He is done, say, "Amen!"

Get your brush out, paint this, let us meet God face-to-face on our faces! Here in Gen. 17:18 we have the first recorded prayer in the form of a father praying for his son: *"And Abraham said unto God, Oh that Ishmael might live before Thee!"* I believe Ishmael is a believer in the LORD and is lying on the ground right next to his father with his face in the dirt too. However, this was asking far more than God had offered to do, and he also received an immediate answer in v.20. A beautiful example of prayer for your children to God, *El Shaddai,* the Almighty God, the All Sufficient One; the Strengthener and Satisfier of His people; the One Who enriches and makes fruitful.

El Shaddai promises a 100-year-old man and a 90-year-old woman that He would bless them and multiply them exceedingly and make them fruitful (v.16). The name used for God primarily before the law on Mt Sinai was *El Shaddai*, the All-Sufficient One. Then it was *Jehovah*, the Self-Existent One (*YHVH*). Job uses *El Shaddai* 31 times, so Job chronologically fits right here in Gen. 17. So Abraham met *El Shaddai* face-to-face, on his face, and listened intently, speaking briefly (and probably wished he could take those seven words back, although they came from a father's heart). "*El Shaddai,* Sustainer, Strengthener, Satisfier of all mankind -- we believe your Word and we say, 'Amen!' to Your promises. LORD we seek Your will in this coming year, may You strengthen us, sustain us, and satisfy us. LORD teach us to cultivate the lost art of listening in our prayer closets and lives." I trust you were able to mix a few pigments on your palette and apply a few brush strokes to your canvas on portraits of prayer. We have some more palette work to do before we jump back into Isaac, Jacob, Joseph and the matriarchs, so walk with me.

(**Prayer** - *"Lord, let us take something from this lesson today and apply it to our prayer lives, just a brush stroke or two. It does not have to be a finished project, just something to enrich our lives and strengthen our prayer lives for You, God, to make them more alive and vibrant. There is so much in this lesson to add to our canvas of prayer life, so much to learn from Your giants of faith who have gone* *before us. Teach us, Lord, as we bow before You. In Jesus' name. Amen!")*

Principles for Prayer:

- In prayer we need to meet God face-to-face and take Him at His Word literally!
- God will do what He has promised in His own time frame, but He will do it!
- What we need today is the "<u>Amen</u>" <u>of faith in our prayers</u>, like Abraham had.

"I have never known a child of God who acted according to Matthew 6:33 in whose experience the Lord did not fulfill His word of promise."

George Müller

"More Prayer Paint Pigments" #36
Gen. 18:1

Got your palette and brushes ready? Because God is going to pay another visit to His friend, Abraham, and you may want to add some more shades to your masterpiece. Gen. 18:1 says, *"The LORD appeared unto him* [Abraham] *in the plains* [or by the oaks] *of Mamre."* There should be no doubt in your mind Who one of these men is who visits Abraham in the plains of Mamre in the heat of the day. Gen. 18:1 says, *"The LORD* [Jehovah –YHVH] *appeared unto him."* Well, He is omnipresent, isn't He? <u>Everywhere present at once</u>! Then in v.10 He says, *"I will certainly return unto thee according to the time of life; and lo, Sarah thy wife shall have a son."* It is the LORD Who gives life, because He is omnificent; He is unlimited in creative power (one of His omni-attributes seldom discussed.) Then in v.13, *"The LORD said to Abraham, wherefore* [why] *did Sarah laugh…?"* showing the LORD knows everything about everyone (even the things we whisper in secret, proving He is omniscient).

But the real cap-stone is in v.14, a verse we should inscribe on our hearts: ***"Is anything too hard for the LORD?"*** The answer is NO! Not even for a 90 year old woman to give birth and nurse her son for three years. Why? <u>Paint **omnipotent** on your canvas</u>, right over <u>omnificent</u>, <u>omnipresent</u> and <u>omniscient</u>. That's the God Who meets you in your prayer closet in the morning or in your prayer garden before the cock crows, before the dew dampens your manna, and before the sun warms the crust of the Earth. What a God we serve!

Now this meeting in Gen. 18 is more than meeting God in your quiet time. Abraham gets a personal visit from *Yehovah*. He is in Mamre (fatness) in Hebron (communion) residing near the altar he built in Gen. 13:18 and God personally pays him a visit. There is fellowship and communion here we know little of today, *(YADA)* spiritual intimacy, spiritual intercourse, on a level few of us will ever encounter. Abraham was, "a friend (*ahav* – a lover) of God." Can that be said of you? Can it?

What sweet communion they enjoyed together, close intimate fellowship. A friend, a real friend, a true friend will share the inner personal thoughts and intents of their hearts. Someone once suggested, "When we lose a friend we die a little." However, when we lose our best friend we die a lot, and we may never recover. A friend is a gift we give to ourselves. Here is one of my favorites statements, "Friends are the chocolate chips in the cookie of life." I don't know who said it, but I could eat a dozen of them. But a real, true friend will share the thoughts and intents of their heart and the LORD, *Yehovah* in v.17 said just that, *"Shall I hide from Abraham* [My friend] *that thing which I do?"*

Oh, to have that kind of relationship with *Yehovah* God, that He chooses to share with you His cares, His intents, and His will. It makes me well up with tears as I type these words right now, I can hardly see my screen. Oh God, please help me to finish painting this portrait for my readers. I am not worthy. Please God, stay Your hand, LORD. I am trembling by the power of Your very presence in this room, at this very moment, please Jesus help me……I need to focus. Thank You. (Sorry) As I tremble!

Isn't that what He has done in Christ and in His Word – reveal His will and His intents for us to pray about (I John 5:14-15; Eph. 5:17)? Oh to see God, to talk with Him, to walk with Him, to share the burdens of our hearts and have Him share the burdens of His heart! Could we even bear to hear it? But He does reveal His heart to us and His burdens, in His Word. That's where He talks with us, and <u>we can share our hearts with Him in prayer</u>. In our quiet time, our secret place, our prayer garden (Matt. 6:6), but remember to shut the door! He is waiting for us in the secret place -- patiently, longingly, lovingly, calling tenderly, "Come unto Me," in our *Mamre*, (fatness) our *Hebron* (communion). Do we enter or do we walk away empty? God, please hear me now!

In Gen. 18:20, The LORD shares that burden with Abraham, *"...Because the cry of [outcry against] Sodom and Gomorrah is great, and because their sin is very grievous..."* He goes on in v.21, *"I will go down now, and see whether they have done altogether according to the cry [**zah-ak**; shriek, outcry, to cry for help in a time of distress] of [against] it."* Most frequently this cry is directed to God. In Gen. 19:13, it was a tortuous cry or prayer from those being abused in the city. It could have been the neighbors surrounding the city. Whoever it was, God had enough and He had heard enough! And enough is enough! So, He sent messengers down to check it out, along with His Son, and to destroy it if necessary. God never acts over or against any of His creation without a full understanding of all the circumstances, never! What God heard and saw is found in every large and small city today world-wide, namely the noon-day of Hell!

But He heard the outcries, the tortuous shrieks against Sodom and Gomorrah and there lies the key: **"against!"** Can our prayers, shrieks, cries, tears, outbursts, **against**, abortion, perverse sexual sin, alcohol, drugs, crime, sin, gambling, pornography, child abuse, etc., etc., make a difference? I believe it can, and just like Sodom and Gomorrah, God will come down and see America and judge it, if our outcries against it are genuine and loud enough and great enough for Him to hear. But I don't believe we loathe it enough yet! I don't think we hate it enough yet! Our outcry, like theirs, must be tortuous and painful; and our prayers must literally shriek to heaven's throne room! As someone once said, "If God does not judge America soon, He will have to apologize to Sodom and Gomorrah." Do you believe that? Then pray like you really hate sin!

*(**Prayer** - "Oh God, help us to hate sin like You do, to loathe sin, to detest sin, to abhor sin, all sin, any sin, every sin. May our prayers be a tortuous outcry **against it**, and may You remove it from our midst and heal our land. LORD, we long to be Your friend like Abraham. Help us to have fellowship like he had, and to have a prayer life like he had. Teach us, O LORD. In ha Shem Yeshua we pray, Amen!")*

Principles for Prayer:

- God has revealed His will and His intents in His Word so we can pray for them, with Him.
- Sometimes God meets with you because He has something special for you to pray about.
- Remember, it's the omnipotent, omniscient, omnificent God who meets with you for prayer.

"Prayer is either a prodigious force or a disgraceful farce. If a farce, you may pray much and get little;
if a force, you may pray little and get much!"

A.T. Pierson

"Brush Strokes for Prayer" #37
Gen. 18:23

*"...But Abraham stood **YET** (od – longer, still, more, yet) before the LORD."* (Gen. 18:22-37). One of the greatest prayers of **intercession** between man and God in all the Bible (for mankind) takes place right here. Here is a gap-man of the rarest sort. Oh, if God would only raise up more gap-men like Abraham, "father of a multitude." America might even stand for another hundred years if we had more Abrahams. The two angels left for Sodom, but Abraham stands before the Judge of all the Earth and levels with God in Gen. 18:23. *"Wilt Thou also destroy the righteous with the wicked?"* Obviously not! Here we see the importance, the supreme importance, of the righteous in contrast to a wicked, sinful world or family! Like Abraham, we need to be honest with God in our prayers. Phil. 4:6 *"In everything...let your requests be made known unto God."* As Josh McDowell said, "Get it in the light or be honest with God." He knows your heart, your desires, your wants, and your intentions anyway.

Abraham answers his own question or reason in v.25, he also recognizes one of God's eternal attributes. *"Shall not the Judge of all the earth do right?"* Can you imagine for a moment the relationship this man had with the Judge of all the Earth? To enter into this kind of a dialogue? Pure, unadulterated friendship! These two, Abraham and *El Shaddai* were more than intimate friends, they were (*ahav* – lovers). God willingly, lovingly directly answers Abraham's question in v.26. He will spare the city for the sake of the righteous, **"America Take Note!"** Now Abraham realizes he has God's undivided attention, but he also realizes Whom he is talking to and humbles himself in v. 27, *"I ... am but dust and ashes."* Humility is the key to intercessory prayer. We need to be open and honest, yes, but we also need to be humble. These two go hand in hand in prayer: humility and honesty.

We must not only recognize who God is: sovereign, supreme, immutable, omnipotent, omniscient, omnipresent and omnificent, etc. <u>But we must remember who we are: dust and ashes.</u> Gen. 2:7 says He created us out of nothing (*Ex-Nihilo* – Latin). We, like Abraham, need to remember Heb. 4:16, that God's throne is a throne of GRACE! And that we have access only because of Heb. 10:19, the blood of the supreme sacrifice *Yeshua*/Jesus. And we must come humbly before Him remembering the only way up to God is by being down on our knees and faces. I Peter 5:5-7. There can never be true intercessory prayer without true humility, true holiness of our spirit, and true honesty. <u>Humility is the first essential element of intercessory, efficacious prayer; and honesty is the second</u>.

This is beautiful. Abraham continues to **intercede** with the LORD and the LORD continues to **concede** to his requests. I am speaking reverently here, please don't misunderstand me! God has given us the <u>ministry of reconciliation</u> (II Cor. 5:18); He has made us ambassadors (II Cor. 5:20); and He has declared us righteous because of what Jesus Christ has done (II Cor 5:21). Therefore, let us still stand before the LORD, before, the Judge of all the Earth, and <u>intercede for our wicked cities</u>, towns, nations, continents and leaders! <u>God has given us the ministry of reconciliation and intercessory prayer, and we squander it. Shame on us!</u>

Listen, the only time you are in perfect unity with the Tri-Unity of the God-Head is when you enter into <u>intercessory prayer</u>. Then you are praying to the Father, through the Son, by the power of the Holy Spirit. Only three individuals have the privilege of the ministry of intercession on behalf of others: the Spirit (Rom. 8:27), **the Son** (Heb. 7:25), and **the saints** (I Tim. 2:1). "LORD help us to see how vital our ministry really is on this **dirt ball** spinning in space to oblivion. LORD, call the righteous to their knees before it's too late; and teach us to pray for America, for Israel and for the world before we destroy ourselves." In Jesus' name, Amen!

"Suppose there were five less than fifty righteous, would You destroy the city for the lack of five?" Abraham asks this of God (v. 28). Abraham is desperate now. His nephew, Lot, and his family are in that city. If you knew that God was going to destroy the city your family lived in, would you become desperate and intercede? Listen carefully, ***God does not answer prayer***! Let that sink in.... In fact let me say it again for emphasis, ***God does not answer prayer***! **He answers desperate prayer**! **Determined prayer**! **Destitute prayer**! He answers prayer that sweats, prayer that moans, prayer that cries, prayer that bleeds! And Abraham was at that point: desperate, destitute, despairing, and determined to save Lot and his family -- 50, 45, 40, 30, 20, 10... He thought he was safe; why not?

Surely, there was saved Mr. & Mrs. Lott, his two saved married daughters and their two saved husbands and his two saved single daughters who were dating two saved God-fearing men. That would make 10! Surely, none of them would be unequally yoked, right? Wrong! Listen, even if he went to five and threw in the milkman and mailman, it still would not have been enough! We don't ever want to stop short in our intercession with God, **NEVER!** This is definite, determined, detailed, demanding, desperate, PRAYER! The key to intercession is **don't stop short!** If you are going to go for it **go for it!** God wants to know just how serious you are about a certain person or need. How badly do you want your loved one saved? How badly do you want that revival? How badly do you want unity? How badly do you want that healing? How badly do you want that job? How badly do you want that ...?

This kind of prayer, intercessory prayer, **COSTS** blood, sweat, tears, sleep, and pleasure. We have lost the concept of **praying through** in prayer, and in intercessory prayer that is vital. We must never stop pleading until the guilty party is acquitted. Now either Abraham thought there were at least ten righteous people in Sodom, or God stayed his hand from praying any further. When God finally decides to destroy a place, He forbids it to be prayed for anymore (Jer. 7:16; 14:11). Jeremiah was forbidden to pray, cry or intercede for Judah anymore. Now, we don't know His determined will many times, unless we pray or study His Word. We know it is not His will for any to perish (*apollumi* – die and go to hell). So we can plead for anyone.

The telephone company used to have a slogan, "**Don't hang up**!" Jer. 33:2-3 tells us to call on Him and He will answer. That's His promise, and God can't lie any more than a rock can swim or a duck can chew gum. It's against His nature. Our problem is we hang up to soon; we cut Him off before He is done talking. We need to cultivate a principle in our prayer life, our intercession, to pray through, not stop short, and not hang up. Got it? Why am I not so sure?

(*Prayer* - *"Oh LORD, make us gap-men and gap-women for America, for Israel, for the world, for our Churches, and for our families. Oh LORD, take us, break us, fill us, remold us, and use us to never stop pleading with You, the Judge of all the Earth, until the guilty are acquitted. In Your Son's holy name we plead. Amen!*)

Principles for Prayer:

- We need to be open, honest and humble when we pray. Humility and Honesty are key in prayer!
- God doesn't answer prayer! He answers desperate, determined, destitute prayer. Prayer that sweats, bleeds and cries!
- The key to prayer is "don't stop short - don't hang up - don't quit" and pray through, until you get an answer from God!

"The secret of Judson's profound influence and endurance is found in the fact that he gave so much time to prayer. He kept his iron red-hot with prayer."

E. M. Bounds
(speaking of Adoniram Judson's impact on Burma)

"One More Brush Stroke" #38
Gen. 19:13

"...The cry of [outcry against] them is waxen [has grown] great before the face of the LORD." Gen. 19:13. The torturous cries or shrieks were either from people within Sodom who were being abused, or people without who were crying out for God to do something. If Lot and his two daughters were the only ones spared, then there were no other righteous people in Sodom. The age old question comes up again, "Does God answer the prayers or cries of anguish from the unsaved?" Psalm 65:2 says, *"O thou that hearest prayer, unto thee shall all flesh come."* Like Jonah chapter one, I don't believe it is a question of whether God hears the prayers of the unsaved heathen for salvation. We know He hears their prayers for salvation (II Peter 3:9). <u>In our text we are talking about outcries against sin</u>!

Now God is omnipresent (everywhere at once), and He is omniscient (He knows everything anyway). Therefore, all speech, all cries, and <u>all prayers</u> are heard and noticed by Him. <u>Hearing is one thing; answering is quite another</u>! Whoever it was who was crying out against Sodom, it came up before the face of the LORD (Gen. 19:13), and He sent two angels to check it out (Gen. 18:20-22). In Gen. 19:19-20, Lot pleads for mercy for a little city to flee to, and the angels grant his request of intercession. Even in his sinful state, God heard Lot's cry for mercy and answered it. Abraham had interceded for Lot and his family and, *"...God remembered Abraham."* (Gen. 19:29.) If it wasn't for Abraham, Lot's uncle, Lot wouldn't have made it. <u>Does intercessory prayer work? Ask Lot when you see him</u>, or Abimelech, Pharaoh, Ishmael, Isaac, Hagar, or the Kings of the vale, or even Melchizedek.

Lot lost his daughters, his sons-in-law, his wife, his testimony, all his possessions (which were great - Gen. 13:6), and almost his life. He then committed incest with both of his single daughters. How low can you go? But Lot's family died, due to one word, "LUST," and poor judgment. Remember, as far as we know Lot did not have a wife before he went into Sodom, so his wife was probably from Sodom. <u>She didn't just turn around to look back; she turned around to go back</u> (Luke 17:32 - *"Remember Lot's wife."*). But the prayers, the intercessory prayers of a friend (and a friend of God) prevailed; 50-45-40-30-20-10. <u>Praise God for **prayer-warriors** who will stand in the gap</u>. Genesis 19:27 says, *"Abraham gat [got] up early in the morning to the place where he stood before the LORD."* The place (Gen. 18:22) where he bartered with the LORD but stopped short! However, even 5 would not have saved it!

When was the last time you stood before the LORD for a backslider who was living in Sodom, who lost all he or she had, including their testimony? Galatians 6:1 fits in here like a piece of a puzzle. Let us learn a valuable lesson (**or prayer principle**) from this, less we slip away, or worse, get lost and fail to intercede for one who has slipped away - 50-45-40-30-20-10-
5-1. Don't stop short; don't hang up; **pray it through** -- until you have your answer. (Gen. 18:32 *"I will not do [destroy] it for ten's sake."*)

God promises to answer prayer (Gen. 19:29, *"And it came to pass, when God destroyed the cities of the plain, **that God remembered Abraham,** and sent Lot out of the midst of the overthrow..."*) *"God remembered Noah."* (Gen. 8:1); *"God remembered Rachel."* (Gen. 30:22) – "remember (*zaw-kar* – to mark, so as to be recognized." <u>Does God remember you? Better yet, are you known in Hell as a man or woman of prayer (Acts 19:15)</u>? "Oh LORD, may we be intercessors for those who have pitched their tents outside of the gates of Sodom; for those who have fallen away and lost everything including their testimony. Help us, LORD, to remember that <u>prayer does make a difference</u>, and that You do remember! Oh LORD, remember us, our prayers, and our Lots! Amen!"

"...For he is a prophet and he shalt pray for thee, and thou shalt live." (Gen. 20:7). I love this verse, and this principle and promise from God, don't you? God could have healed Abimelech without Abraham's prayers, but He chose not to

(Isa. 45:11). *"Ask of me things to come concerning my sons, and concerning the work of my hands, command ye me."* Now there is a principle to wrap your heart and hands around and to paint on your canvas!

Abimelech was innocent. In the integrity of his heart and in the innocence of his hands he took Sarah as his wife. Abraham and Sarah lied to him (they told him half truths, which is a lie). But God closed all the wombs in Abimelech's house. Then God told Abimelech, he was a dead man, he and all his house, unless Abraham prayed for him, because God called him a prophet (Gen. 20:7)! Interesting! <u>Unless Abraham prayed, God would not heal!</u> Wow!

<u>God has chosen to be somewhat limited by our prayers</u> (I say that reverently). In fact, God's blessings are dependent upon man's prayers; we have already seen that. There is no such word as **"FAIR"** in God's vocabulary, only justice and mercy; and He decides which is dished out to whom. So Abraham prays to God and God heals Abimelech, his wives, and his maid servants; and then they bear children (v.17). Oh, how dependent the unsaved world is upon our prayers for their blessings and fruitfulness, and they are not even aware of it (nor are we many times)! Too often we fail both God and the world because of our lack of and desire for prevailing intercession on the part of mankind in general. In church we are fortunate if we see 25 people come to Christ over the year. Why? No prayer! <u>C.H. Spurgeon had 500 men praying in a room in the basement while he preached on Sunday.</u> **500!** How many do you have?

<u>The costliest service and most fruitful a Christian can enter into is intercessory prayer</u>. It means to judge, to entreat, to make supplication, to intervene or interpose. The traditional explanation of this word is to "invoke God as Judge," "break oneself," "be contrite" "pray;" "act as a mediator," or to "seek assessment or consideration." An interesting verse where this word is used twice (once for God and once for man) is found in I Sam. 2:25, *"If one man sin against another, the judge will*

*judge (**intercede**) him, but if a man sin against the LORD, who shall intreat [**intercede**] for him?"*

You could write a book on the word "intercession." It is used 30 times in I Kings 8 and II Chron. 6, when Solomon dedicates the Temple. However, what is really interesting is how some writers view the origin of this word. It is an Arabic word meaning "to notch the edge of your sword" or "**to cut or wound oneself**" (such as the priests of Baal did on Mt. Carmel). In another place it means "to fall, emphasizing prayer or prostration." Or it comes from the word meaning "to break or cut, or to pass judgment." I guess they are all right, as true intercessory prayer will take blood, sweat, and tears. It will require prostration of the heart, soul, and body at times. It is to call God into judgment. It does speak of estimating or assessing a situation at times. It does mean to intervene, interpose, entreat, intercede and to stand in the gap!

And failure to do so is **SIN** (I Sam. 12:23)! John Knox cried, "Oh God, give me Scotland or I die!" Jonathan Edwards prayed for three days, "Give me New England!" and God did! We need to enter into intercessory prayer for our Pastors, our churches, our leaders, our country, our families, our fellow men, and our enemies!

"The LORD, needs intercessors today, gap-men and women, not just prayer-buddies. Men and women need to tarry, prevail, stand in the trenches. They need to fight the good fight, stand in their places before God and not let go until He blesses them (and those for wom they are interceding). Want to sign up? There is still room for a few. The little hand is on the 12 and the big hand just left the 11, so we don't have much time!"

(**Prayer** - "Lord we need intercessors, prayer warriors, mediators, arbitrators, gap-men, to make up a hedge, to stand between us and You, to take the incense off the altar and run between us, before it is too late. Do it now Lord, do it now! In Jesus' name. Amen!")

"Now unto Him that is able to keep you from falling, and to present you faultless before the presence of his glory with

exceeding joy, To the only wise God, our Saviour, be glory and majesty, dominion and power, both now and [for]*ever. Amen."* Jude 24-25.

Principles for Prayer:

- <u>Does intercessory prayer work</u>? Ask Lot when you see him or Abimeleh, or Isaac, etc.
- Memorize Isaiah 45:11, *"and concerning the work of my hands, command ye me."*
- The costliest service and the most fruitful a Christian can enter is, <u>intercessory prayer</u>.

"I wish I could pray for something new every day, while there are so many things in the treasury of God."

A. Bonar

"Commune with God Alone" #39
Gen. 24:63

Abraham was 99 years old and God said, "You are going to have a son," and he fell on his face and broke out in <u>laughter</u>; not in tears, **laughter** (Gen. 17:17). Isaac or *Yitzhak* was born in Gen. 21:1-8, circumcised on the 8th day, and weaned from his mother on his third birthday. That's how it was done. The next day Hagar and Ishmael, Isaac's half brother, were driven out, expelled, with nothing more than a loaf of bread and a bottle of water.

Thirty-seven years passed between Gen. 21:14 and Gen. 22:1. Thirty-seven years between that period and the beginning of the next chapter, the account of Abraham's sacrifice on Mt. *Moriah*. So, we know nothing about Isaac's early life as we do Ishmael's. Isaac's early life is a mystery, just like the early life of *Yeshua, Jesus*. However, we do know he stayed on Mt. *Moriah* with the Angel of Jehovah when his father Abraham left to return home to his mother Sarah in Gen. 22:19 with the two servants, as seen in the Hebrew text, why? To commune alone with the LORD like Joshua did in Ex. 33:11. Do you take time to commune alone with the LORD, in prayer? Do you? What does it mean to commune with the LORD? Could this be where Isaac learned to meditate on the LORD (Gen. 24:63)?

In Gen. 23, Sarah, Isaac's mother died, whom he loved very much, and he mourned her death and lived in her tent. He was very close to Sarah, as Ishmael was very close to Abraham and Hagar. How do we know this? <u>Gen. 24:67 says he is finally comforted</u>, (*na-cham*) consoled, eased of grief following his mother Sarah's death. Question: where did he take Rebekah? Into his mother Sarah's tent. He was living there while Abraham his father was living with *Keturah*, his new wife (which means incense), who bore him six more sons, at 140. The ancient Rabbis believe this is Hagar who came back after Sarah died.

In Gen. 24, Abraham's eldest servant, probably *Eliezer* (God's helper) of Damascus went to Iraq to get Isaac a wife, namely Rebekah the second matriarch. Her beauty and character were captivating, like a noose around your neck, and Isaac's grief was immediately lost in his love for his newly-arrived bride. The first time we find Isaac as an adult other than on Mt. *Moriah* is in Gen. 24:63, where we find him meditating in the field near Lahairoi. *"And Isaac went out to meditate in the field at the eventide: and he lifted up his eyes, and saw, and, behold, the camels were coming."* His father taught him well, or the Angel of the LORD did. The next time we find Isaac is in Gen. 25:19-23 where he **entreats"** the LORD for children for his wife at the age of 60. Four things stand out here, (**C**ommune**; O**ffer, **M**editate, and **E**ntreat) and they form the acrostice C.O.M.E.: **1** – He knew how to **commune** with the LORD; **2** – he knew how to **offer sacrifices** to the Lord; **3** - He knew how to **meditate** on the LORD; 4 – He knew how to **entreat** the LORD. Have we learned those three vital prayer principles for a vital prayer life with the Creator of life?

Abraham is still alive and 160 years old when his grandsons Esau and Jacob are born. They are about 15 years old when Abraham dies, so he had time to influence their lives. There is another famine, and the LORD tells Isaac to go to *Gerar* (not Egypt), and confirms Abraham's Covenant with him in *Lahairoi*, which we know as the Gaza Strip today. Abraham is dead at this point. Isaac becomes the new patriarch with the confirmation of the covenant, just like Abraham did when his father Terah died in Haran in Gen. 11:32. Isaac lies about his wife Rebekah being his sister (she is about 60 years old and very beautiful). Like father like son, or as they say, "The apple doesn't fall far from the tree!" What is ironic is the only verse in the Bible like this is Ezek. 16:45 which basically says, "Like mother like daughter." But we will leave that one alone for now.

Then Isaac enters a new career, a new occupation, a new calling if you will. So far we have had Adam the garden-tiller; Enoch the God pleaser; Noah the ship builder; Abraham the altar builder; Hagar the runaway; Moriah the God seer; Ishmael the great archer; and now, Isaac the well-digger. Here's something to put on your frig: "A person's prayer life should encompass more than his/her prayer list!" Ponder that thought for a moment!

Wells are very important, especially in the desert where water is very scarce. To name a well denoted the right of property and to stop or destroy one was a mark of territorial conquest or encroachment. Just keep that in mind! A dug well many times was a source of living. You paid or bestowed gifts on the owner to drink. Esau married Judith, whose father *Beeri* (well), owned a well, which made him rich (Gen. 26:34). Water is essential to life. You need it to cook, clean, drink, irrigate. Dr. Shelton, who studied fasting, stated that a man can go without food for 40 days, without water for three days, without air for 8 minutes, and without hope for 30 seconds. Starvation begins on the 41st day, when the stored food reserves in your tissues are used up. (Interesting that Moses, Joshua, Elijah, and Jesus all fasted for 40 days, not 41). We take water for granted (we just turn a faucet), but in Isaac's day you either lived by a river, dug a well or died of thirst and dehydration. A dug well indicated that you liked the area and that you planned on staying there for a while with your family. Now Abimelech and the Philistines envied Isaac. They filled his father's wells with stones and told him to move on; to get out of their territory (Gen. 26:14-16). Does this sound familiar? So, he departed from *Gerar* City and dwelt in *Gerar* Valley. By the way, *Gerar* is the Gaza Strip and is the modern city of *Umm*. The root word for *Gerar* means, "to drag off or away."

Sometimes, my friend, God has to drag us off or away from something so we can hear His voice and know His will. We like security; the unknown is a scary thing. Most of us don't like to live "by faith!" He was, "at ease in Zion," to use a common phrase, and God dragged him off to the valley where He could use him and speak to him. We don't live on the mountain top of transfiguration; we live in the valley with the demons (Matt. 17). Question: where has God dragged you off to today? Do you feel lonely, lost, destitute, hopeless, and helpless? Then you are right where God wants you, in the valley where the enemy has chased you! Isaac could have stayed and fought, but it was God's will for him to move on. He had something to do for God and something to hear from Him.

There are times in our lives when circumstances cause us to move on, to make changes, and to adjust to whatever God is allowing to happen to us. Remember, God led him to *Gerar* during the famine, and then he became great (Gen. 26:13), *"And the man waxed [became] great, and went forward, and grew until he became very great."* Sometimes God's servants stay too long in one place and sometimes they don't stay long enough to make a difference. Isaac could have gotten mad at the Philistines, but instead he just moved on, and on, and on....

It is no different with us today either. Sometimes God allows circumstances to occur in our lives in *"Gerar,"* and drags us out kicking and screaming; or He has to use the enemy to shove us out the door, so He can speak to us and use us for His glory. So don't get mad, get moving. Pitch a tent, not a fit. Grab a shovel, dig a well. Dip your cup in, try some living water. Be still and listen to that small, still voice and wait on Him! That's what I had to do in the fall of 2006, when He said, "Step out of the boat!" I've never looked back, not one time. And I've never, ever regretted stepping out of that boat!

*(**Prayer** - "Abba, Father, thank You for leading us along the way, showing us the way, teaching us the way, even when we have to come kicking and screaming. You know what's best. Abba always knows best, because only God knows the end from the beginning. Show us, Abba, the way in which we should walk, the right paths, so we may commune with You and Your Son, meditate on You and Your Word, and entreat with You and Your Spirit." In ha shem Yeshua we pray, Amen!)*

Principles for Prayer:

- Know how to commune with God; meditate on God and entreat God.
- A person's prayer life should encompass more than their prayer list.
- Always remember to take time to commune alone with God; Jesus did, and He **was** God!

"No circumstances in which we can ever find ourselves can be called 'impossible circumstances' while the God of the impossible is on our side and dwelling within us."

John Harrison

"Digging Up Old Wells" #40
Gen. 26:17-18

Isaac begins his new vocation by digging up his father's old wells, a good place to start. <u>Always start with the familiar</u>. Gen. 26:17-18 says, *"And Isaac departed thence [from there], and pitched his tent in the valley of Gerar, and dwelt there. And Isaac digged again the wells of water, which they had digged in the days of Abraham his father; for the Philistines had stopped them after the death of Abraham: and he called their names after the names by which his father had called them."* Isaac began to dig up his father's wells which the Philistines had stopped up.

<u>Arabs believe destruction shows possession</u>! (Go figure!) Question: has God dragged you off, my friend? Are you discouraged, distressed, down in the dumps? Have you lost all hope? Then maybe, just maybe, you need to roll up your sleeves and do something for God, like dig a new well (or an old one) to refresh yourself and others. Maybe that's what *Yeshua*/Jesus meant when He said, *"Occupy till I come."* (Luke 19:13.) The word in Greek is (*pragma*) where we get pragmatic from, or practical. In other words, do something practical; don't just occupy space or a pew in church.

The Interpreters Bible Commentary says, "Isaac turned back to what were proven wells." He could have looked for a new oases, but why bother? Solomon said, "There is nothing new under the sun." We are heirs of our ancestors whether we like it or not. I see pictures of my father and sometimes it's scary. We are ancestors in culture, customs, character, features, knowledge, nature and experience. In fact, those lessons of life teach us about man, God, duty, prayer, worship, sacrifice, etc. I am amazed at just how much my parents did teach me about life. But many times the only thing we learn from life is that we didn't learn anything from life, and we have to keep repeating our mistakes. Benjamin Franklin once said, "<u>Experience is our best teacher, but fools learn from no other method</u>."

Isaac was dragged out of *Gerar* and cast out into the desert. He needed water (a lot of it), and he needed it right away! So his servants dug a well in the valley (Gen. 26:19) and found a *"well of springing water."* (***Beer-Chay-Mayim***); fresh, flowing, running water, an artesian well. However, there was contention with the Philistines, and they said it was theirs, so he named it "***Esek***" (contention) and moved on. Then they dug another well and this time there was strife and fighting over it, so they named it "***Sitnah***" (strife) and moved on again. What problems are facing you today? Are there contentions and strife in your life? Have you lost your spiritual joy? Maybe, just maybe, you need to put those old Philistines behind you and move on. Let them have that old well. It may not be worth the fight, but sometimes it is. So weigh the odds, count the cost, and make your choice, but choose wisely and always on the LORD's side. God has a place of rest and enlargement just for you, Jabez!

In v.22 Isaac left *Sitnah* and dug another well; and for that one the Philistines strove not. He named it *"Rehoboth"* and said, *"For now the LORD hath made room for us, and we shall be fruitful in the land."* The common interpretation for *"Rehoboth"* is "wide places or streets." However, when you look at the root in "Paleo-Hebrew," the Hebrew prior to the Babylonian captivity, the (*Resh*-is a head; the *Chet*-is a fence or inner-room; and the *Beth*-is a tent or house). So, you have the "Head person of the private, inner-room, of the house or family." Or, the "Head, offering security to the family." *Rehoboth* is more beautiful and picturesque in ancient Hebrew than just a wide place, and I believe that is what Isaac is offering his family.

Finally he is far enough away from the Philistines to obtain peace from without, but not peace from within! Peace from his enemies, yes! But not from himself, nor from his God! You see there is **peace with God** (Romans 5:1); there is **peace from God** (Romans 1:7); there is the **peace of God** (Phil. 4:7); and one day there will be **peace on Earth** (Luke 2:14). Do you possess the first three? You can have peace on the inside and peace on the outside **only** if Jesus Christ is living on the throne of your heart! Peace with your enemies is only good if you have peace with yourself and with God!

So, Isaac's unrest caused him to move again; or is it the Spirit of God moving him, (v.23)? *"And he went up from thence to Beer-sheba."* He went home to the place where he grew up (Gen. 21 and 22), where his father dug a well, built an altar, planted a grove, and called on *"El-Olam,"* "the Everlasting God." That night the LORD appeared to Isaac and spoke to him (v.24), making a covenant promise to bless him and his seed for Abraham, His friend's, sake. Do you get the impression that God was leading him along the whole time to get him to the place where God could bless him and use him for His glory? *Beer-La-Hai-Roi, Gerar, Ezek, Sitnah, Rehoboth, Beer-Shebah*! God had a plan for Isaac as He does for every one of us if we will just trust Him and obey His Word. How does that old hymn go? "Trust and obey, for there's no other way, to be happy in Jesus, but to trust and obey."

Six things happen in Gen. 26:24-25: two happen **to** Isaac, and four are done **by** Isaac. It is important to note their sequence: **One** – (v.24) Isaac had a personal encounter with the LORD! Have you? Before you can know God's will and direction, you must know *"YADA"* God. (Ps. 46:10 -- that's, spiritual intimacy.) To do this, you must be willing to spend time in prayer alone with Him, seeking His divine direction and intervention. Isaac was in the habit of **communing alone with** the LORD (Gen. 22); and **meditating alone with** the LORD (Gen. 24); and **entreating alone with** the LORD (Gen. 25). Are you in the habit of doing those three things on a regular basis? Remember, a person's prayer life should encompass much more than a person's prayer list. Prayer is a two-way street. **Two** – (v.24) God promises Isaac divine assurance and divine blessings; *"I am with thee, and will bless thee, and [I will] multiply thy seed..."* He receives a three-fold blessing: assurance, blessing and multiplication.

Isaac does four things as a result of this encounter. Note them in v.25: **First** – He builds an altar for family and corporate worship of Creator, Jehovah-Elohim. **Second** – He calls upon the name of the LORD in prayer (asking for protection and provision). **Third** – He pitches his tent and establishes his homestead (he settles in for a "long winter's night" -- about 80 years worth). **Fourth** – He digs a well to provide his family refreshment and remuneration, and he takes possession of his area.

Where are you today? On the back-side of some desert? Has God dragged you out from among the Philistines? Is there contention and strife among your peers? Do you have more to bear than you can bear? Then you need to build an altar; you need to call on the LORD; you need to pitch your tent; you need to dig a well. But first you may need a Bible, a blanket, a canteen, a cabin and Psalm 46:10, *"Be still and know (yada) God."* (The *"I am"* is in italics, which means it's not in the Hebrew text.) So can you do that? Just be still and *"yada"* God, have spiritual intimacy with Him, <u>some one-on-one time with God</u>? It's not as easy as you think. Adam had *"yada"* with Eve in Gen. 4:1 and she gave birth. God is looking for that same kind of intimacy, but on a spiritual level (Hos. 6:3). Isaac found it; but he had to come full circle and so do we (Rev. 2:4), "We have left, not lost, **LEFT** our first love!"

*(**Prayer** - "Father, we have stepped out of the circle. You are waiting in the inner-room of our tent, our Rehoboth, with open arms, wooing us. 'And the Spirit and the bride say, Come. And let him that heareth say, Come. And let him that is athirst Come. And whosoever will, let him take the water of life freely.' God of Heaven and Earth, You want to know if there is room in the Bethlehem of our hearts today for the Son of God, Your Son, to be born afresh. Because, 'He who testifieth these things saith, "Surely I come quickly."' Yes LORD, there is room in our hearts for You, for Jesus and for the Holy Spirit. 'Even so come Lord Jesus.' Amen!")*

Principles for Prayer:

- "Occupy till I come." This is the Greek word (*pragma*) which means, put feet on your prayers – *practicology*!
- Spiritual intimacy means having some one-on-one time with God. A time out with Jehovah!
- Is there room in the Bethlehem of your heart for Jesus to be born afresh today?

"May all fear as to our being able to fulfill our vocation vanish as we see Jesus, living ever to pray, and standing surety for our prayer life."

Andrew Murray

"Commune, Offer, Meditate, Entreat – Which?" #41 Gen. 25:21

In Gen. 26:26-31 *Abimelech* and the Philistines show up for dinner. Sure, right after all the work is done! Because that's what Philistines do, show up after the work party... to party! They cut a covenant, swear an oath, eat a meal, and depart in peace; yeah, right! Then Isaac's servants find a new well and he names it *"Shebah,"* the well of the oath or covenant. *Beer* means well and *Shebah* means oath. *Beer-Shebah* is an area south of *Gerar* or *Gaza* on the trade route, so a well would be very valuable in that location to travelers. Many times a well was about four feet wide and about six to ten feet deep in a dry river bed and would form a pit!

The wells in Genesis were very significant and associated with special events; *Beer-lahai-roi*, was the well of Him who lives and sees me (Gen. 16:14; 24:62; 25:11); *Beer-sheba*, was the well of the oath or covenant (Gen. 21:25-33; 22:19; 26:23-25; 46:1-5); *Esek*, was the well of contention (Gen. 26:20); *Sitnah*, was the well of hatred (Gen. 26:21). Those last two were Isaac's own attempts at well digging, after that he chose to live by the wells of his father Abraham. *Rehoboth* was the well of enlargement, as most would have us believe. The *Paleo-Hebrew* says, "The head of the inner-room of my heart and home who offers my family security." (Gen. 26:22). When Isaac returned to *Beer-Sheba*, the LORD of his father, Abraham, made Himself known to him and established His covenant with him; and Isaac built an altar for sacrifice, worship and prayer, pitched his tent and dug a well. He was staying put!

In Gen. 27, Isaac is 100 years old and blind, and we have the story of the stolen blessing of *Easu*. First he traded his birthright for a bowl of lentils in Gen. 25. The first-born always got the farm. With the Amish the youngest gets the farm. So he gave away the farm for a bowl of soup. Then Jacob stole his blessing in Gen. 27 with an old goat (or was it *from* the old goat)? The moral here is don't wait till you are old and blind to bless your *kids*, because you might bless the wrong ones. Isaac lives 80 more years and dies in Gen. 35:27-29. He is gathered unto his people and buried by Jacob and Esau. Isaac is alive for 60 years after Jacob returns to the Promised Land with his family from Laban's labor camp, but nothing is known of Isaac's later years (or of his earlier years for that matter). Rebekah's nurse, Deborah, dies and her death is recorded in Gen. 35:8. <u>Rebekah's death is never recorded</u>. <u>She died in silence</u>, during Jacob's 20 year absence, of a broken heart. She sent away her favorite son, never to see him again! So sad.

Now, what prayer principles can we glean from this well digger's life? Isaac learned about altars from his father, Abraham, the altar builder. In fact, he built one with him in Gen. 22 on Mt. Moriah and then laid on it! It was there Isaac learned to commune with God. That is our **First principle** for prayer. The word "**commune**" in its earliest form meant to have in common (both in giving and in receiving) in <u>thought, word and in deed</u>. In fact, from it come the words, commune, communicate, communion, community, and even **communism**. In Ps. 4:4, the word "commune" is (*amar*) "to say in your heart." To commune with your heart upon your bed and be still. In Ps. 64:5, the word for "commune" is (saw-far) "to recount, reckon, rehearse, enumerate, go over and over." In Ps. 77:6 the word for "commune" is (*see-akh*) "to muse, ponder, consider, to put forth in thoughts. (I communed with my own heart). When you commune with God no words are uttered; the giving and receiving takes place in your heart, soul and mind. ***Listen, you always commune <u>with</u> some<u>one</u>!*** Not with **some<u>thing</u>**.

The **Second principle** Isaac taught us about prayer is **offering sacrifice.** Isaac had learned from his father, and from his life experience, how to offer sacrifices to the LORD.

The **Third principle** Isaac taught us about prayer is **meditation**, Gen. 24:63, *"Isaac went out to <u>meditate</u> in the field at eventide..."* He was in the field meditating when his wife arrived. ***Listen, you always meditate <u>on</u> someone or something!*** The word (*soo-akh*) means to go over a matter in one's mind, to rehearse silently or aloud. To speak, mutter, utter, moan, or growl. The main difference between commune and meditate is the audible part. One is always silent (commune), and the other can be silent or it can be audible (meditate). Ps. 119:15, 23, 48, 78, and 148 use the same root word showing pious meditation and devotion. Psalm 1:2 and Josh. 1:8 use a different, but similar word (*hāḡâ*). Again, you meditate on someone or something.

The **Fourth principle** Isaac taught us about prayer is **entreaty** (Gen. 25:21), *"And Isaac intreated [entreated] the LORD for his wife, because she was barren:"* He **entreated** the LORD for his wife. The word here is (*athar*) "to pray, to supplicate, to plead, to intercede, to stand in the gap." The root of this word means abundant, plentiful, and to multiply. I get the idea he did a lot of entreating, for a very long time! Amen? How does that verse go, "The effectual, fervent prayer of a righteous man, avails..." Twenty years is a long time to be barren. Now why was she barren (*aw-kawr*)? Listen carefully, this word means she was sterile! How is that for a prayer request? Pray for me I want a child, and oh yeah, by the way I am **sterile!** *Oi vei!* Then she receives a double portion, "Red and Fred." You see, faith is not believing God **can**; faith is believing God **will!** Now she is pregnant and the twins are struggling and she inquires of the LORD (Gen. 25:22), (*da-rash*) to seek or consult. But Isaac made abundant, plentiful entreaties (*athar*) on her behalf -- to plead, to supplicate, to intercede, to stand in the gap. There is a big difference in their prayer lives, a big difference. Where did they grow up? Hmmm? One in the Promised Land; and the other in Padanaram.

You commune **with** someone; you sacrifice **to** someone; you meditate **on** someone; you entreat **for** someone! Did you learn anything from Isaac? How to dig a well? How to run from God? How to lie about your wife? Or how to walk with God? I trust you learned some more principles about Isaac's prayer life that you can apply to your own. Communing is from your heart to God's heart. Entreating is uniting your spirit with God's Spirit. Meditating is from your mouth to God's ears. And all of it is directed to your LORD! Which will it be for you today, a shovel to dig a hole and look for water, a pair of running shoes to find a place to hide, an old prayer altar to lay those burdens down, or a quiet place to hear that still, small voice; <u>to commune, meditate, ruminate</u>, and to take a fresh look into the face of *Yeshua/Jesus?* When was the last time you took a fresh look into the face of *Yeshua/Jesus*? Isn't it about time you did it again?

*(**Prayer** - "Father, some of us have been running a long time and we are tired and we want to hang up our running shoes. Some of us have worn out our shovels and we want to turn them in. We just need an old altar to lay our burdens down and to call on You, our 'Burden-Bearer.' Please, LORD, help us to commune with You, to meditate on You, and to entreat for those around us. In Jesus' name we pray. Amen!") "Now unto the King eternal, immortal, invisible, the only wise God, be honour and glory for ever and ever. Amen." (I Tim. 1:17)*

Principles for Prayer:

- Have you shown up for the work party today to <u>party</u> or to <u>PRAY</u>?
- Have you sold your birthright or blessing for some beans and an old goat's opinion on <u>prayer</u>?
- To commune is to have in common in thought, word and deed; in giving and in receiving.

"When God is going to do something wonderful, He begins with a difficulty. When He is going to do something miraculous, He begins with an impossibility."

Charles Inwood

"Desperate, Destitute, Determined Prayer" #42 Gen. 25:21

I don't think we lowered our buckets deep enough in the well at *"Beer-Sheba."* So, let's go back and give our buckets a little more rope and take another sip. Genesis 25:21 says, *"Isaac intreated (pleaded) with the LORD for his wife, because she was barren (sterile): and the LORD was intreated of [by] him (or granted his request) and Rebekah his wife conceived."* Isaac was 40 in v.20 when he married Rebekah, and 60 in v. 26 when Jacob and Esau were born. So Rebekah was barren for the first 20 years of their marriage, and barren again for the remainder of their marriage. <u>Isaac entreated or pleaded with the LORD for his wife</u>. This word means <u>to burn incense in worship</u>, to intercede, pray, or entreat (*a'thar*). Its <u>Arabic cognate means to slaughter a sacrifice</u>; <u>perhaps the Hebrew word has a sacrificial basis too</u>. It means to make an earnest request or prayer, to beseech or implore. Biblical prayer is spontaneous, personal, motivated by a need and unconditioned by time or place. Its marks are childlike, sincerity, simplicity and confidence. The LORD can be approached anytime, anywhere, for anything. With all of Israel's detailed instructions on sacrifice, there is no fixed liturgy for prayer. It is <u>spontaneous, sincere, and simple</u> and child like (like a child talking to their mother or father). Isaac pleaded with the LORD for his wife, *"He intreated the LORD for his wife... and the LORD was intreated of him."* God listened to his prayer, and **v.21 tells us the LORD granted his plea**.

God listened to his prayer, He hearkened, (*shama*) listened with understanding, and was intent on doing something about it. Why? Isaac was <u>desperate, destitute, and determined</u>. Interesting how God withheld children from Sarah, Rebekah, Rachel, Hannah, Elizabeth and others. Remember, Isaac is living near the well, *"Beer-La-Hai-Roi"* (The Well of the One Who Lives and Sees Me). Sixty years of Isaac's life is gone; now he comes to God with an <u>urgent prayer request</u> and God listens and grants it. I believe <u>he had been praying for 20 years</u>; but now he is <u>desperate, destitute, and determined</u>. God answers that kind of prayer, and that's what God has been waiting for. Psalm 127:3 says, *"...the fruit of the womb is his reward."*

There was strife in Rebekah's womb (*rasas*); a struggle, to crack in pieces, to break, bruise, crush, oppress. This word is used to describe maltreatment and oppression. There was trouble in her womb from conception, abnormal movement, and one baby was trying to break the other in pieces. In Romans 9:10-13, God said (while the babies were in Rebekah's womb), *"...Jacob have I loved, but Esau have I hated."* Two nations struggling (*rasas*) in the womb. Was one trying to eliminate the other before birth? I believe he was! So, Rebekah inquired (*daras*) of the LORD. To seek with care, to consult for knowledge, advice or insight into a particular problem. That's just what Rebekah had, a problem! Her two boys were trying to break each other into pieces in her womb. They were born for contention, as sure as sparks fly upward, and their lives bore this out. Two answers to prayer: <u>one an entreaty, the other an inquiry</u>, and God answered them both. Why? They were <u>desperate, destitute and determined</u>! It does not matter what your problem is, or how big it is, bring it to God. <u>He is the God of the impossible</u>; in fact <u>His middle name is impossible</u>! The moment you say, "I can't!" He says, "I Can!"

In Gen. 26 Isaac follows the same route as Abraham, his father, even by running to Gerar and lying to Abimelech about his wife. But God chooses to bless him anyway. Not <u>because</u> of him but <u>in spite of</u> him, and because of His promise to Abraham. We have a covenant-keeping God; One who never breaks His promises, One who must keep His word. That is a key principle to remember in prayer. We have a tremendous transformation in the life of Isaac in this chapter, and it is brought about by prayer. <u>You don't see much of Isaac's prayer life</u>. He runs (v.1); God speaks to him (v.2-5); He lies (v.7); God blesses him (v.12); He digs wells (v.18ff); God reveals Himself to him (v.24); God confirms His covenant with him (v.24); He builds an altar and finally calls on the LORD (v. 25) at Beer-Sheba the "Well of the Oath," where Abraham and Abimelech made a covenant (Gen. 21:31).

Despite all the promises, protection, and blessings of God; we don't read about any sacrifices, prayers, or altars of Isaac until now! It wasn't enough just to live in his father's past and dig up his father's wells and receive blessings due to his father's faithfulness and obedience. He had to return and worship <u>for himself</u> his father's God, ***El Shaddai, El Olam, Elohim***. God appears to him in Beer-Sheba and Isaac finally builds an altar and calls upon the name of the **LORD JEHOVAH**, the self-existent, eternal One, and he builds an altar to the God of Isaac! Gen. 26:25 says, "And he builded an altar there. and called on the name of the LORD, and pitched his tent there..." Sounds pretty decisive! Remember, Abraham never built an altar in Beer-Sheba; he planted a tamarisk tree (Gen. 21:33) to the "Everlasting God, ***El Olam***." Isaac's servants dug a well there and called it *Sheba*.

Isaac is about 80 years old at this point, and it took him that long to begin to practice the presence of Almighty God, ***El Shaddai***. When he did, the Philistines knew it (v.28), and they said, *"We saw certainly that the LORD was with thee:"* It is exciting when the unsaved say that about the saved. Amen? They saw it and they feared it; <u>what a testimony to practicing the presence of God in the midst of your enemies</u>. We need to pitch our tents, build our altars, and call on the name of our LORD in the midst of our enemies. We need to stop riding on the sleds of the past, stop bowing to the demigods of yesterday, strike out on our own, and discover that God the LORD is a covenant keeping God. One who never breaks His promises and must keep His Word if we (v.5) obey His voice, keep His charge, His commandments, His statutes, His laws, stay in His Word and let His Word stay in us and obey it. The God of Enoch, Noah, Abraham, Isaac, Moses and David is the God of Roger, Mary, Jane, Frank, Eden, and John. He is our personal God. So, let's pitch a tent, build an altar, dig a well, call on the name of our LORD, and practice the presence of God in the midst of a heathen society. Amen? I said AMEN? Better!

(**Prayer** - *"Oh LORD, may we daily practice Your eternal presence so that You might manifest Your power through us among the unsaved around us and bring glory to your name. And may they see and know that we have been with Jesus by our words and actions." In Your Son's name we ask. Amen!)*

Principles for Prayer:

- Biblical prayer is spontaneous, personal, motivated by need and unconditioned by time and place.
- The Lord can be approached anytime, anywhere, for anything, in a sinner's simple childlike manner.
- Prayer should be like a child talking to their father or mother and asking for something they need.

> ***"Prayer is but the touch of an infant, put on the arm of the Almighty."***
>
> ***Thomas Scott***

"The Stolen Prayer Blessing" #43
Gen. 27:35

Yitzhak (laughter) or Isaac, the well digger is also known for his blessings. So, we have named this devotional, "**The Stolen Prayer Blessing.**" Is a blessing a prayer? It is if it is invoking God's promises or blessings upon an individual, family or nation. Gen. 27:35 says, *"Thy brother came with subtilty, and hath taken away thy blessing."* Esau could not get the blessing back, even though it was taken away deceitfully by Rebekah and Jacob. They didn't have to do this, because God promised her in Gen. 25:23 while she was still pregnant and praying to God (when the twins struggled in her womb), *"The elder shall serve the younger."* (Rom. 9:12). In other words, Esau will serve Jacob, why? (Rom. 9:13) *"As it is written, Jacob have I loved, but Esau have I hated."*

God is omniscient. He knew you before you were born, before you were conceived, <u>before you were a gleam in your father's eye, before you were a thought in your mother's heart</u>. In fact, He knows what you are thinking right now, so be careful (John 2:24-25). An oath or blessing with God is a permanent thing (Gen. 27:33) *"...yea, and he shall be blessed!"* Ecclesiastes 5:2 says, *"Be not rash with thy mouth, and let not thine heart be hasty to utter any thing before God: for God is in heaven, and thou upon Earth: therefore let thy words be few."*

The word "bless" (*barak*) or blessing is all over this chapter, vv. 4, 7, 10, 12, 19, 23, 29, 33, 34, 35, 36, 38, 41: Isaac tried to reverse God's order, will and plan to have Esau serve Jacob (v. 40) *"...and it shall come to pass when thou shalt have the dominion, that thou shalt break his yoke from off thy neck."* Esau was angry because of the blessing and vowed to kill his brother Jacob after Isaac died. <u>The family blessing was a powerful thing in those days as it is today</u>, but it has been forgotten in most cultures. Jacob later blessed his twelve sons in Gen. 49, but in chapter 48:13-22, he blessed Joseph's two sons, Ephraim and Manasseh, in reverse order. Ironic? No, God's perfect will! You see, it took him about 100 years to understand God's plan and purpose. How long will it take you?

Isaac didn't walk as close to God as his father Abraham did. Isaac only built one altar that we know of, in *Beer-Sheba*, and he stayed there. Little is said about his walk or talk with *El Shaddai*. The promise was to come through him and it did. God keeps His promises. If he had walked closer to God I believe he would have recognized God's plan and he would not have tried to reverse it. You don't hear any more about Isaac from this point on. Gen. 28 picks up with Jacob's life, and Isaac is about 150 years old. In Gen. 35:27-29; Isaac dies at 180 and, Jacob and Esau are between 80-100 years old. Isaac's first blessing in Gen. 27:29 was intended for Esau, *"...be lord [master] over thy brethren...,"* but God said Esau will serve Jacob. Isaac tried to reverse God's will, but in v. 40 he says, *"And by thy sword thou shalt live, and shalt serve thy brother..."* Do you ever try to reverse God's will in prayer, or bargain shop with Him? Sometimes we seem to think God shops for prayer requests on E-bay and the answer goes to the highest bidder, but He doesn't.

Isaac gives Jacob a final blessing in Gen. 28:3-4, and asks God Almighty to give him the blessings of Abraham. He calls on *El Shaddai*, the Strengthener, the Satisfier; really He is the All-Sufficient One. He not only enriches, but He makes fruitful. Listen, to Isaac's blessing, *"And God Almighty [El Shaddai] bless thee, and make thee fruitful, and multiply thee, that thou mayest be a multitude of people; and give thee the blessing of Abraham, to thee, and to thy seed with thee; that thou mayest inherit the land wherein thou art a stranger, which God gave unto Abraham. And Isaac sent away Jacob..."*

El Shaddai is a God of fruitfulness. This is the God Isaac prays to, the God of his father Abraham. Jacob was a supplanter, a heel catcher, a conniver, but he was obedient. Esau was honest but rebellious, disobedient, hateful, and seditious. *Yeshua/Jesus* spoke of a similar situation in the parable of the two sons in Matt. 21:28-32. Which of the two son's did the will of his father? The first who said he would not go to work in the field, but did? *"Jacob have I loved, but Esau have I hated."* (Rom. 9:13; Mal. 1:2-3) A statement that has perplexed theologians since it was written. Jacob, like his father Isaac and his grandfather Abraham, would eventually meet *El Shaddai, Elohim, YeHoVah*; and He would become the personal God of Jacob or Israel when he returned to *Bethel* in Gen. 33:20.

For now though, what has happened to, **"The Blessing of the Blessing?"** That may sound redundant, but it's not meant to be. It's meant to be a probing question. I believe our children and our children's children have missed out on spiritual and material blessings because we believe "blessings" are an "Old Testament" tradition that should be packed away in the attics of our minds in moth balls. When was the last time, **fathers,** you laid your hands on your children and seriously prayed a blessing over them and for them? That was a regular, weekly tradition in the orthodox Jewish home, and the church was birthed out of the womb of Judaism. Children are a blessing from God, not a curse or a punishment. The fruit of the womb is His reward and happy is the man whose quiver is full, and <u>**a warrior's quiver in the Older Testament held 13 arrows**</u>!

I have eight children (four by birth and four by marriage), and each one makes my heart sing. I also have fifteen grandchildren and one great-grandchild who make my heart smile; what a blessing! (There is still room for more grandchildren and a brood of great-grandchildren!) As the patriarch of your family you need to reclaim that **"stolen blessing"** which belongs to your family, and re-establish once again the blessing the enemy has snatched. By the way, who stole it: Your neighbor, the deacons, God, or Satan?

Every church service used to end with a benediction or a blessing. Now they end with announcements, a song, a screen saver or, "You're dismissed!" What, are we still in the fourth grade? God instructed Moses to instruct Aaron and his sons to bless the children of Israel and put His name on them so He in turn could bless them in Num. 6:27. Could you apply that to the church, and if not, why not?

You have the word "bless," "blessing," or "blessed" 500 times in the Scriptures; **500 times**! Is it important to God, is it? It would do us all well to memorize Numbers 6:24-26, "The Aaronic Blessing," and use it whenever needed. You see it on walls and plaques everywhere, so let's steal it back and use it for God's glory! *Amen?*

*(**Prayer** - "Abba, Father, please, Bevakasha, help us as fathers and pastors to re-establish the blessing which You gave to us as heads of our families and churches to give to them. To bless them and cause them to be fruitful, to multiply, to fill the Earth, to inherit the land and to worship You, the only true God! Lord, please allow us to study and claim the "Blessing of the Blessing" once again for our families and churches, for it has been stolen from us. Father, it is ours by right of inheritance and we claim it back." In Yeshua's name. Amen!)*

Principles for Prayer:

- When was the last time, Dads, you laid your hands on your children/grandchildren and prayed a blessing over them?
- Pastors, when was the last time you prayed a blessing over your congregation at the close of a service? A blessing!
- Husbands, when was the last time you laid your hands on your wife and prayed a blessing over her?

"I am hoping to give special time to prayer and Bible study on this voyage. I want our life to be an ascending plane, not resting in anything we have learned or felt or attained, but pressing on and up to Him."

Hudson Taylor (to his wife)

"Praise for Answered Prayer" #44
Gen. 24:26-27

In Gen. 2:18, *"...the LORD God said, It is not good that the man should be alone; I will make him an help (ezer) meet (or fit) for him."* Actually, it is repetitive, so it would be (*ezer - ezer*) for him. One of the best definitions I have found for this ancient Hebrew word is "life-saver."

I was a lifeguard, and what is their function? They sit on a stand with a whistle and a buoy, watch the people in the water, wait for someone in distress, and immediately rush to their aid and save their lives. They wrap their arms around the one in distress and bring them to safety at the peril of their own lives. They have one purpose -- the safety of others, the protection of others, and the life of another at the cost of their own life. When I put up my sign, "Lifeguard on Duty," you were safe to go in the water. Before that, you took your life in your own hands. My son, Adam, was a lifeguard, and he actually saved the lives of others. The name *"Eli-ezer"* means, "God's Lifeguard."

In Gen. 14:13-16, Abram (with only 318 men) delivered Lot, his goods, the women and the people of Sodom from four kings: *Amraphel, Arioch, Chedorlaomer*, and *Tidal* (and their armies) out of Damascus. How? Simple: Eli-ezer (Gen. 15:2) was from Damascus; he knew the way in and the way out, and he became the heir of Abraham's household, "God's – Helper." So when Abraham was ready to arrange a marriage for his son Isaac, whom he left on Mt. Moriah (Gen. 22:9) after the *"Akedah,"* the binding, he called his most trusted servant, the heir of his household, "God's – Lifeguard" to go fetch her (Gen. 24). Abraham made him put his hand under his thigh and swear an oath. Eli-ezer traveled to Mesopotamia, to the city of *Nahor* and arrived in the evening at the well, at the time of watering, when the women come out to draw water (v.11). You see, it was the woman's job to draw water, men never carried water pots, except on very special occasions.

Eli-ezer stood and prayed (Gen. 24:12-14), *"O LORD God of my master Abraham, I pray thee, send me good speed this day, and shew kindness unto my master, Abraham."* Specific, pointed, determined prayer -- that's what the servant of Abraham, Eli-ezer of Damascus, used. We are not even sure it's his God he is praying to at this point. We can assume it, but he never addresses Jehovah personally but only as the "God of my master." In v.14, he says, *"And let it come to pass, that the damsel (na-arah – young woman) to whom I shall say, Let down thy pitcher, I pray thee, that I may drink; and she shall say, Drink, and I will give thy camels drink also: let the same be she that thou hast appointed for thy servant Isaac; and thereby shall I know that Thou has shewed kindness unto my master."*

Do you pray like that? Do you? Then how will you ever know if you are getting answers or not? Specific requests get specific answers and God gets the specific glory! All five Hebrew words for "woman" are found in this chapter for a reason: to clarify, I believe, Isaiah 7:14; **Ish-ah** --woman in contrast to man (v.5); **Na-rah** -- young woman (v.14); **Bethu-lah** -- young virgin woman (v.16); **Al-mah** -- young virgin woman contracted in marriage (v.43); **Bat** -- daughter (v.23). What happened between v.16 and v.43? Rebekah took the nose ring (*nezem*) in v.22, saying she was under a marriage contract.

Rebekah came to the well, and with her came those specific answers (vv.16-21). Rebekah was born to *Bethuel*, who was born to *Nahor*, Abraham's brother (v.4, "go to my country, to my kindred, and take a wife for my son."). Does God answer specific, desperate, pointed, prayer? Ask Eli-ezer when you see him (and you will see him). Then why don't we pray that way? Because we are afraid to. He might not answer, and then again, He just might. Verse 26 says, *"[He] bowed down his head and worshipped the LORD."* I get the feeling here that Abraham's LORD is Eli-ezer's LORD. Do you get that feeling too? Bowing is a form of worship. The word means to shrivel up, to bow low. He probably fell to his knees with his face to the ground. Verse 52 sheds more light on this verse, *"he worshipped the LORD, bowing himself to the earth."*

Prayer is also a token of thanksgiving. He blesses God for His goodness to his master (v.27). I love this principle in v.27, *"**I being in the way, the LORD led me** to the house of my master's brethren."* The principle here is availability, not ability! Are you in the way **for** the LORD like Eliezer or are you in the way **of** the LORD, like Judas? It makes a big difference! Do you hear His voice saying, *"This is the way, walk ye in it..."* (Isaiah 30:21)? How would you know, if Psalm 46:10 is not on your **"to do"** list?

The place or posture of prayer is not as important as the spirit and attitude of prayer. In John 4:20-24 *Yeshua/Jesus* said that His Father seeks those who worship Him in spirit and in truth. Eli-ezer stood to pray (v.13). Later he bowed to worship (v.26) right next to the kneeling camels, next to a public well, in the busy evening when the women were drawing water (v.11). What a beautiful picture. Can you see it? Close your eyes. Now do you see it? What a beautiful principle. Can you feel it? Do we bless God that quickly for answers to prayer, do we? Maybe that's why we get so few answers. He's still waiting for the, **"Thank You."** for the last one He gave you! How quick are you to continue to give to a thankless or unappreciative child? Have you thanked God for yesterday yet, today? In fact have you thanked Him for today yet? (This thought brought tears to my eyes as I proof read my book.)

Eli-ezer said, *"...Blessed be the LORD God of my master Abraham...."* (v.27). He blessed God, *(barak)* which means to kneel or bless God as an act of adoration. This is a servant! Do we bless God on a regular basis? King David did (read Psalm 103 and many others). This is one area that seems to be missing in our prayer lives: adoration to God, blessing God! Just try to spend 60 seconds adoring God! Not thanking Him for what He has done, but praising Him for Who or What, He is! We need to take the time to adore the One Who created us, and swam out into our cesspool and drowned, to save us from drowning.

Eli-ezer went on in v.27 in his prayer to God, *"...who hath not left destitute my master of his mercy and his truth...,"* meaning,

"Who has not forsaken His mercy and His truth toward my master." These are attributes and characteristics of God that can never be denied or diminished -- NEVER! His mercy and His truth for all His children are only a prayer away. Eli-ezer was a prayerful servant, just like his master, Abraham. His prayer life was specific, definite and precise; and God answered his prayer specifically, definitely and precisely. Therefore, he could do nothing else except fall on his knees, worship the LORD his God, and cry out (as we should).

(**Prayer** - *"Father, we praise Thee above Heaven and Earth. Blessed art Thou, O LORD, our God, Creator of Heaven and Earth. Hallowed be Thy name, above every name in heaven, on Earth and under the Earth. Help us O God, to pray specifically, so that we would have great cause to worship and adore You specifically. Your mercy and Your truth are great and beyond all human understanding. You are the God of mercy and the God of truth. Blessed be Thy holy name, forever and ever." Amen!*)

Principles for Prayer:

- Availability is more important to God in our prayer lives than ability!
- Are you in the way **for** the Lord like Eliezer, or are you in the way **of** the Lord like Judas?
- Spend 60 seconds in your prayer time just adoring God, for His attributes. Nothing else, just adoration!

"We prove the value which we attach to things by the time we devote to them. The Kingdom of God asks for our time."

Andrew Murray

"Answered Prayer Key – Obedience"
#45
Gen. 24:27

There are at least 10 Eliezers mentioned in the Scriptures that I am aware of, and that is why Moses has chosen to label Abraham's, "Eliezer of Damascus." Moses had a son named Eliezer (Ex. 18:4). Benjamin had a grandson named Eliezer (I Chron. 7:8). There was a priest that helped bring the Ark back to Jerusalem named Eliezer (I Chron. 15:24). A prophet named Eliezer rebuked Jehoshaphat (II Chron. 20:37). In Ezra 8 & 10 you have a chieftain, a priest, a Levite and a son of Hiram all named Eliezer. In Luke 3:29 you have an ancestor of Joseph, Mary's husband, named Eliezer.

Genesis 24 is beautiful in so many ways; you could spend a lifetime bisecting, trisecting, and dissecting it, and never really plumb its depths. Verse 27 seems to be the centerfold of the chapter. This is where Rebekah literally runs off to her mother's house with the news and the ring. Eliezer falls on his face, prostrate, and cries out to the God of his master Abraham, *"Blessed be the LORD God of my master Abraham (JeHoVaH Elohim), who hath not left destitute my master of his mercy and his truth:* **I being in the way, the LORD led me** *to the house of my master's brethren."*

Now the key here to answered prayer (and you need to note it is) **OBEDIENCE**! Are you in the way or are you *in the way*? As I stated a few pages ago, availability is important and much more important than ability many times! Eliezer could say of himself, *"... I being in the way the LORD led me!"* He praised the LORD for His guidance and direction. This is simply the case today: many Christians are in the way **of** the Lord even in their prayer lives and service. They are preventing His work, His will, and His servants because of their opinions, their desires, their likes and dislikes. We need to be, in the way **with** the Lord, in the center of His will, obedient to the Master (and His leaders who are obedient to Him).

Eliezer was blessed due to his obedience, which is always better than sacrifice (I Sam. 15:22). Isn't that the main lesson God wants us to learn here on Earth? "Trust and Obey, for there is no other way." In v. 42-44, Eliezer repeats his prayer to God for Rebekah and her family. In v.45 he tells us this prayer was in his heart. In v.48 he repeats his praise to God for directing him to Rebekah. Principle for prayer -- God won't lead His children astray, and He leads us in the way of truth. Remember v.27, where the servant praised God for His mercy and truth? Now here we see where God leads us in the way of truth. It reminds us of John 14:6, where *Yeshua/Jesus* said, *"I am the way, the truth and the life..."*

In v.52 the servant immediately worships the LORD in response to their answer to his question, but really in answer to his and Abraham's prayers. Instantly, immediately, publicly, he prostrated himself, holding nothing back, no reservations. He was trained well by Abraham. Then Laban, her brother, and Bethuel, her father, said, *"The thing proceedeth from the LORD."* Did they know the LORD? Remember, Abraham's father Terah, left Ur of the Chaldeans in Gen. 11:31 to go to the land of Canaan with his family, but died in Haran, making Abraham the patriarch.

First, they try to hinder Eliezer's departure for ten days, and he says in v.56, *"Hinder me not, seeing the LORD hath prospered my way;"* Eliezer is on a mission and nothing can turn him to the right or to the left. So they ask Rebekah if she will go with this man and she says, *"I will go."* Then they "bless" Rebekah in v.60, and give her a nurse Deborah (Gen. 35:8). *"Thou art our sister, be thou the mother of thousands of millions, and let thy seed possess the gate of those which hate them."*

"WOW!" What a blessing they give to Rebekah! "May your descendants possess the gates of those who hate them." That is still true today! What a chapter! This servant exercised faith, the faith of his Master (Galatians 2:20). He had a correct view of God's character, mercy and truth. He had a specific answer to a specific prayer, to indicate God's specific presence. His prayer was simple, specific, direct, intercessory and childlike;

and that is the kind God answers. The obedience of a servant and the faith of a friend of God. Wow! What a combination -- together they are unbeatable.

"I being in the way, the LORD led me...who had led me in the path of truth and mercy." *Yeshua/Jesus* said in John 14:6, *"I am the way, the truth and the life: no man cometh to the Father, but by Me."* In Matthew 4:19 He said, *"Follow me..."*

Will we be obedient servants, like Eliezer (God's helper), and follow our Master in prayer, in service, in life, in suffering, and in death? What a chapter! You could spend years plumbing its depths and never reach its ocean floor.

We are not done yet, Isaac is in the field, in the evening, meditating **on** someone, his Master. He is in the way of "Beer-La-hai-roi" (The well of the One Who lives and sees me) and he is communing in his heart **with** the LORD. However, he is also praying and interceding **for** himself and **for** his bride to be, he is aware of Eliezer's mission, he is also interceding for comfort concerning his mother's death, v.67.

Rebekah asked Eliezer who was in the field. He said it was his master's son and she veiled herself and got off her camel. Eliezer told Isaac the whole story and he took Rebekah into his mother's tent and she became his wife and he loved her and Isaac was finally comforted after Sarah's death. Eliezer's mission was complete and he moved off the scene, his job was to exalt the son, to lift up the master's son, to find a bride for the son and deliver her as a chaste virgin at eventide (3:00 pm on the new day).

C.I. Scofield points out that this chapter is highly typical of a king who would make a marriage for his son, Matt. 22:2; the servant is a type of the Holy Spirit who "does not speak of Himself" but takes the things of the Bridegroom to win over the bride (John 16:13-14).

This servant is also a type of the Spirit enriching the bride with the Bridegroom's gifts (I Cor. 12:7-11; Gal. 5:22-23). He then brings the bride safely to a meeting with the Bridegroom (Acts 13:4; 16:6-7; Rom. 8:11; I Thess. 4:14-17). <u>Rebekah is a type of the Church</u>, "the called out" virgin bride of Christ (Gen. 24:16; 2 Cor. 11:2; Eph. 5:25-32). Isaac is a type of the Bridegroom "whom having not seen" the bride, loves her through the testimony of this servant (I Pet. 1:8). Isaac is also a type of the Bridegroom who goes out to meet and receive His bride in the evening, (Gen. 24:63; I Thess. 4:14-17). There is so much doctrine, so much theology, so much eschatology, and so much typology in this chapter that you could write a book on it, let alone a devotional thought! Enjoy your prayer time with the Lord!

*(**Prayer** - "Oh, LORD, may we be obedient like Eliezer, Your helper, and be found faithful, "walking in Your way." Quick to pray and continuously praising You, trusting You, obeying You, and serving You! LORD, help us to learn from Eliezer's life that, if we walk in Your ways, You will lead us and guide us. We will be successful in Your eyes, and that's all that really matters in this life, on this journey, for Your glory alone." Baruch ha shem!)*

Principles for Prayer:

- One of the major keys to answered prayer is obedience, and God can't stress it enough.
- God never leads His children astray, He leads them in the way of truth.
- The servant had a specific answer to a specific prayer to indicate God's specific presence.

"Prayer is the fire that warms the frigid soul, the ship that carries away our wants, and comes back with a cargo of divine help."

Dewitt Talmage

"Pillows Become Prayer Pillars" #46
Gen. 28:17-18

The first time we find Jacob/*Ya'akov* he is wrestling with his brother Esau in his mother Rebekah's womb, before birth (Gen. 25:22), and this struggle would never cease, NEVER! In fact, his name *Ya'akov* in Hebrew means, supplanter, heel catcher, or leg puller. As it says in Gen. 25:26, *"...his hand took hold on Esau's heel; and his name was called Jacob..."* Rebekah was told by the LORD **(YHVH)** in v. 23 that from the womb, *"...the elder (**Esau**) shall serve the younger (**Jacob**)."* So, the battle lines were drawn in the womb and would continue even till today. As they grew Esau became a cunning hunter and Jacob a tent dweller and a great cook. Esau wanted some of his red lentil stew, for which Jacob made him swap his birthright, at the age of 15. The birthright encompassed three things: the family priesthood, the Messianic promise from Adam, and the Abrahamic promise of the Promised Land and blessings of fruitfulness. Basically, the first born got the farm and Esau wasn't interested in farming at that time. He was a hunter, not a farmer, and he even despised his birthright (v. 34).

The "Arahamic Covenant" is confirmed to Isaac in Gen. 26 and a famine strikes *Gerar/Gaza*. After the famine they leave, dig some wells and settle in *Beer-Sheba*. Then Esau marries Judith, the daughter of Beeri a Hittite, in Gen. 26:34, which seems strange since Judith means, "*Jewess or Judahite*" a, "Person of Judah, a Judean, a Jew, or Jewish." Now, Judah and the Jewish people are not on the scene yet so this can't be a descendant of Judah because he hasn't been born.

Isaac was 60 in Gen. 25:26 when Esau was born and now he is 100 in Gen. 27, and physically blind when he is ready to give his blessing to Esau. So, he asks Esau for savory food (v. 4), so his soul can bless him -- *his will, not God's, and he knew it*. Rebekah overhears him and devised her own evil plan and she and Jacob fix two goats and steal Esau's blessing from a 100 year old blind man (Gen. 27:28-29). Of course Isaac tries to reverse it but you can't. What's done is done! So Isaac calls Jacob in Gen. 28:1-5 and blesses him one last time with the "Abrahamic Blessing" and sends him to "Laban's Labor Camp" to get a wife from his mother's family.

Esau overhears the plan and goes to his uncle Ishmael and takes one of his daughters, *Mahalath* a Canaanite for a wife because he knew it would hurt his father and mother. Rebekah will never see Jacob again. The "few days" of Gen. 27:44 become the rest of her life, as she sat in the tent door and watched and waited for his return. In fact, we never hear of Rebekah again after this scheme. I think God was really upset with her evil plan.

Then Jacob/*Ya'akov* went out from *Beer-Sheba* and stopped at *Bethel* (God's house) and laid down to rest. There he had a dream of a ladder reaching into Heaven and angels ascending and descending on it, with the LORD standing above it giving him the "Abrahamic Covenant." So, he took the stone he used for a pillow and used it for a pillar, poured olive oil on it, called the name of the place *"Bethel"* and vowed a vow to God and promised to give Him ten percent (**a tithe**) of all God gave him. This is 600 years before the law.

What's interesting is that this is the passage Nathaniel was meditating on under the fig tree in Galilee, when Phillip found him and said, *"We have found Him, of whom Moses in the Law, and the prophets, did write, Jesus of Nazareth, the son of Joseph."* (John 1:43-51). Jesus said, *"Because I said unto thee, I saw thee under a fig tree believest thou? Thou shalt see ...the angels of God ascending and descending on the Son of man."*

You see He knows the thoughts and intents of your heart right now (John 2:24-25). Whenever, you read His Word, you may think you received nothing out of it, but He knows exactly what you read because He wrote it through His (*nabi*) prophets and He knows what you are reading. So, read it to Him. You only remember **7%** of what you read and **38%** of what you hear, so if you read His Word out loud to Him you will remember **45%** (makes sense), no? It will be a lot more enjoyable too, trust me, to have your quiet time with the Author. (Try it. I think you will like it.)

So, Jacob the heel-catcher leaves everything he knows: family, friends, servants, environment, occupation, life, for a strange place, *Padan-aram*. On his first day this "angel wrestler" bumps into a ladder of angels ascending into heaven. He has a dream (*kalam*) (now in my circle we don't talk about them, so we call them "**DMI's**" -- Dynamic Mental Impressions.) Joseph actually is the "Dream-Catcher" who we will catch-up with later. Now, this word (*kalam*) also means to grow strong, so I get the feeling this was a strong "DMI". Again I like to use the "Paleo Hebrew" when looking at Hebrew words (it paints a better portrait), and this root is made up of three letters (*chet* – fence, inner room; *lamed* – prod, goad; *mem* – mighty, strong). So, this dream or "DMI" in Jacob's inner heart and mind was used to goad him and it was very strong. In this dream the LORD confirms the covenant He gave to Abraham (and to Isaac) with Jacob and promises to bring him back to the land He promised his father and grandfather.

He wakes up from his sleep, believes he is in the house of God, the gateway of heaven, takes his **pillow** and makes it a **pillar** or an altar, and names the place ***"Bethel"*** "The House of God." Before that it was called *Luz*, the "Almond Tree." Then he makes a vow to the "God of *Bethel*" and this is the last time he builds an altar (at least that it is mentioned) until he prays 20 years later when he is on the bank of the *Peniel* River. Then after wrestling all night with God or The Angel of the LORD, he limps to *Shechem* and builds an altar in the Promised Land, calling it *Elelohe-Israel*, "To God, the God of Israel or Jacob." (Gen. 33:20)

Except for the possibility of prayer in Gen. 31:1-3, where Jacob is fearful for his life after 20 years of swindling and God tells him to return to Canaan and He will be with him, Jacob's vow seemed to be a bargain with God. "God, if You will do this for me, then I will do this for You!" God is not a bargain hunter. He doesn't shop for prayer requests on E-bay or Craig's List and neither should we. It seems to me (and I might be wrong) that <u>the only place they build altars to YeHoVaH is in the Promised Land,</u> not in foreign countries. They may pour oil on a stone, or plant a tree but not build an altar.

God also spoke to Jacob in a dream (*kalam*) (v.12) and God usually only speaks through dreams to those who don't or won't speak to Him or who <u>don't or won't read His Word</u>. Now that is not always the case, like Joseph and Daniel and others, but many times that is the way he gets the attention of the hard hearted and unbelievers like Pharaoh, Nebuchadnezzar, etc.

"*Beth-El*" the house of God, or the "Gate of God's Heaven" is anywhere God is, your prayer closet, your prayer garden, your secret chamber, etc. Oh, my friend, let us not make deals with God, let us just lay hold of His promises and hang on with both hands in prayer. Let us take our **pillows** at night and consecrate them to God and make them **pillars** and pray with David in Psalm 63:6, *"When I remember thee upon my bed, and meditate on thee in the night watches."* So when we awake in the morning we can say with Jacob, "<u>Surely the LORD is in this place!</u>"

(**Prayer** - *"Oh LORD, may we be open and honest with You, but obedient as to Your will and not a bargain hunter in our prayer lives. May Your will be done in our lives as it is in heaven; You choose, LORD, and we'll choose what You choose. We love You, LORD. Let our closets, our gardens, our hearts, be Your Beth-El!"* **In ha Shem Yeshua we pray. Amen!**)

Principles for Prayer:

- Don't make deals with God; lay hold of His promises, and then hang on with both hands and <u>pray</u>!
- They built altars in the "Holy Land;" outside of it they planted trees, poured oil on a stone, or piled up rocks.
- You can't reverse God's blessings; what's done is done! Just accept it and deal with it.

"The Lord Jesus is still praying. Thirty years of living; three years of serving; one tremendous act of dying; and nineteen hundred years of praying. What an emphasis on <u>prayer!</u>"

S. D. Gordon (of Christ's intercession)

"Prayer of the Barren Womb" #47
Gen. 30:17

We left *Ya'akov*/Jacob in *Bethel* pouring oil on his **pillow** and making it a **pillar**, and making his father Isaac's God his God. Now he comes to the land of the people of the east, to his mother's people in *Paddan-aram* and stumbles upon Rachel and his mother's family in a field. <u>If you believe that, I have a bridge in Brooklyn for sale!</u> The God he vowed a vow to in *Bethel* is guiding his every step. And if He is your God and you made your pillow a pillar last night, then He hears your payers and He is guiding your steps right now too. Psalm 37:23 says, *"The steps of a good man are ordered by the LORD, (YHVH) and He delighteth in his way."* Or as George Mueller used to say, "The stops too!"

He first happens upon Rachel and Gen. 29:17 says, *"Rachel was beautiful and well favored."* In fact, she is so beautiful the writer needs two words to describe her beauty and form, and both words are compound words. It wasn't only her face that was beautiful, lovely and fair to look upon but her form was also beautiful. She is described as "well-favored" (you will have to do further research yourself). This word is used only one other time in the scriptures, in Deut. 21:11, when referring to a captive woman. In fact she was so beautiful that when Jacob first saw her he <u>lifted up his voice and wept</u>. You might say, <u>"Well he met a relative,"</u> <u>but he didn't weep when he met Leah</u>.

Now, Leah was "tender-eyed," soft, gentle, tender, she could melt chocolate on the table by just looking at it. She had a look about her, have you ever met a child like this, who looks up at you with those big brown eyes, and maybe there is a tear in the corner of her eye and she has a little dirt on her cheek and she hands you her doll with a torn arm and says trembling, "Please!" That's Leah, got the picture now? Get the cross-eyed girl out of your camera lens, which is not what this word means. It means gentle, smooth, soft, delicate, silky like velvet, smooth like satin, you just want to hug her and hold her in your arms. But v.18 says, *"And Jacob loved Rachel;"* yeah obviously, the flesh was attracted to the flesh. But Laban, her father, loved both of his daughters, and especially his little Leah! So, *Ya'akov*/Jacob makes a deal for Rachel and promises to work for Laban for seven years for her, which seems like a few days. But on the wedding night Laban slips in "Little Leah" instead of "Ravishing Rachel" and when Jacob wakes up in the morning he has the wrong daughter (or does he)? You see, God's plans are accomplished in spite of our schemes. So he ends up getting Rachel after fulfilling Leah's week, and works another seven years without wages. (Too much wine on the wedding night could be a problem in the morning).

We entitled Gen. 29 & 30 "Prayer of the Barren Womb." You have two marriages, four sons (Reuben, Simeon, Levi and Judah), and no mention of prayer or altars. In vv. 31-35 Leah gives birth to four sons. Is it possible she was in prayer to *El Shaddai*, the One who enriches and makes fruitful? Why do I say that? Look at the names of her sons, Reuben (v. 32) "looked on my affliction" or "see a son;" (v.33), Simeon, "hearing" or "the LORD has heard;" (v.34), Levi, "attached;" and finally (v.35), Judah, "praise," or "now I will praise the LORD." Gen. 30:17 says, *"And God hearkeneth [listened] unto Leah, and she conceived, and bare Jacob the fifth son."*

God listened to Leah. He heard her prayers, her pleas, her cries for children; and she conceived and bore children. I am convinced that Leah, being the first wife and being rejected, cried out to *El Shaddai* and He heard her and blessed her womb and gave her four sons (including Judah, through whom the Messiah was to come) and closed Rachel's womb. In fact, it is Leah who is later buried in the cave of *Machpelah* with Jacob, along with Isaac and Rebekah and Abraham and Sarah, not Rachel.

Does prayer work? Does *El Shaddai* give children in answer to prayer? Can He make the blind to see, the lame to walk, the deaf to hear? Does He open the womb of a woman who has dried up or is sterile? Ask Leah, ask her mother-in-law Rebekah, ask Rebekah's mother-in-law Sarah, ask Hannah, ask

Rachel, or my wife or her friend Dee or millions of other mothers who prayed, "LORD open my womb!" Ask David who wrote Psalm 127:3, *"...the fruit of the womb is His reward."* **"Prayer of the Barren Womb**." Are you barren? Does your womb ache for children? Have you born any spiritual children lately? I don't mean last year; this year, this month, this week, this day? **THEN PRAY**! Pray to the God of the womb, *El Shaddai,* the many breasted One, this name means fruitful! <u>He is the God of the womb not the God of the tomb</u>!

In Gen. 30 the ladies are at it again, but not *Ya'akov*. Rachel cries out to Jacob at first instead of God, so he goes in unto *Bilhah* and she conceives and bears Dan (v.6). Rachel says, "God has heard my voice," or "He has judged my case" and "Given me a son." Has God heard your voice, has He judged your case, has He given you a son? Have you cried out to Him for one, for ten, for fifty, for a hundred? <u>What is your soul goal for this year, do you even have one</u>? Rachel learned form Leah, the answer for children is *El Shaddai!* In Gen. 30:17, God listened to Leah and she conceived again, and again, and again. These ladies knew the pattern; they were on track. In verse 22 God listened to Rachel and opened her womb. Fourteen years have passed and as far as we know Jacob is still not praying, but his wives sure learned how to get a hold of God in prayer for children.

Oh my friend, are you barren? Are you without spiritual children? Then pray, NO! **Cry out to God, to *El Shaddai*.** He desires to give you spiritual children more than you desire to birth them. He is waiting to open your womb. If a Christian is childless it is not because they are sterile, it is because they don't know their God. Now Jacob has waited 20 years, a few days have turned into many years and still no altars, no prayers, no worship, no spiritual blessings, physical yes but no spiritual blessings! We'll see this when he crosses the *Peniel* River (the face of God) and wrestles with the Angel of the LORD in Gen. 33 and enters back into the Promised Land.

*(**Prayer** - "El Shaddai, our wombs are barren, empty, dry, but not dead. Lord, give us children, lest we die. Open our wombs, increase our faith, strengthen our testimonies, and give us boldness to proclaim Your truth. Keep us close to You, LORD, as we worship You daily, praise You continually, and speak of You unceasingly. **In ha Shem Yeshua we pray. Amen!**")*

Principles for Prayer:

- God's plans are always accomplished in spite of our sneaky schemes.
- Is your womb barren for spiritual children? Then you need to pray to *El Shaddai* for souls!
- Leah was in prayer to *El Shaddai*, the One who enriches and makes fruitful!

"God does nothing but by prayer, and everything with it."

John Wesley

"The Prayer of Fear" #48
Gen. 32:6-7

I entitled this "The Prayer of Fear" for a good reason. In Gen. 31:1 Jacob is scared and in fear for his life and his family's and that seems to be the only time he prays. In chapter 28 he is afraid and running from Esau when he runs into God at Bethel. Here he is running from Laban's sons when he is reminded of his vision at Bethel and his vow. He ends up running into Esau again in Gen. 32. Question: do you pray when you are scared? David did, Daniel did and Paul did. It is not wrong to pray due to fear; in fact it is very natural and normal. Many avowed atheists pray just before they die due to "the core of man's existence," which is the fear of death (Heb. 2:15), and their prayer is, "Oh, God!" But it's too late for them. No, there is no problem with praying when you are in fear. You do have a problem, though, if that seems to be the only time you pray! **It's too late!**

In Gen. 31:3, the LORD tells Jacob to return to the Promised Land. Twenty years have passed since Jacob was in intimate communion with the LORD. Remember, this is not the LORD's trip, it's Rebekah's. In v.11 the Angel of the Lord appears to Jacob, the *"God of Bethel"* (v.13), so he takes off for Canaan. Notice God speaks to Jacob through dreams and visions, not through His Word or Jacob's prayer life. However, there were not too many versions of the Bible on the market at that time, just the originals. Even the KJV wasn't out yet, but we are without excuse today, Amen? God usually has to speak to people in dreams and visions who don't or won't speak to Him in prayer. (Like the unbelievers, the hardhearted, the Labans, the Jacobs, the Pilates, etc.) However, not all dreams and visions were to the hardhearted and unbelievers. You have the Josephs, Daniels, Ezekiels, and Pauls, too. If dreams and visions make you uncomfortable lets call them (DMI's) for **Dynamic Mental Impressions**. Feel better now?

In Gen. 31:44-49, a covenant is made (or cut), a pillar or a heap of stones becomes a witness between two arch enemies. *"The*

LORD watch (Mizpah) between me and thee, when we are absent one from another." They didn't trust each other, v.53 *"The God of Abraham, and the God of Nahor,* [his brother] *the God of their father,* [Terah] *judge betwixt us."* Did they originally worship Jehovah? It appears to be so! In Gen. 31:54, Jacob builds an altar and offers a sacrifice. Remember, an altar should have three things: <u>sacrifice, worship and prayer</u>. Jacob, not being a godly man at this time, prays only when in fear or when it is for material gain. Here he desires protection and gain! Sounds like the average gim-me prayer of Christians today! How much time do you spend in praise and thanksgiving in your prayer time compared to asking God for things? Jacob hasn't had his "Water-loo" yet; it's coming in Genesis 32 on the banks of the Peniel River, "The Face of God!"

He is still worshiping the God of Isaac and Abraham, not the God of Jacob. There is no personal part in his prayers or worship yet! How about yours? Do you pray to "God the Person" or do you pray to the "Person of God?" Think about it -- it makes a big difference. Prayer is on an intimate, personal level from your heart to the heart of God! We need to enter into His almighty presence by the blood that was shed to give us access into the Holy of Holies. Praise God! In spite of our spiritual state or condition, God always remains faithful and true, even if we don't. God always keeps His promises. He is not only "The God of the Word," He is "The God of His Word!" He said it, that settles it, and I believe it! It's wonderful and fearful at the same time to know that He keeps His Word! <u>For the Christian it's wonderful; for the non-Christian it's fearful!</u>

Now we come to Gen. 32, and here comes Esau with 400 men to kill him, so Jacob prays! Note, Jacob is still a crisis prayer, even though he just met the *"Mahanaim"* the band of angels (v. 2), he is still scared. He does not know God yet in a personal, intimate way so he prays, *"O God of my father Abraham, and God of my father Isaac, the LORD which saidst unto me, Return unto thy country, and to thy kindred, and I will deal well with thee:"* (v.9). It's the God of his ancestors, the God he makes deals and bargains with, his **E-bay God** he prays to. The God he goes to when he is in need of something (but we never do that do we, come to God only when we are in need?). I am afraid too many Christians pray this way all the time; in fact I would say a vast majority of born-Again, blood-bought Christians are just that -- crisis prayers, to our shame and God's.

It has been 20 years now since Beth-el and the ladder, the pillar, the vow, the vision, (the DMI) the oil, the angels. WOW! Twenty years between chapters 28 and 32. But notice the first three words in Gen. 32:12 as Jacob prays, *"And thou saidst..."* (referring back to v.9, "The LORD which saidst..."). He held God to His Word, to His promises! That's why God heard and hearkened, not because of Jacob's flawless character or his intimate friendship with Jehovah, but because the LORD is a God of His Word. He keeps His promises and He is not a covenant breaker. We too need to hold God to His promises and to His Word. Jacob did and so did George Mueller, D.L. Moody, Roger Boguski, etc., and God blessed them. So Jacob is coming back to the land, back to the God he left, back to the prayer life of his ancestors. Twenty years have elapsed and we have the same God, but a different Jacob; Jacob the heel catcher, the supplanter, the conniver is becoming "Israel," the "Prince with God!"

We have a lesson to learn here in prayer, a principle for prayer. When we pray, we should hold God to His Word. He glories in that, **"for You said!"** Those are the sweetest, most beautiful words in prayer, **"for You said!"** God said it, and that settles it, whether you believe it or not! Amen, Amen! The answer to this prayer of Jacob comes in Gen. 33:4, when Esau runs, meets him, embraces him, falls on his neck, kisses him and weeps! There is the power of God! Esau was coming to kill Jacob, not kiss him. So, what changed his mind, the 550 goats, sheep, camels and bulls? No! It was the power of prayer and, **"for You said!"** The promises of God, they are there for you and me to, **cash in on**! Or as one saint put it, "They are like bank drafts on Christ's account waiting to be cashed in." Oh my friend, we need to spend time in the Word finding those precious promises and then get on our knees (and faces if possible) **and cash them in**. Let us determine from this day forward to hold God to His Word, to put Him to the test (Mal. 3:10), to pray back His promises, **"for You said…"** He delights in that kind of praying. In fact, He is glorified by it. Try it; I do!

Maybe our crisis isn't severe enough. Maybe we need to pray for God to send an enemy with 400 warriors who wants to kill us and our families first. Maybe that's what it will take to see the *Mahanaim*, before we take God at His Word. Remember God does not answer prayer, He answers desperate, destitute, determined prayer! **"For You said…"**

*(**Prayer** - "Oh God, help us to search Your Word to find Your promises and then hold You to Your Word when we pray. Thank You, LORD for Your faithfulness, even when we are not faithful, or walking close to You. LORD may we not just come to You for things, or when in a crisis, but to worship, praise and adore You for Who You are. And may those three words become part of our prayer life, **"For You said…"**) In ha Shem Yeshua we ask. Amen!")*

Principles for Prayer:

- May those three words become a part of our "Prayer Life"– "**For You said!**"
- Do you pray to "God the person" or do you pray to the "Person of God?" It makes a big difference!
- God is not just the "God of the Word;" He is the "God of His Word." He wrote it, He signed it, He believes it, so Pray it!

*"Someone has said Job keeps up his communion with God, and conquers Satan upon the dunghill.
Adam loses his communion with God, and falls before Satan in paradise."*

George Müller

"Wrestling God in Prayer" #49
Gen. 32:24

I should have entitled this, "Wrestling in Prayer." In Gen. 32:13ff. Jacob sends a gift to his distraught brother Esau (550 animals), a gift to appease his enemy (and the bigger the better)! There is a principle between the lines here for us, if we look carefully, and it works. You can't dislike or hate someone you are doing a kind deed for, and it's hard to dislike or hate someone who is doing a kind deed for you. However, in v.24 *Ya'akov*/Jacob (the heel catcher, the supplanter, the conniver, the swindler) was left alone. His family is gone, his possessions are gone, his servants are gone, his protection is gone, and the verse says, *"And Jacob was left alone;"* Have you ever been alone with God? Just you and God, in a cabin with a Bible, a blanket, a canteen and maybe a Strong's concordance for a pillar? That could change your life forever and that of those in your inner circle, trust me. I have been there more than once!

Anyway, it says, *"And there wrestled a man with him until the breaking of the day."* All night he wrestled with this "Man of God" and the angel did not prevail. Jacob was wrestling for his life and the lives of his family also. This "Man of God" did not prevail against Jacob and the sun was coming up. I guess Jacob had him in an **angel-lock**, so he dislocated Jacob's thigh and he still wouldn't let go and said, *"I will not let thee go, except thou bless me."* Praise God! Now, that my friend is persistent, desperate, sacred praying. Jacob is destitute. In Gen. 32:28 Jacob gets a new name, "Israel, Prince with God" because as a prince he struggled with man and with God and prevailed.

Wow! Can men say that about you... can they? Have you struggled with men and with God, and have you prevailed with both? Do you bear the marks, do you walk with a limp? Read II Cor. 11:23-33 and 12:1-10 and tell me if Paul bore the marks, struggled with men and with God and prevailed? Tell me if he fought a good fight, kept the faith, finished his course. If you think a vibrant, effectual prayer life is easy, read on.......

The word "wrestled" is the Hebrew word (*abaq*) and means to float away as a vapor, to be dust, to grapple, to be light dust particles. The idea is one of fierce wrestling, being ground into powder; this is the only place this word appears in the Older Testament. In Gen. 30:8 Rachel wrestles with Leah (*patal*), meaning to twine or struggle. There a different word and meaning is used altogether than you have in Gen. 32:24. Here the struggling is intense, in the dirt; dust is flying, grinding each other into powder. This wrestling match is so fierce bones are dislocated, and no one is yelling, uncle. **Wow!** What a beautiful picture of persistence in prayer, of not letting go until God blesses you, hanging on tenaciously until death or blessing! Persevering in prayer! In Luke 11:5-10, *Yeshua/Jesus* tells us about importunity in prayer with the parable of the persistent friend, and again in Luke 18:1-8 with the woman and the judge. Importunity means to request or beg for urgently, to be persistent in a request or demand, to be troublesomely urgent. Jacob is troublesomely urgent, Esau is coming to kill him and his family with 400 warriors. He's scared, desperate and destitute, just where God wanted him.

He is at his wits end, or in "wits end corner." Have you ever been there? He is wrestling, not with Abraham's God, and not with Isaac's God. He is wrestling with the God of Jacob, the God of Israel (you will see that in Gen. 33:20 when he builds an altar to *El-elohe-Israel,* "to God, the God of Israel"). But here he meets God "face-to-face" and names the place, *"**Peniel**"* which means, "The Face of God." Have you wrestled with God all night in the dust lately? Do you have your *"**Peniel**?"* (Gen. 32:30 uses Peniel, and Gen. 32:31 uses Penuel.) Yes, Jacob was a scoundrel and a conniver, but he had his Water-loo on the *Jabbok River* and he received a new name, "Israel – Prince with God" (He will rule as God).

This is the first time Israel is used in the Bible. Oh that we might have our own Waterloo with God, our own *Jabbok River*, and have it soon. I wish that every one of us could wrestle (*abaq*) all night for a blessing from God (and cry out in the night, "I won't let You go unless You bless me!"), then get up limping. Just how desperate are you? Jacob is east of the

Jabbok River; he has not entered the Promised Land yet, and before he does he must meet God face-to-face. If he is to become the nation of Israel and rule as God would have him, he must know Him personally. Gen. 32:31, *"As he passed over **Penuel** the sun rose upon him, and he halted* [limped] *upon his thigh."*

Just as he crosses the river, the sun rises on him, the dawn breaks, and he limps into the Promised Land ready to meet his brother, broken and humble, but a "Prince with God." What a change, what a transformation a night of prayer can make in our lives, but more importantly in the lives of others in our inner circle. I cried as I wrote this picturing Jacob/Israel limping into the Promised Land a new man. Let this soak in a minute, don't rush on! Just let it soak in!

Gen. 33:1, *"And Jacob lifted up his eyes, and looked, and, **behold, Esau** came, and with him 400 men."* The moment he crossed the *Jabbok River* he faced his greatest fear. Prayer doesn't always remove our fears; it gives us the strength many times to face them head on. And God is always with us in the midst of them (Isa. 43:1-7). Here comes Jacob's greatest fear, **ESAU** (Gen. 33:4). *"And Esau ran to meet him, and embraced him, and fell on his neck, and kissed him: and they wept."*

Oh my, I bet Jacob was not expecting that reception. Again, Esau set out to kill him, not to kiss him (you don't take 400 warriors to a kissing party). What changed Esau's heart? The 550 animals, seeing all the women and children, his limping, humble brother bowing seven times? I believe the same angel, the Angel of the LORD, that touched Jacob's thigh that night while wrestling in prayer, touched Esau's heart while wrestling in sleep. Not to belittle the gift to the offended party (and the bigger the better), but your prayers many times will do as much, if not more to soften the heart of the offended party to the touch of the Master's hand than anything else. In fact, 25 years later, Jacob and Esau together bury their father, Isaac, who is 180 years old in Gen. 35:29 in the cave of *Machpelah* with Rebekah, their mother. Was that prayer on the *Jabbok River* (or *Peniel*) is still working 25 years later, or was it the gift of 550 animals? One thing is sure; Jacob was still limping on that hip!

*(**Prayer** - "Oh LORD, may we have our Peniel and may we have it soon. We want to wrestle with You or Your Angel and prevail. May we know both the presence of Your almighty power and the power of Your almighty presence in a new and personal way, like Jacob." In ha Shem Yeshua we pray. Amen!)*

Principles for Prayer:

- Many times our prayers do more to soften an offended heart than a large gift, though the gift still helps.
- Prayer does not always remove our fears; it gives us strength to face them, head on, with God by our side.
- Persistence in prayer, importunity, persevering until we get an answer – that is what is vital!

J. C. Ryle was a powerful prayer warrior and wrote a lot on the subject. I have several of his books in my library. He stated that prayerless people are not genuine Christians. Without a vibrant private prayer life, you are just an outward member of Christ's church, not a living member of Christ.

R.T.B.

"Prayer: Preparation for Battle" #50
Gen. 35:1-28

Jacob safely arrives in *Shechem* (Gen. 33:18), which is in the land of Canaan, the Promised Land. There he erects an altar and calls it, "*El-elohe-Israel* -- to God, the God of Israel." Now *Jehovah, Elohim, El Shaddai* is no longer just the God of his fathers, Abraham and Isaac. He is the God of Jacob! He is the personal God of Israel, the "Prince with God!" This has been true since the *Peniel* River experience (where he met God face-to-face, God changed his name from Jacob to Israel, and he found favor in the eyes of the LORD and in the eyes of Esau, Gen. 33:4). Remember, it wasn't the gift that softened Esau's heart, although it may have helped, it was the all-night prayer meeting on the *Jabbok River* that changed the "Isaac brothers" for life.

Now Jacob becomes an altar builder like his ancestors before him, and builds one in Gen. 33:20. Notice in v.18 he pitched his tent and in v.20 he built an altar. Sound familiar? Just like his grandfather, everywhere Abraham had a tent, God had an altar! Prayer, worship, and sacrifice: the necessary components of an altar to the God of Israel. "I love it!" No longer is he dependent on man, but on God. *Shechem* is the same place Abraham stopped on his way to the Promised Land in Gen. 12:6, and he also built an altar there. The word *Shechem* means neck, shoulders, place of burden, and comes into play quite a bit in the Older Testament. It is a good place to rest after the long, hot journey through the desert, but Jacob camped and settled there, **ouch**!

He pitched his tent, he built his altar, he bought some property, and he unknowingly sold his daughter! Be careful about camping outside the city gates of pagans. Your children will be *in*fected, not *af*fected -- infected like Lot's. You may have the power and strength to resist the temptation but they may not. Jacob's sons Levi and Simeon slew all the men of *Shechem* and took their sister Dinah out of *Shechem's* house. However, the point of this chapter is prayer, and that God obviously became very personal to Jacob on the bank of that river, and he began to build altars to "*El-Elohe-Israel*." El means strength or might, especially the Almighty, All Powerful One. *Elohe* is the singular form of *Elohim* which is the personal name for God. And Israel is two words, **El** being the name for <u>Almighty God</u> again and the first part meaning to prevail or to have power as a prince. So, Jacob built an altar and prayed to, "<u>El-the Almighty One, *Elohe*-the God of, *Isra/el,* the Prince with God or God's Prince</u>" or "<u>To God, the Almighty God of Israel</u>."

"And God said unto Jacob, Arise, go up to Bethel, and dwell there: and make there an altar unto God, that appeared unto thee when thou fleddest from the face of Esau thy brother." (Gen. 35:1). That's where he started when he fled to *Paddanaram* over 20 years earlier. He makes a full circle, back to *Bethel*, and back to the "House of God." God always brings us back to the starting place, back to the point, or place or person we ran from. Jacob tells his family and his household to put away their foreign gods, their earrings, change their clothes, and purify themselves for <u>they are going to worship the true God in *Bethel*</u>. There Jacob builds a second altar "*El-Bethel*" or "To the God of the house of God." God was a personal God to Jacob since the river of *Peniel*, and remember an altar must have three things: <u>sacrifice, worship, and prayer</u>.

What a time of communion and reunion this must have been for Jacob and Jehovah! This is actually the first recorded **"revival"** we have in the Scriptures, and it has all the earmarks of a revival. <u>It is preceded by gross iniquity, it's initiated by a word from God, there's a forsaking of all that is displeasing to God</u> (followed by <u>obedience to God's will and Word</u>), <u>God's past blessings are remembered</u>, it's accompanied by <u>a new revelation of God's character, God's promises are renewed, and a higher spiritual life is sought and given, and many commit their lives to the LORD's service and are protected and provided for</u>. Wow! Now that's **revival**!

Deborah, Rebekah's nurse, dies, is buried, and they mourn for her (Gen. 35:8). She must have been with Jacob, although no mention is ever made of his mother. His name is officially changed to Israel by God (v.10), God speaks to him and blesses him as *El Shaddai* (vss.11-13), and He confirms the Abrahamic covenant which God also gave to his father Isaac. *"...be fruitful and multiply; a nation and a company of nations shall be of thee, and kings shall come out of thy loins; and the land which I gave Abraham and Isaac, to thee I will give it, and to thy seed after thee will I give the land. And God went up from him..."* Just like He did from Abraham.

Then Israel sets up a pillar/altar and pours oil and wine on it and called the place, *"Bethel* – God's House," and since our Lord called God's house **"The House of Prayer"** we have those three elements of an altar: **sacrifice (v.14), worship (vss.2-3), and prayer (vss. 13-14)**. What an experience! God is fine tuning this heel-catcher, this conniver, this sly businessman! Oh, he could make the speckled bear striped and the striped bear speckled and turn two *shekels* into four like magic, but could he get his children to follow his God, or his wives to stop fighting like cocks?

Deborah dies in v.8, Rachel dies giving birth in v.19, Isaac dies in v.29. There is a lot of mourning and prayer in this chapter. Jacob sets up a pillar on Rachel's grave (v.20) and mourns. The heartache he must have felt. When it rains it pours. Two of his sons kill all the males in *Shechem* and Dinah, his daughter, is raped in Gen. 34. Reuben commits adultery with *Bilhah* one of his concubines, Wow! How much can a frail human being take? What could have prepared him for all of this? *Paddanaram,* Laban's labor camp, *Galeed/Mizpah?* No, the *Peniel* experience, where he met God face-to-face, where the God of Abraham and Isaac became the God of Jacob or Israel, *"El Elohe* Israel" (his personal God) and Jacob became a *"Prince with God"* **"Israel."** He knew how to wrestle with men in business, how to make a *shekel* or two and always come out on top; but there on the river bank, alone, scared, in the night, desperate, and destitute he learned how to <u>wrestle with God in prayer and to give God His way and let Him come out on top!</u> He learned how to commune, how to trust, how to hang onto God, how to wrestle, how to pray like his life depended on it because it did! What has happened to that tenacity in our prayer lives today? Why don't we **pray through** any more or have prayer vigils or pray and fast? Instead we have a moment of prayer, or we mention others in prayer, or we bring them up in prayer, or put them on a prayer list. Jesus said, *"...My house shall be called of all nations the house of prayer..."* Mark 11:17 & Isa. 56:7. Then why is there so little importance put on it in our churches today? Why? It's an afterthought.

*(**Prayer** - "Father, help us. Prepare us for what the future holds. We are desperate and destitute like Jacob, and scared. Teach us to pray, to wrestle, to hold on until You bless us. And as tribulations come our way (and we know they will come), may we cling closer to You and hold on tighter and not let go until You bless us." In ha shem Yeshua we pray. Amen!)*

Principles for Prayer:

- Gen. 35, the first recorded revival in the Bible, began with prayer at an altar in Bethel, "The House of God." ***Oi Vey!***
- Jacob knew how to wrestle with man, but he needed to learn how to wrestle with God in prayer, and not let go!
- What has happened to tenacity in our prayer lives? Why don't we pray through any more? We quit too early!

"I used to lay down a great many points on how to get people to pray, but I have made up my mind that the only way to get them to do it is to do it myself."

John R. Mott

"The Silent Prayers" #51
Gen. 37:24

Esau humbles himself after his father Isaac dies. He takes all that he has and leaves Canaan, the Promised Land, for another country, because he and Jacob/Israel are too great and have too much to dwell together. Why did he leave graciously when he had vowed to kill his brother after his father died in Gen. 27:41? That prayer on the river bank is still working 25 years later. The God of the Peniel River is still as real as the day Jacob met Him. Jehovah is now the God of Jacob, the God of Israel (the prince with God), and Esau becomes Edom.

The power of prayer linked with the promises of God are a force and a source of strength and help we know too little of, my friend. Gen. 32:12 says, *"And thou saidst..."* and v.26 says, *"I will not let thee go, except thou bless me."* In Gen. 28, thirty years earlier at Bethel, God promised Jacob this land he was standing in and a multitude of descendants. God gave him the same promise He gave to Abraham and Isaac. Then in Gen. 31:3 God promises him His presence "**IF**" Jacob will return to the Promised Land. Jacob claimed those promises, he held God to His word, and he held onto the God of the Word, (Gen. 32:26) until God blessed him again.

Oh my friend, to claim the promises of God in prayer and not let go until God blesses us is the greatest source of strength and help known to mankind. Pray back His promises. Hold Him to His word. He is waiting for you to do it, so **"do it!"** I did 6/8/25 and He is still blessing!

In Gen. 37:1 it says, *"Jacob dwelt in the land wherein his father* [Isaac] *was a stranger, in the land of Canaan."* His son, Joseph, was 17 years old, just a teenager, loved more than his brothers. He was a snitch, had a coat of many colors, was hated by his ten older brothers; then he had a dream of sheaves bowing to him, and was hated even more. All that in just five verses! So he is off to a stellar start as a Bible character. Then he had a second dream of the sun, moon and eleven stars bowing down to him and his father rebuked him. His brothers envied him, but his father quietly observed the dream.

Later Joseph goes on an errand for his father to check up on his brothers and they conspire to kill him, but instead they strip him of his coat and throw him in a dry pit, thanks to Reuben. I bet Joseph spent that night in prayer, wouldn't you? I could have entitled this, "**Prayer in the Pits**." Judah then gets a brain storm when he sees the Ishmaelites approaching. "Let's sell Joseph and be free of his blood." So they sell him for 20 pieces of silver to be traded in Egypt and when Reuben returns he is furious. So they devise another plan, dip his coat of many colors in blood and tell Isaac a wild animal killed him.

Can you as a Christian see God's hand in all this -- His providence, His plan -- maybe in your life? This is a horrible chapter in Joseph's life but God hasn't finished writing the whole story yet. I believe that at the age of 17 Joseph, being the apple of his father's eye, worshiped and prayed to the God of his father, *Jehovah Elohim*. It was obvious God was with Joseph because of his dreams, his coat and his blessings from God, but was he able to see God in the pit, in Egypt, and in prison?

In the last chapter of Genesis, Joseph is speaking to his brothers and said, "You meant it for evil but God meant it for good." But did he see that in chapters two and three of his life story? Only if he was as close to God in the pit as he was in the field.

God has a plan for each and every one of us and we need to trust Him. In Gen. 37:34, Israel tears his clothes and puts sackcloth on his loins and mourns for Joseph many days (7,300+) because he thought he was dead. This is a form of prayer, mourning *(abal)* to bewail, lament, grieve, the emotion and attitude of sorrow. It is not stated that he prayed to God but I am sure he did, wouldn't you? Biblical mourning for the dead involved emotion, usually expressed audibly and visibly. I am sure Jacob asked God 1,000 times, WHY? However, God never told him why, and God knew he was still alive. Jacob heard only silence from God. There are some things God just doesn't choose to tell us. God had a plan, a purpose, and He would bring good out of this evil. Twenty years would pass, and the sackcloth would get pretty itchy, but he would embrace Joseph once again. May we too learn to trust God more when we are <u>in the pit of despair</u> and not just <u>on the pinnacle of jubilation</u>.

Joseph's prayer life is never revealed, although his sons' names in Gen. 41:51-53 mention his family's toil and his afflictions. He had a good teacher his father Jacob/Israel. His life was lived in the very presence of God (Gen. 40:8; 41:16, 25, 28, 32, 39; 45:5, 7, 8; 50:20, 24; 39:9), and is a lesson to us all about sin and God's presence. *"How... can I do this great wickedness and sin against God?"* Joseph would not do evil because it was to sin against God. He had a close, intimate relationship with the God of his fathers. God's plan and purpose for his life is revealed in Gen. 50:20, *"...<u>Ye thought evil against me; but God meant it unto good</u>."*

The LORD was continually with this servant. He was the first born of Jacob and Rachel (Gen. 30:22-24). He was loved more than his brothers by his father (Gen. 37:3). God revealed His will to him through dreams -- the sheaves, the sun, moon and stars. He was hated by his brothers and sold to Midianite traders, then into Egypt, then thrown into prison and <u>he wouldn't see his family for 20 years</u>, but all this time the LORD was with Joseph. Gen. 39:2 - *"And the LORD was with Joseph, and he was a prosperous man..."* Gen. 39:5 - *"...The LORD blessed the Egyptian's house for Joseph's sake."* Gen. 39:21 - *"...The LORD was with Joseph, and showed him mercy, and gave him favour in the sight of the keeper of the prison."* Gen. 39:23 - *"The LORD was with him, and that which he did, the LORD made it to prosper."* <u>Everything he touched prospered</u>.

In Gen. 40:8 he gives God the glory for the interpretations of dreams. He knew what his dreams of earlier years meant, but I'm sure he wondered why all this was happening to him. In Gen. 41:16, he gives glory to God in response to Pharaoh's dreams, *"God shall give Pharaoh an answer of peace."* In v.25 he says, *"God has shewed Pharaoh what He is about to do."* Pharaoh recognizes Joseph as, *"<u>A man in whom the Spirit of God is,</u>"* (Gen. 41:38). Joseph marries Asenath, the daughter of the priest of On, and has two sons: Manasseh, *"For God... has made me forget all my toil and all my father's house,"* (v. 51), and Ephraim, *"For God hath caused me to be fruitful in the land of my affliction,"* (v. 52). <u>Joseph is always careful to give God the glory, even in naming his children</u>. Deut. 4:24 says, *"For the LORD thy God is a consuming fire, even a jealous God!"* If I have learned one thing in walking with God since 1972, it is that God shares His glory with no one! And especially not with me.

Joseph knew this was the ticket to spiritual blessings from God. He also had a reverential trust in and fear of God since childhood, instilled in him by his father (Gen. 42:18). In Gen. 42:6 we see the fulfillment of his first dream of the sheaves bowing down to him referenced in Gen. 37:7. Why did he bind Simeon and imprison him? Was it his idea to throw him in the pit and kill him 20 years earlier? In Gen. 43:29 he blesses Benjamin, his brother, but in Gen. 45:4-9 he reveals to his brothers his true identity, *"I am Joseph your brother, whom ye sold into Egypt...God did send me before you to preserve life."*

The spiritual perception of the sovereignty and providence of God by Joseph is unbelievable! Joseph walked with God from childhood and always gave God the glory! He realized sin was against God. The LORD was always with Joseph, blessing him, and even the pagans observed the Spirit of God working in him. He feared and recognized God in all things. He even named his children after God's faithfulness. Nothing evil is recorded about him.

He closes his father's eyes and his own bones are carried out of Egypt (Ex. 13:19). <u>However, nothing is recorded about his prayer life, nothing</u>! A man who walked this close to God and gave God all the glory and trusted Him completely had to be a man of prayer. The silence of his prayer life speaks louder than his life! Maybe we talk too much about our spiritual lives and walk too little. **Maybe we should walk more and talk less!** Your walk talks and your talk talks, but your walk talks louder than your talk talks! (The Silent Prayer).

*(**Prayer** - "Abba, Father, may we learn from Joseph to trust You and glorify You in everything. Let the silence of our chambers and closets speak volumes. May everyone know, Christian and pagan alike, that we have been with Jesus. May they see His image in our lives and smell His aroma in our presence, and may the dust of His garments fall on us. In His name we pray. Amen!")*

Principles for Prayer:

- Your walk talks and your talk talks, but your walk talks louder than your talk talks.
- Maybe we talk too much and walk too little. Jesus said, "Sell it all, and follow Me!" That's pretty simple!
- The power of prayer, linked with the promises of God, is a force to be reckoned with!
- God is waiting for a man/woman to pray back His promises and hold Him to His word! Are you that person?

"If thou art not a praying person, thou art not a Christian."

John Bunyan

"Pray Back His Promises" #52
Gen. 46:3-4

"Israel took his journey with all that he had, and came to Beer-Sheba, and offered sacrifices unto the God of his father Isaac." (Gen. 46:1). In v.2-4, Israel gets a vision in the night from God (a **"D.M.I."** for those who prefer, **"DMI's**). God is going to make a great nation out of his 70, and he is going to die there. First, let's go back to Gen. 43:14 for a moment, *"And God Almighty give you mercy before the man." El Shaddai,* the All Sufficient One, the One Who Sustains, Satisfys, Enriches, and makes Fruitful! Also the One who chastens His people to make them more fruitful (John 15:2, Ruth 1:20; Heb. 12:10). This is Israel's God, *El Shaddai,* the Almighty One of Whom he says, "May He give you mercy before the man," (not knowing that Joseph, his son, is the man). Joseph is gone, Judah is in prison, and now he has to send Benjamin away. So, he prays a rich blessing on his sons! Do you think he prayed while they were down in Egypt, in *Mizraim*? Would you have been praying, would you have gotten off your knees?

Now he gets word that not only has Judah been released and Benjamin been returned but "JOSEPH" is alive (Gen. 45:26-27), and *"the spirit of Jacob revived."* What a time of rejoicing! So, Israel stops at *Beer-Sheba*, where Abraham planted a tree in Gen. 21:33, and calls on *El Olam* the Everlasting God. That's where Abraham and Isaac left from and returned to when they went to *Mt. Moriah* to offer Isaac as an offering, and that's where Isaac settled, dug a well, and built an altar in Gen. 26. That is also where Jacob/Israel departed from when he ran from Esau in Gen. 28:10.

Ninety years have passed since he left Beer-Sheba, where he stole Esau's blessing and robbed his birthright. He is leaving a lot of memories as he leaves the Promised Land at 130 years old to go to Egypt to grow a nation and die. However, before he leaves the "Holy Land" he builds or rebuilds one more altar and sacrifices one more time to the God of his father Isaac. God gives him a promise in response to his <u>sacrifice, worship</u>

and prayer at the altar in *Beer-Sheba*. In Gen. 46:3-4, God tells him not to fear, that He will bring him down into Egypt and back again, and make a great nation of him, and he will die there. Verse 4 says, *"Joseph shall put his hand upon thine eyes."* (You die with your eyes open, someone else closes them for you.)

Israel is still a man of prayer, "A Prince with God," and God is still blessing him. God keeps His promises and His word! This is the last altar and the last word from God in Genesis. It isn't until 400 years later that God speaks to His servant Moses on the back side of the desert in a burning bush in Exodus 3. The Jewish people could not build altars in Egypt, or offer animal sacrifices, because that was an abomination to the Egyptians (Gen. 46:34; Ex. 8:26). **The Egyptians worshiped the creation, not the Creator**.

Oh, what a precious time that must have been, between God and Israel at that final altar, knowing that it would be over 400 years before it would be repeated again. But Jacob/Israel was still building altars, "to the God of Israel – *El Elohe-Israel.*" The banks of the *Peniel* River and the face of God were as real to him then as they were 65 years earlier. What a precious patriarch or saint of God Israel became -- supplanter to supplicator! But it took time (many, many years) and much heartache. "Oh God, what will it take to make us a prince or princess with You? Thank You for the example of this saint who began as a supplanter and ended up as a supplicator. We need a *Beer-Sheba* every day as we enter our *Mizraim* to work, live, serve and die.

"Jacob [Israel] *blessed Pharaoh,"* (Gen. 47:7). He does so again in v.10 as he is leaving his presence; he invokes God's favor upon him and his country, *"Jacob* [Israel] *blessed Pharaoh."* Jacob/Israel was very grateful for Joseph and the provision for his family. We can bless the unsaved, but they can't bless us (from God, that is). We have discussed blessings already and how important they really are and how much we and our families miss by neglecting them.

In Gen. 47:31, Jacob/Israel makes Joseph swear to him that he will bury him in the *Cave of Machpelah* with Leah, his first wife, and Joseph agrees. Then Jacob/Israel bows himself on the head of the bed. King David does this same thing in I Kings 1:47 after Solomon was anointed King. David was old and advanced in years and cold (I Kings 1:1), so he could not get out of bed. The same is true here with Jacob/Israel. He is 147 years old (v.28-29) *"the time drew near that Israel must die." "And Israel bowed himself upon the bed's head."* (v.31). I don't believe he was worshiping Joseph, I believe he was doing obeisance to *"El-Elohe-Israel"* to "the God of Israel." Remember, the supplanter became the supplicator. Even on his death bed, unto his last dying breath, he worshiped, praised, and prayed to the LORD.

What an example in the second half of his life. Remember, he was 45 when he left Isaac, and was with Laban for 20 years before he met God at the *Peniel*, and it was 10 more years before he returned to *Bethel* to build an altar to *El Bethel*. That is 75 years. He is now 147 years old and they have been in Egypt for 17 years, but here on his death bed he gets Joseph to promise that he would bury him in the Cave of Machpelah with Leah, Isaac and Rebekah, and Abraham and Sarah. In *Mamre* (fatness) of *Hebron* (communion) and he worships and prays to his God. May we be faithful to God unto the very end like Israel. From the womb to the tomb, guided by the hand of the LORD. Prov. 16:9 - *"A man's heart deviseth his way, but the LORD directeth his steps."* Jer. 10:23 – *"It is not in man that walketh to direct his steps."* Ps. 37:23 says, *"The steps of a good man are ordered by the LORD."*

George Mueller said, "The stops, too!" Not only the steps of the LORD but the stops too are ordered, established or ordained by the LORD. That was true in Jacob/Israel's life and it is true in ours. Are we able to recognize God's hand directing our lives -- our steps, and our stops? Can we, like Jacob, in our later years, in our last days, bow our heads on our beds and worship Him? Can we do it now? Jacob became a man of prayer, a prince with God, a real prayer warrior, but it cost him dearly! Are you willing to pay the price, to count the cost, to weigh the odds, to walk that close to God? How are your hips? Any limps, lately? Are you ready for your Waterloo, your *Peniel* or *Penuel* experience? Are you ready to meet God face-to-face, whether in life or in death?

May we not only bow ourselves on our beds at 147, but may we bow ourselves in our closets and churches at 14, at 47, at 74! There are over 2,930 characters in the Bible, and less than 100 of them made it to the ribbon. The vast majority fell out of the race after the age of 60. How about you? Paul said, "I fought a good fight, I finished my course, I kept the faith!" How about you? One verse drives me on and I want it on my tombstone: **John 17:4 - *"I have finished the work which thou gavest me to do.*"** How about you? It's easy to start a race (anybody can), but it takes real guts, courage, spiritual grit, and intestinal fortitude to finish (and to finish strong). Just look over your shoulder -- where are they? The ones that started 10-20 years ago. What happened to them? Why did they fall out? Is a mere profession all that is necessary? Raise your hand, fill out a card, walk an isle, say a prayer, get wet! What did Peter mean in II Pet. 1:10, *"Brethren, give diligence to make your calling and election sure."* Or Paul in II Cor 13:5, *"Examine yourselves, whether ye be in the faith; prove your own selves."* There is a new game on the market today called, "Born Again." Don't play it; you can't win! Jesus said, "You must be born again!" It's serious business, so take it seriously, and make sure my friend. Make absolutely sure you are a blood-bought, born-again baptized child of God! Don't play the game!

*(**Prayer** - "Father, Christianity is not a game, Your Son gave His life so we could have eternal life, and that is so that we might know You, the only true God, and Jesus Christ Whom You have sent (John 17:3). Thank You Father; In Jesus Christ's name I pray. Amen!"*

"And every creature which is in heaven, and on the earth, and under the earth, and such as are in the sea, and all that are in them, heard I saying, Blessing, and honour, and glory, and power, be unto him that sitteth upon the throne, and unto the Lamb forever and ever. And the four beasts said, Amen. And

the four and twenty elders fell down and worshipped him that liveth forever and ever." Rev. 5:13-14.

Principles for Prayer:

- Pray that you will be faithful right to your very last breath, like many of the faithful patriarchs.
- If God can change a supplanter into a supplicater – imagine what He can do with you, if you let Him!
- Jacob/Israel, with his last dying breath, worshiped, praised and prayed to God. How about you?

"Prayer, secret fervent, believing prayer, lies at the root of all personal holiness."

William Carey

"Death Bed Prayer Blessing" #53
Gen. 49:1-33

Jacob/Israel is dying and calls for Joseph's children first so he can bless them. Jacob/Israel places his right hand on **Ephraim** (the younger) and his left hand on **Manasseh** (the elder), which is wrong. This is interesting, since Jacob was younger than his brother Esau and ended up with the blessing and the birthright. In Gen. 48:14, even though Jacob is old and blind, it says he did this knowingly and wittingly, guiding his hands. It was intentional. It displeased Joseph and he tried to switch his father's hands back, but it was to late. Jacob said in v.19, *"I know it, my son I know it."* He told him that Ephraim (the younger) would be greater than Manasseh and become a multitude of nations. Remember, it was *Reuben, Gad and Manasseh* that stayed on the east side of the Jordan and did not settle in the Promised Land, but on its border, on the banks, on the threshold.

Note if you will Jacob/Israel's prayer of blessing in v.15-16, he prays to the God of his fathers; the God Who fed them; the Angel Who redeemed him to *"bless the lads."* He asks for his name, the name of Jacob/Israel to be named upon them. That means all the promises to Jacob are available to Ephraim and Manasseh, plus the promises to Abraham and Isaac. **WOW**! What a blessing! Have we lost sight of the magnitude of the blessing? I think we have! We bless our food, our buildings, our plans and trips, our endeavors, our money, motorcycles, boats, cars (you name it, we bless it!), even our sneezes! But we don't invoke blessings on our children, neighbors or friends regularly. Why? I think there is more to this principle than we realize. It was God in Genesis one and two Who first established the blessing, especially for multiplication. (Gen. 1:22) *"Be fruitful, and multiply,"* (fish and birds); v.28, *"Be fruitful, and multiply,"* (mankind). Then here in our text (v.16) *"Bless the lads...and let them grow into a multitude in the midst of the earth."* Jacob blessed them; and God did bless and multiply them.

Jacob/Israel invokes a blessing on only these two grandchildren here, and Joseph receives a double blessing here. In verses 22-26 Joseph gets his blessing. This double blessing should have been Reuben's but he blew it, so it passed to Joseph, the first born of Rachel, not Leah. Ephraim and Manasseh replace Joseph in the tribal breakdown, making twelve tribes. The blessing seems to have a tremendous impact and significance (can I say power without causing a problem?). Further personal study would seem appropriate on this matter, but in the context of our study, this prayer of blessing is of tremendous importance as these two sons of Joseph form the tribe of Joseph.

Jacob/Israel continues in Gen. 49:1-33 to bless all of his sons; **Reuben** the first born, unstable as water, shall not excel because he committed fornication with his father's concubine on his couch. **Simeon and Levi** were instruments of cruelty when they slaughtered the men of *Shechem* for raping Dinah. They will be divided and scattered. **Judah's** brothers shall praise him; he is a lion's whelp. The *Scepter* shall not depart from Judah; it is through him the Messiah will come to establish His Kingdom. **Zebulon** will dwell by the sea and become a haven for ships. **Issachar** will be strong like a donkey, and serve and see that the land is pleasant, and love it and serve it. **Dan** shall judge his people like a serpent in the road way. **Gad** shall triumph over his enemies like a troop and be victorious at last. **Asher** shall yield bread and baked goods to feed the people. **Napthali** is like a deer let loose who gives words of beauty. **Joseph** is a fruitful bough by a wall of water, and is to grow strong and multiply. **Benjamin** is a ravenous wolf to devour the prey and divide the spoil. v.28, *"And [Jacob] blessed them; every one according to his blessing, he blessed them."* Wow! The blessing of the Blessing!

Oh, my friend, are we negligent in this vital area of our prayer life? Do we neglect to seek God's will for our children to give them a rich blessing and heritage? Is it the money that we leave them that's important, or a rich spiritual heritage that is more important? In the world today it's money that's important. How much did your parents leave you in the will? Who got the house, the cars, the boat, the gold, the guns, and the library? In the Scriptures those things are never mentioned once with Abraham, Isaac, Jacob, Moses, etc., never once! How many sheep or goats did you get?

Our priorities and valuables are way out of focus. This saint of God, this <u>supplanter turned supplicater,</u> learned what was most important; and it was <u>the spiritual blessings, not the material</u>. Jacob did not discuss how many sheep or shekels each son was to get, but what God was going to bless each one with. Then he charges them to bury him in the Cave of *Machpelah*, where Abraham, Sarah, Isaac, Rebekah and Leah are buried. Interesting -- he wants to be buried with Leah, not with Rachel; God's choice I believe, was Leah, who bore him Judah through whom the Messiah would come. Jacob's choice was Rachel due to her physical beauty, and it cost him dearly. She was so beautiful it made him weep, but Leah was God's *Beshertah (soul mate)* for him. It just took him 147 years to figure it out!

The power of blessings is something we need to consider in our lives and ministries. <u>The last thing this saint would do was to give his sons his blessing,</u> draw his feet into the bed and die! Are we that at peace with God that after we have blessed our children we can draw our feet into the bed and breathe our last breath and die? What a beautiful scene this must have been. Jacob/Israel is 147 years old, surrounded by his 12 sons (who ranged in age from about 70 for Benjamin to about 95 for Reuben).

"And Joseph fell upon his father's face, and wept upon him, and kissed him." Then Joseph ordered the servants and the physicians to embalm Jacob/Israel, and the Egyptians mourned (*bakah* - to weep, bemoan, make lamentation with tears) for 70 days. Although weeping is usually associated with distress or sorrow it is also a sign of joy, and all of the occurrences of this usage are found in the life of Jacob: Gen. 29:11 when he met Rachel; Gen. 33:4 when he met Esau after 20 years; Gen. 46:29 when he met Joseph again.

It may be said that there is no genuine repentance apart from a bitter sense of sorrow over one's sin, a sorrow so deep that it may quite properly issue in weeping. No indication of prayer other than who are you weeping or mourning to? In Deut. 34:8 they wept and mourned for Moses for 30 days. Gen. 50:10-11 tells us that they mourned again for seven days (*sitting Shiva*) in Canaan at the threshing floor of *Atad* before committing Jacob to the Cave of *Machpelah*. <u>This is not prayer; it is mourning, wailing and lamenting.</u>

*(**Prayer** - "LORD, may we be able to impart to our children a rich spiritual inheritance. And may we fully understand the importance and impact a prayer of blessing may have on an individual or a nation. May we continue to bless the Jewish people as well as the Jewish Nation in our prayers daily, Gen. 12:1-3; Ps. 122:6. In ha shem Yeshua's name we pray. Amen!")*

Principles for Prayer:

- The power of blessings is something we seriously need to consider in our prayer life.
- There is no genuine repentance apart from a bitter sense of sorrow over one's own sin against God.
- Jacob's prayer blessing on Joseph's sons was the transferring of his own name and promises unto them.

"Make me sensible of real answers to actual requests as evidences of an interchange between myself on earth and my Savior in Heaven."

Dr. Chalmers (from his diary)

"Portraits of Prayer in Exodus"

"Groaning in Prayer" #1
Ex. 2:23-25

"And it came to pass in process of time, that the king of Egypt died: and the children of Israel sighed by reason of the bondage, and they cried, and their cry came up unto God by reason of the bondage. And God heard their groaning, and God remembered His covenant with Abraham, with Isaac, and with Jacob. And God looked upon the children of Israel, and God had respect unto them." Exodus 2:23-25

The children of Israel **sighed** (*anah*) groaned, moaned, mourned, and they **cried** (*tza'aq*) to call out to, weep aloud, howl, and God **heard** (*shema*) hear, listen, obeyed their groaning. They were afflicted and in bondage (*boda*) slavery, forced labor and about to be exterminated (Ex. 1). So they sighed, cried, groaned, moaned and shrieked to God; wouldn't you? They were desperate, destitute and in distress; and they finally turned to the One who could help, God! The word "groan" (*ne-aqa*) means to sigh, moan or groan, and comes from a word meaning to weep in sorrow, usually referring to mourning for the dead. Could it be this mourning was for the dead male children in Exodus 1:15-22, who were being killed by the Egyptians, even being fed alive to the crocodiles in the Nile? Yuck!

"They cried," (v.23). The word here is *zā'aq* - to shriek out from anguish, fear or danger; to cry out for help in time of distress; but more frequently it is a cry directed to God! This is a cry of those approaching the breaking point! Have you been there, at the breaking point that is? Then you know this kind of prayer; <u>prayer that groans, prayer that moans, prayer that cries, prayer that sweats drops of blood</u> if necessary (*hematohidrosis*)! God's response to Israel's <u>groaning prayer</u> is seen in vss. 24-25. He responds in four specific ways, and you need to note them: **1st** – He heard (*shema*) their groaning -- to

hear intelligently, to hearken with obedience, diligently; like the *shema* in Deut. 6:4; to hear and do something about it: **2nd** – He remembered (*zakar*) His covenant with Abraham, Isaac and Jacob. The word "remembered" refers to an inward mental act accompanied by an appropriate external act. To bring to mind, and to do something about it: **3rd** – He looked (*ra'a*) -- to see, plain and simple; to look, view, see, to inspect. He looked, He saw, He gazed upon from heaven: **4th** – He knew (*yada*) their plight, their problem, their dilemma, He acknowledged the problem. To know and ascertain by seeing, feeling, and hearing. To have first hand knowledge, to acknowledge their acquaintance, become a familiar friend, to know intimately. God heard their groaning, remembered His covenant, saw their need, and acknowledged their acquaintance. They were His people! His covenant people!

Are you or someone you know at the breaking point today, right now? I am. It's interesting that I should be writing this today, as my wife was diagnosed with cancer last week. Groaning in prayer is not so unfamiliar, is it? **No** it is not! In fact, my wife had to go for a Thermography today and my daughter, Rebecca, also!

God hears our prayers and cries today, and remembers His promises not only to us but to His Son, Jesus, the Christ, as well. He sees us and our needs and He acknowledges us, not only as familiar friends, but as sons and daughters as well. Prayer is no different today for the Christian than it was for the Israelite yesterday, except it is even more intimate today because we have an Advocate, *"Jesus Christ the Righteous"* (I John 2:1).

Exodus 3:7-9 are a repeat of Exodus 2:23-25 with a tremendous promise added on for Israel's benefit and ours. Exodus 3:7 says, *"I have surely seen the affliction… and have heard their cry… I know their sorrows."* Verse 8 says, *"And I am come down to deliver them out of the hand of the Egyptians, and to bring them up out of that land unto a good land and a large, unto a land flowing with milk and honey."* He will snatch them away, deliver them, defend them and rescue them; He will do whatever it takes to save His children. Wouldn't you, to save yours?

Psalm 65:2 tells us He hears the prayers of all mankind. This is true, but He especially hears and answers the prayer that groans, prayer that moans, prayer that cries and sweats. James 5:16 says, "[It is] *the effectual, fervent prayer of a righteous man* [that] *availeth much."* It's that hot, glowing, fervent prayer, picked up with those tongs by one of His angels off the incense altar before God that will really move that mountain for God. Amen?

It's only recorded that Yeshua/Jesus groaned twice in His spirit, at Lazarus' grave (John 11:33; 38). Paul refers to the whole creation groaning in Rom. 8:22, and all of us groaning within ourselves in v.23. He also refers to the Holy Spirit making groanings in v.26, *"But the Spirit itself* [Himself] *maketh intercession for us with groanings which cannot be uttered."* Christ receives our sighs, groans and moans in His prayer censer, because He Who made them knows what they are all about. In fact the Holy Spirit (Who also makes them) knows what they are. The Spirit makes groanings for us and God answers them, because we don't know what to pray for as we ought, and He knows the mind of God and the hearts of saints.

So, many times, spiritual groanings are the perfect answer to our spiritual dilemma when the request is to heavy for words. Think of Job in 23:2, or David in Ps. 6:6; 38:9, or Hannah, Eliezer, Daniel, Isaiah, Jeremiah, etc. In I Sam. 1:9-18, Hannah (the mother of Samuel) prayed in her heart so fervently that Eli the priest thought she was drunk; but she, <u>*"poured out* [her] *soul before the LORD."*</u>

Mental prayer is not unheard! When the heart is so full of grief that it can only groan in prayer, God writes it down in His prayer book. <u>C. H. Spurgeon once said, "Groanings which cannot be uttered are often prayers which cannot be refused."</u> I like that! Don't you? Wow, there is so much in these three verses you could write a book on them! *"God looked upon the children of Israel, and God had respect unto them* [knew their plight]," as He does yours and mine.

*(**Prayer** - "LORD, thank You that You hear, see, know, remember, and deliver us out of our dilemmas every moment of every day. You are truly our (ezer-ezer) our Life Saver! And whether we verbally cry out to You or groan from the depths of our hearts, You know and hear our every need and word (expressed or unexpressed) through the groaning of the Holy Spirit. What a comfort. In ha shem Yeshua we thank You, Amen!")*

Principles for prayer:

- God hears, God remembers, God sees, and God knows your problem!
- God sees, God hears, God knows, and God delivers His people!
- Groanings which cannot be uttered are <u>prayers</u> which cannot be denied!

"Prayer is the hand that moves the world, but the fingers of that hand are consecrated men and women."
Robert Moffat

"Barefoot Praying before God" #2
Exodus 3:5

"...Draw not nigh [near] hither: put off thy shoes from off thy feet, for the place whereon thou standest is holy ground." Ex. 3:5. **WOW**! Holy ground! This is the first appearance of the word "holy" (*kodesh*) in the Scriptures -- holy, sacred thing or place, set apart or dedicated to God. A Sacred place, consecrated, dedicated, hallowed, holy; its root means to be clean and pure (apartness, holiness, sacredness). God, Who is holy, calls men to be holy also, I Peter 1:16, *"Because it is written, Be ye holy; for I am holy."* Where is it written? Lev. 11:44-45, *"For I am the LORD your God: ye shall therefore sanctify yourselves, and ye shall be holy; for I am holy..."*

The International Standard Bible Encyclopedia (ISBE) states holiness as, "Man was made in the image of God and capable of reflecting the divine likeness. And as God reveals Himself as ethically holy, He calls men to holiness resembling His own." Holiness is something you do not hear much about today from our pulpits, because the prophets of old can tell you, "The fruit of a ministry of holiness is loneliness." It is not a popular subject, ministry or calling today. That is why prophecy conferences have kind of died out or last only one or two days any more, and true prophecy speakers, true prophets of the Word, are as rare as **hen's teeth**.

Prophecy should always lead us to a life of holiness, but you don't see that happening today. Why? Just more prophecy, more end times, more Revelation, but no change in the lives of the listeners. No deeper prayer life, walk with God, worship experience, missionary service, zeal for soul-winning, No change! Just, "When's the next conference?"

I would venture to say that 90-95% of the students I teach never re-study the teaching material I give them. Prophecy conferences should lead right into revival, renewal, renovation of the heart and spirit but they don't. Why?

Maybe we should take off our shoes, like the Muslims, as we enter the house of worship. After all it is called a *"house of prayer"* (Isaiah 56:7), is it not? In many Synagogues, on the front wall or on the *"Aron Ha-Kodesh"* (the doors of the Holy Ark in which the sacred scrolls are kept) are these words in Hebrew, **"Dah Lifnay Me Attah Omed."** (Know Before Whom You Stand!). This idea came from the experience of Moses and the burning bush in Ex. 3:5. This saying reminds us to have a reverent, focused attitude while attending the worship service, and to be filled with respectful awe over the presence of God as we approach His Word. But do we? Stand up while it is being read – show respect! Do we?

Blaise Pascal said, "There are two kinds of people – saints who know they are sinners and sinners who think they are saints." Which category do you fall into? Remember, pride is the deadliest of all sins because it distorts reality. Sometimes we come to church to meet "Joe" instead of *"Jehovah,"* and we dress like it too! We have lost the sense of His holiness in our churches today. Our sanctuaries are more like night-clubs, studios, and theaters than holy, sanctified, purified places of worship. They have lost their aura, their ambiance, their atmosphere of worship.

He said, "Sanctify, purify yourselves and you shall be holy, for I am holy." It is not just a good idea to be holy, we are commanded to be holy. So, *"put off thy shoes from off thy feet."* Paul tells us to walk "circumspectly" like we are in a mine-field, feeling every little blade of grass under our feet, every grain of sand, every twig. In Eph. 5:15 the word "circumspectly" is (*akribos*). Guess what word we get from that word, and watch what acrobats put on their feet, or not! This word in Hebrew means to be set apart exclusively for the presence of God, so take off your shoes!

"For the place whereon thou standest is holy ground." The word for "ground" is (*adamah*) soil, earth, land, dirt, redness in color. Its root is (*adam*) to show blood. Gen. 2:7 says, *"God formed man of the dust of the ground."* The substance God used to form man from, He is now standing on and it is holy!

Why? Because, God is standing on it! So, *"put off thy shoes from off thy feet."* Do we realize when we enter into prayer or worship that it is holy ground that we tread upon? Do we?

You call upon the <u>name of God the Father</u>, in the <u>name of God the Son</u> through the power of <u>God the Holy Spirit</u>. Do you really believe you have an audience with the God of the universe? Of course you do! Then what do you think you are standing on? Dirt, cement, carpet, wood, what? **"HOLY GROUND!"** Do we take off our dirty shoes from off our feet? Our dirty clothes and stand before a holy, perfect God, bare-naked? How can we come to God with any defilement, any dust from the road of life and expect to be accepted?

I know the blood of *Yeshua/Jesus* washes away all our sins. Just read <u>Isa. 64:6 in the Roman Catholic Bible</u> for a good description of our good deeds and righteous garments, sometime. Jesus washed the disciples' feet. Mary washed Jesus' feet, the widows washed the saints' feet (I Tim. 5:10), but if Aaron and his sons did not wash their feet before stepping into the Tabernacle, <u>they died instantly (Ex. 30:17-21)</u>. Why? It was **"holy ground!"** That was the purpose of the "Laver." However, the point here is not, "Wash your feet, Moses", but, *"Put off thy shoes from off thy feet, for the place whereon thou standest is holy ground."*

We cannot, we must not come before His holy presence defiled, polluted, desecrated, and impure! Take off your shoes, your hat, your coat, whatever is defiled. You are on holy ground as you stand before His presence. Joshua, Moses' successor had the same experience in Joshua 5:15 - *"Loose thy shoe from off thy foot; for the place whereon thou standest is holy." <u>And Joshua did so</u>."*

As we get into the Tabernacle and the priesthood, the word "holy" is stamped on every board, every curtain ring, and every utensil. A veil separated the Holy Place from the Holy of Holies. If even the high priest himself made a mistake in the Tabernacle <u>he was killed instantly</u>. Why? He was on holy ground! But we have permission to enter that Holy of Holies;

the divine presence of God, if we are indeed washed by the precious blood of the Lamb of God (Heb. 10:19) - *"Having therefore, brethren, boldness to enter into the holiest <u>by the blood of Jesus</u>..."*

Think for a moment of the implications of John 13 when the Messiah was washing the defiled, polluted feet of His followers in light of this passage! Oh, the beauty and love of our precious LORD and Savior for us! Let us bow and worship Him in the *"<u>beauty of holiness</u>,"* (Psalm 29:2; 96:9). Oh, my friend let us, too, turn aside like Moses and see why the bush burns but is not consumed. But let us take our sandals off our feet as we enter our prayer closets to worship the God of the living. "Be ye Holy for I the LORD your God am Holy."

*(Prayer – "Lord, thank You for this beautiful passage of Scripture and thought today. May we walk before You bare-footed and bare-hearted. May we seek Your Shekinah Glory and turn aside to see why the bush burns, but is not consumed. LORD, we love You so much. Draw us into Your bosom, and never let us go. Hold us, lead us, and guide us with Your everlasting eye and teach us what it means to pray and worship on holy ground. May we, **"Dah Lifnay Me Attah Omed – Know Before Whom We Stand!"** As we pray, as we worship, as we praise, as we confess, as we adore, we thank You Father, for the blood Your Son, Jesus the Christ shed on Calvary! Amen!"*

I leave you with a verse a young man gave me over 45 years ago at an altar, bare-footed, after he kicked off his shoes at Lakes Pond Baptist Church in Connecticut. Lev. 6:13, *"The fire shall ever be burning upon the altar; it shall never go out."* God starts the fire, but you stoke the fire with five things: Bible, prayer, worship, fellowship, amd witnessing." In II Tim. 1:6, Paul told Timothy to stir up the gift of God that was in him, or "fan the flame." That's our job; God starts the fire; we stoke the fire and we fan the flame so it will never go out. NEVER!

Got your shoes off? Good, now stand with me before the bush that burned with fire but was not consumed. Ex. 3:2 tells us that in the bush was the Angel of the LORD (*the YHVH*), Who said in v. 14 that His name was *(Ehyeh Asher Ehyeh)* *"I Am That I Am."* The One Who causes to be or exist; the One Who causes to breathe or live; the uncaused cause; the "Is-ing One. It's not a question of, "Who am I to go?" (v.11). It's a command -- "I Am has sent me to you!" (v.14). Then He told him, "Now go!" (v. 16).

Are you still standing? Where is it the Great I AM wants you to go? Let's ask Him right now, "Father, where would You like us to go?"

Principles for Prayer:

- Know before Whom you stand before you begin to pray!
- Holiness leads to Godliness and opens the door into God's presence!
- *"Dah Lifnay Me Attah Omed"* "Know Before Whom You Stand!"

"God hears the heart without words,
but He never hears the words without a heart."
Unknown

"Prayer is a Two-Way Street" #3
Exodus 4

We speak to God and He speaks to us, or vise-versa. Where do we get this idea that when we pray we do all the talking and God does all the listening? Did you ever have a conversation with a person, especially a close friend, who never let you get a word in edgewise? They kept talking, and talking and talking and asking you more questions and giving you more requests and directions and requests; and talking, and talking and then say something like, "Well I have to go, so I'll see you tomorrow?" Very frustrating, isn't it?

How do you think God feels when we come to Him in prayer with our shopping lists and read them off, item by item, as if He can't read or remember; and ask Him a lot of questions and then say, "Amen!" Then go about our business and sometimes, never even giving a second thought to all we just told the God of Eternity. Do you ever think that God gets frustrated with our prayer life, our prayer lists, our prayer journals, our prayer agendas or our "Five Point Prayer Plans?"

Note Exodus 3:2. Here the LORD Jehovah, the God of Redemption, the Angel of the LORD called unto Moses out of the midst of the burning bush and said, "*Moseh, Moseh!*" Several times you find God calling someone's name twice to get their attention, and it usually works. Like "Abraham, Abraham," on Mt Moriah as he was about to kill his son, Isaac. And *Moseh* answers, "Here *am* I!" [(*hinneh*) behold, see, look, here, "It's me!"] And the dialogue continues for two chapters.

God talks and Moses listens, or Moses talks and God listens: v.11, Moses said to God, *"Who am I?"* v.12, God answers Moses, *"Certainly I will be with thee; and this shall be a token unto thee:"* v.13, *"Moses said unto God, "Behold, when I come unto the children of Israel, and shall say unto them, The God of your fathers hath sent me unto you; and they shall say to me, What is His name? what shall I say unto them?"* v.14, "God said unto Moses, "I AM THAT I AM: ...Thus shalt thou *say unto the children of Israel, I AM hath sent me unto you."* v.15, *"And God said moreover unto Moses, "Thus shalt thou say unto the children of Israel, The LORD God of your fathers, the God of Abraham, the God of Isaac, and the God of Jacob, hath sent me unto you: this is my name forever;"* Chapter 4:1, Moses answers God and says, *"...Behold, they will not believe me, nor hearken unto my voice;"* v.2, *"The LORD said unto him, "What is that in thine hand? And he said, A rod."* v.3 *"And he* [the LORD] *said, "Cast it on the ground. And he cast it on the ground, and it became a serpent..."* A bad one because Moses fled from it, (smart man – they bite!).

Now v.4 is the faith verse. Anybody can throw a rod on the ground, and anybody can run from a poisonous snake, but to bend down and pick it up by the tail, takes one of two things, mountain-moving faith or <u>blatant stupidity</u>. Now I don't have a doctorate in serpentology but I know one thing about bad snakes, good snakes, and any snake: <u>never pick them up by the tail</u>! Go to the garage, get a shovel and whack off their head first, then scoop them up with the shovel and bury them! <u>The only good snake is a dead snake</u>. Anyway, enough about snakes, back to our prayer lesson. This prayer dialogue between God and *Moseh* continued on throughout chapter four and the Pentateuch.

So, "What we see is prayer is a two-way street!" We speak to God and He speaks to us, very much like a normal conversation between two close friends. Jonah in chapter 4:9-11 has a similar dialogue with God. God says to Jonah, *"Doest thou well to be angry for the gourd?" And he* [Jonah] *said, "I do well to be angry, even unto death* [ouch]*." Then said the LORD, Thou hast had pity on the gourd, for the which thou hast not labored, neither madest it grow; which came up in a night, and perished in a night. And should not I spare Nineveh, that great city, wherein are more than sixscore thousand persons that cannot discern between their right hand and their left hand; and also much cattle?"* So, again we see this two-way dialogue going on between God and one of His saints, which we call **prayer**. How much of this goes on in your prayer life? Do you take time to allow God to get a word in edgewise or put in His <u>two shekels</u>?

Can you imagine having lunch or coffee with the president of the United States of America (I don't care what your political persuasion is or whether you would or wouldn't have coffee in the White House. Just bear with me, OK? *oi vey!*) Anyway, you are asking him a lot of questions and doing all the talking, never giving him a chance to answer. Then you get up, thank him for the coffee and leave. Do you think he would invite you over again? Be honest – Rude Dude!

We need to cultivate a fine crop of listening in our prayer lives. How else will we ever know if God is paying attention if we don't take time to listen to Him? List<u>ening is the key to prayer, and an art that appears to be lost today</u>! What did young Samuel say in I Sam. 3:9-10, *"Speak, LORD; for thy servant heareth."* What did young David say in Psalm 46:10, *"Be still, and know (*yada*) that I am God."* Or James, the half brother of *Yeshua*/Jesus, in James 1:19, *"Wherefore, ...let every man be* **<u>swift to hear</u>**, *slow to speak, slow to wrath."* However, Solomon sums it up so beautifully in Ecc. 5:1: **_"Be more ready to hear, than to give the sacrifice of fools."_**

Prayer is much more than just words and lists and journals and talking. It is listening as well; it is a two-way street. Like a coin, prayer also has two sides, <u>one for talking and the other for listening</u>. Chapters three and four of Exodus are a continual prayer between two close friends, God and Moses. God and Abraham, God and Jacob, God and Enoch, God and Adam, God and Noah, God and Isaac, God and David, God and Daniel, God and Isaiah… and the list goes on; but is your name on that list, and if not why not? I have said it before: the words "listen" and "silent" have the exact same letters, but in order to listen you must be silent.

That is why I like Psalm 46:10, *"Be still (*rapah*) and know (*yada*) God."* Ask God to teach you to listen in your prayer life as well as to pray. It is a learning process, <u>like teaching a grandchild to listen while hunting</u>. Like I said about fishing, it's the same with hunting. You can go hunting or you can take a grandchild hunting, but you can't do both at the same time. (But it's way more fun to teach a grandchild to hunt than to hunt.) God would love nothing better than to teach you to listen as you pray. Just ask Him and see what He says. I dare you – I double dare you!

*(**Prayer** - "LORD, God, thank You for this thought today from Your precious Word on listening in our prayer time. LORD, teach us to listen as we pray, and teach us that prayer is a two-way street, a two-sided coin, and that both are very important. We love You, LORD, Thank You for today's principles. In ha shem Yeshua's name. Amen!")*

Principles for Prayer:

- Listening is the lost art in the science of prayer.
- It takes far more patience to listen in prayer than to speak.
- The words "silent" and "listen" have the exact same letters.

"If we would pray aright, the first thing that we should do is to see to it that we really get an audience with God; that we really get into His very presence. Before a word of petition is offered, we should have the definite consciousness that we are talking to God, and should believe that He is listening and is going to grant the thing that we ask of Him."

R.A. Torrey

"Get Down and Pray" #4
Exodus 4:31

Aaron spoke all the words of the LORD and Moses did all the signs of the LORD and the children of Israel believed. When they heard that the LORD had visited them and had looked upon their affliction, they bowed their heads and worshiped the LORD. They recognized His messengers (Aaron and Moses), His message, ("Let My people go,"), and His divine presence. So, they "got down and worshiped!" It has been a long time and the affliction had been very severe, but the LORD had finally visited the children of Jacob and looked on their affliction. In Exodus 2:23-25, God said He heard their groaning, remembered His covenant, looked upon them, and acknowledged their plight. Then in Exodus 3:7, God said that He saw their affliction, heard their cry, knew their sorrows, and He had come down to deliver them and bring them to a land flowing with milk and honey.

So now, in Exodus 4:31, they bow their heads (to contract or bend the body or neck in deference, a sign of humility and obeisance), and they worshiped (to depress or prostrate oneself in homage to royalty or to God). Or to use an old-time expression, **"They got down and worshiped!"** When you finally recognize and realize God's almighty presence and power, what else can you do but fall down prostrate and worship Him? The signs merely verified Moses' position and authenticated his office, and the words of God did the same for Aaron. The Jewish people are referred to as a "stiff-necked" people by nature, according to God's Word, and they require a sign for authentication (I Cor. 1:22; Matt. 12:38). They were going to get signs; one after another for many years to come. However, they bowed, worshiped, praised and prayed to the LORD Jehovah! Sometimes it takes the unusual or supernatural to bring us to the point of prostration and brokenness so we too can, **"Get down and worship!"**

Eliezer got to this point in Genesis 24:26, after finding Rebekah in Mesopotamia in the city of Nahor or Haran (468 miles from Hebron where Abraham was when he sent him to find a wife for Isaac). Imagine traveling for 18 days with 10 camels, coming to a town, kneeling down by a well outside the town and asking God for direction (by bringing you the ***beshertah*** -- the soul mate He had chosen for your master's son out of all the women in the city coming to draw water) and He does just that. No wonder v. 26 says that he got down and worshiped! However, v. 27 says, "...<u>I being in the way, the LORD led me</u>..." The key is, "<u>being in the way</u>." And the key to that is **availability not ability**! The other occurrence of this phrase is in Exodus 12:27 in Egypt on the night of Passover, after the children of Israel got their instructions and just before midnight when <u>over two million people in Egypt will be struck dead</u> for not obeying God's Word. Verse 27 says, "And the people bowed the head and worshiped." **They got down and worshiped**! Wouldn't you?

What will it take for us to "<u>get down and worship</u>?" A rod turned into a serpent? A hand turned into leprosy? Water turned into blood? Frogs covering the land, three days of darkness that can be felt, or the death of the first born? Does it matter what it takes as long as it happens? We must get down on our knees and faces and worship the God who created us and saved us. We must spend time in His Word and in our prayer closets and gardens alone with Him. Without it, we will dry up like an old creek bed in the hot summer sun and be of no use to anyone except to gather some **smooth stones** from our dry river beds. But without <u>His Word</u> and <u>much prayer</u> we won't have the <u>courage</u> or <u>insight</u> to throw them at a <u>grasshopper</u>, let alone a <u>giant</u>.

The Jewish people are accused of being stiff-necked, but are Gentiles any different? At least they "<u>got down and worshiped!</u>" <u>Have you lately</u>? Have you? What will it take? <u>Blood, frogs, lice, leprosy, serpents</u>? We need to bow our heads and our hearts and worship the LORD! The One Who gave us the greatest sign of all, His Son, crucified, risen and coming again! Our sign (the sign for any of today's stiff-necked people, Jew or Gentile) is the **empty tomb**! Now let us "**get down and worship**" the LORD of the empty tomb!

Now watch the next verse, Ex. 5:1 *"And afterward Moses and Aaron went in, and told Pharaoh, Thus saith the LORD God of Israel, Let My people go....!"* And Pharaoh said, "NO!" That went well! And the people just, "got down and worshiped!" So don't think that everything is going to go your way right after you "get down and worship!" The other side won't see it that way. So, Moses returned to the LORD (after both Pharaoh and the Israelites reject him and his message) and he prays in v. 22, *"LORD, wherefore hast Thou so evil entreated [badly treated] this people? [and] why is it that thou hast sent me?"*

So, this is where "Mission Impossible" got its name! Have you ever asked, "Why?" of God before? Even when you know something was His will and it didn't go the way you had expected? "Why, God? Why me, why this, why now, why here...?" Did you realize that the word "**why**" is the **first** step to Disobedience? **Self-will** is the **second**, and **rebellion** is the **third** and final step! You'd better watch this with your children. When you ask a child or someone under your authority to do something and they say "**Why**?" many times they are saying, "I wouldn't do it that way stupid, I have a different idea." Or, "If I were in charge, I would use a totally different plan than your silly plan." But you are not in charge, and Moses isn't God.

So, Moses returns to God and questions Him (but in prayer, like we do). It is not the way Moses thought it should be done. We do this often, too, question God's ways, reasons, and motives. Someone at prayer meeting would think we are the chairmen of the Ways and Means Committee for God. God answers Moses in Ex. 6:1 and reveals why He is doing it His way. Also, God reveals Himself to Moses in a new way and by a new name: (*YHVH*) JEHOVAH, *"The Self Existent One -- He That Is Who He Is*! *The Eternal I AM!* Jehovah is distinctly the redemption name of Deity, and He is about to redeem His people from Egypt. Moses is somewhat impatient with God in chapter 5 because it wasn't working according to Moses' plan.

In Numbers 16:11-15, Moses has the same problem with the people over the Manna *(What is it?)* Just shut up and eat it!

We are no different! God meets our impatience with patience! Why do we get so impatient when it does not go the way we planned? Someone would think we created the universe or we died on a tree for the Church. True Prayer results in obedience to God's perfect will (which we will see in Ex. 7:20). Prayer, real prayer, fulfills the will of God! It doesn't change His will, it conforms us to His will.   Moses had to learn this lesson. He is **80** now and at 120 he is still learning, so don't give up hope.

God had to reveal Himself to Moses as Jehovah, the self-existent, eternal One. He did not need Moses; Moses needed Him! Do you think God could have delivered His people without Moses? Yeah, me too! He could have just used the stick! Listen, when it doesn't go the way you planned, don't go to pieces, go to God! In prayer, seek His face, His will, His grace, ("Why God?") so that He may be ultimately glorified. God shares His glory with no one, NO ONE! Not me, not you, not Frank, no one, got it? Good! Now "get down and pray!"

*(**Prayer** - "O LORD, don't let us rob You of Your glory. If You can use us, use us. If not, let us be patient and don't let us get in the way of Your perfect will for our lives. In Your Word in Isaiah 28:16 You said, "He that believeth shall not make haste." Lord, we believe; help Thou our unbelief. In Yeshua's name we pray. Amen!")*

Principles for Prayer:

- True prayer does not change God's will; it conforms us to His will.
- Remember, "Why" is the first step to disobedience, and rebellion is the final step!
- The key to "being in the way" for the LORD is availability, not **ability**!

*"'Rise up early to pray and meet God. Seek the Son before the sun seeks you!' E. M. Bounds looked for 50 years for two men to adopt his early praying – only two did:
one minister and one layman."*

W.H. Hodge

"Groaning Which Cannot Be Uttered" #5 Exodus 6:5

Although I titled this, "Groaning Which Cannot Be Uttered," sometimes they can be uttered. Whether they are or aren't, they are always heard by God, always! God continues His dialogue with Moses and reveals a new name to Moses, "Jehovah, the Self-Existent One" (Exodus 6:3). He had revealed Himself as "God Almighty" before *(El Shaddai)*, but not as "*YHVH*, Jehovah." He remembers His covenant and then says in v. 5, *"And I have also heard the groaning of the children of Israel, whom the Egyptians keep in bondage; and I have remembered My covenant (My promise, My word on it),"* just like in Exodus 2:23-3:12.

God heard their groaning. Romans 8 says the Earth, the people and the Holy Spirit groan and travail! How bad is our bondage or our affliction from sin? Are we groaning in the Spirit in prayer? Listen to Jesus groaning in His spirit in John 11:33-38 at Lazarus' tomb and then you might get a sense of its deep spiritual depth. In Rom. 8:26-27 the Holy Spirit, *"...maketh intercession for us with groanings which cannot be uttered."* Maybe it will have to get a lot worse before it gets a lot better. What do you think?

God remembered His covenant, His promise, and He never forgets. He waits for us to get to the point where we are desperate enough to groan in prayer and then He answers. Oh God, teach us the beauty of groaning in prayer.

Notice the "I wills" that follow in v. 6-8, these are the four "I wills" attributed to the four cups at the Passover. Some add a fifth "I will" v. 8 because they are back in the land since, May 14, 1948: **One** – I will bring you out from under the burdens (of the Egyptians); **Two** – I will rid you of their bondage: **Three** – I will redeem you with an out stretched arm; **Four** – I will take you to Me for a people and be your God; **Five** – I will bring you into the land I swore to Abraham, Isaac and Jacob and give it to you. "I am the LORD, Jehovah!"

WOW! We have and serve a God who hears and answers prayer (Psalm 65:2 -- *"O Thou that hearest prayer, unto thee shall all flesh come."*) When we are desperate, destitute, and determined enough, and begin to groan in prayer, He will take us seriously! Webster defines groaning as "a deep throated sound expressing grief, pain or disapproval; to be over loaded or over burdened; to call out painfully or urgently." It is a deep inarticulate sound conveying pain, despair, pressure or weight that is unbearable anymore. "I can't take any more!"

How bad do you desire God -- His will, His Spirit, His forgiveness, His presence, His power, His fellowship, or His mercy? Maybe it's not that bad yet? C. H. Spurgeon said, "Groaning which cannot be uttered is prayer which cannot be refused." The Psalmist wrote in 38:9, *"LORD, all my desire is before thee; and my groaning is not hid from thee."* Have you ever come to a place in your life where the pressure or burden was so heavy that you couldn't even pray, and all you could do was groan or moan or sigh before God? That is the point the children of Israel had reached here, and in Exodus 2:23-24 and God heard, remembered His covenant, and said He would deliver them!

Christ receives our groans and moans in our censers of prayer in Heaven, though others may mock and ridicule; yet He who made them knows what they mean. In fact, the Holy Spirit who makes them for us now knows full well what they mean and how powerful they are at the Father's throne. Hannah spoke in her heart; her lips moved but her voice was not heard and Eli thought she was drunk. She was drunk (with the Spirit), and was groaning in prayer, prayer that could not be uttered but prayer that could not be denied either. When your heart is so full of grief that it can only moan or groan, you have God's undivided attention! Robert M. M'Cheyne said, "The most spiritual prayer is a groan that cannot be uttered (Rom. 8:26); or a cry of, 'Abba, Father.' (Gal. 4:6)." In Ezek. 9:4 the "Ink Horn Man" was to go throughout Jerusalem and set a mark (***tav***), an ancient cross on the foreheads to protect the men who, *"sigh and cry for all the abominations"* that were done in the midst of it. My friend, I think it is time for us to learn how to sigh and cry (or moan and groan) against the sin and abominations that are being done in the midst of our Jerusalem before it is too late. I don't know how much time is left for America (or wherever you live) if any, but we do have NOW! We are also commanded to pray for the peace of Jerusalem (Psalm 122:6), *"Sha'alu Shalom Yerushalayim!"*

*(**Prayer** - "Abba, Father, teach us to pray, to groan, to moan for Your very presence and power in our lives and lands; like Hannah, like Job, like David, like Jesus. Holy Spirit, please make groanings for us and for our countries and for Israel, for peace that cannot be uttered. In Yeshua's name. Amen!)*

Principles for Prayer:

- Groaning in the Spirit, in prayer, is a depth few of us know anything about!
- Spurgeon said, "Groaning which cannot be uttered is prayer which cannot be refused!"
- M'Cheyne said, "The most spiritual prayer is a, "groan that cannot be uttered."

"Don't stop reading His word or praying because you are not getting anything out of it. You do it because you are commanded to do it. When you read His word, God talks to you; when you pray, you talk to God. It's a two-way road. Have a pen and notebook handy to write down what He says, but remember to listen -- and to do that, you must be silent! So take some time to sit still and listen to the small still voice of God, He will speak, I promise you!"

R.T.B

"Personal Prayer Dialogue" #6
Exodus 6:11

"And the LORD spake unto Moses, saying, Go in, speak unto Pharaoh king of Egypt, that he let the children of Israel go out of his land," (Ex. 6:10-11). *"And Moses spake before the LORD, saying, Behold, the children of Israel have not hearkened unto me; how then shall Pharaoh hear me, who am of uncircumcised lips?"* (v.12) (slow speech, slow tongue -- Ex. 4:10). Excuses, excuses, excuses. Or was he still carrying his burden of sin from murdering that Egyptian 40 years earlier? He did have a speech impediment, because Aaron became his spokesman. This dialog goes back and forth for a while and finally in Ex. 7:6 they obey. *"And Moses and Aaron did as the LORD commanded them, so did they."*

Sometimes it takes a while and some personal dialog with God in prayer to convince us that His way is the best way (and the only way). Moses is 80, Aaron is 83 and Miriam is 93, so they are not spring chickens. Then sometimes God just has to command us (Ex. 6:13), *"And the LORD spake unto Moses and unto Aaron and gave them a charge [sawah – command] ... to bring the children of Israel out of the land of Egypt."* Enough is enough! No more dialogue. Here is a command!

There is a lot of close personal prayer dialog in Exodus, quite a contrast to Genesis where God did most of the talking. Moses is not being irreverent; he just has a very close relationship with the LORD. Our prayer life should be on an intimate level with Jehovah and we should be experiencing personal, intimate (*yada*) with Him. Prayer should be a two-way conversation. If it is not, there is a problem and you need to fix it immediately (and it's on your end of the line). One of the major problems with our prayer lives is that we do all the talking and God does all the listening (or tolerating), or most of it anyway. We need to pray, "Lord, teach us to listen, when we pray." The Older Testament is a book of recorded conversations between God and man or man and God. The expressions, "The LORD said," or "God spoke," etc., occur no less than 1,900 times in the O.T.

Prayer is a direct address to God. It is an approach to the living God, and He desires us to enter into intercourse with Him often. In Ex. 6:12, Moses asks God how Pharaoh will heed his speech when his own people won't. However, in chapter 7 God reassures Moses he will. God is always there to fulfill His promises, His will and His Word. God told Moses that he would be like a god (*elohim* – Ex. 4:16) to Pharaoh; and his brother Aaron would be his prophet.

Oh my friend, if we will **just ask God what He wants** or what He is doing, **He will show us**. His perfect will is no secret (Rom. 12:1-2; Eph. 5:17). Obedience (let me repeat it) **obedience** is the key to His perfect will! *"...Whom shall I send, and who will go for us? Then said I, Here am I; send me!"* (Isa. 6:8). You have the sovereignty of God and the free will of man in the same verse. Isaiah was privy to a conversation between the Lord, *Adonai,* the LORD *Jehovah* and the Holy Spirit, the *Ruach ha Kodesh*. Isaiah stepped forward and said, "(*Hin-neh Sha-lach*) Behold me, sow me, spread me, send me, stretch me, scatter me." And the Lord said, "GO! *Behold, to obey is better then sacrifice, and to hearken than the fat of rams."* (I Sam. 15:22).

God always chooses to authenticate His men. In Moses' case it was by miracles (that is not always the case), but He always authenticates His men, always. Especially His men of prayer like Mueller, Taylor, Moody, Spurgeon, etc. Now the magicians could imitate but never duplicate God's miracles. In fact they could never counter or stop any of the plagues either. The blood, the frogs, the lice were already coming when they supposedly made more come. Counterfeits, spiritual counterfeits -- the world is full of them today, especially in the church (and even in the fundamental ones).

Moses was a man of prayer, 80 years old and just beginning to serve God. He spent forty years on the back-side of the desert learning how to pray, I wish we all could attend (D.P.I.) "Desert Prayer Institute" before entering into His service. Why is it we fight Him so long and so hard, why not go to Him right now, enter into that two-way street of sweet intercessory prayer and <u>obey Him, His will, His way and His Word</u>! I'm sure there is someone in your life right now that could use a little prayer. So find a quiet place, take a knee, and spend some time with God.

*(**Prayer** - "Father, the most spiritual prayers are a groan or a cry which can only be heard by the Trinity in Heaven. Please help us to express the groanings of our innermost hearts to You and the tears of the depths of our souls at Your almighty feet, Lord. Because only You are worthy to hear them, only You can understand them, and only You can truly answer them. In Jesus' name, Amen.")*

Principles for Prayer:

- Prayer should be a two-way conversation with God. If it is not, fix it immediately!
- Prayer is a direct address to God, an approach to the living God, on an intimate level.
- We need personal intimacy with God (*yada*) for an effective prayer life, we need to (know) Him!

"The most spiritual prayer is a 'groan' which cannot be uttered (Rom. 8:26) or a cry of, 'Abba, Father!' (Gal 4:6)."

R.M. McCheyne

"The Plague of Prayer" #7
Exodus 8-12

"Then Pharaoh called for Moses and Aaron, and said, "Intreat [entreat] the LORD, that He may take away the frogs from me, and from my people;" (Exodus 8:8). The word "entreat" is the Hebrew word (*atar*) -- to burn incense in worship to, to intercede, to pray for, to entreat on behalf of. It was reciprocal, to listen to prayers. It comes from the word for perfume or incense, and of course later the Jewish people had an "Incense Altar" in the Holy Place before the Holy of Holies, where prayer was offered on a regular basis, every day morning and evening.

Pharaoh's magicians could imitate the miracles of Moses, but they could not duplicate them nor stop or counter them. The blood, the frogs, the lice were already coming when they said, "More frogs, more lice, more blood." Also they could not entreat the God of Moses, because they had no access to Him or to His presence. Pharaoh said, "Tomorrow," (v. 10), he was saying, "I need one more day to try and get rid of them myself. I need bigger brooms." We are no different today, when do you want me to entreat for you or intercede for you? Tomorrow! *"And Moses and Aaron went out from Pharaoh: and Moses cried unto the LORD because of the frogs which He had brought against Pharaoh,"* (to cry (*sa-ak*) to keep crying out, shriek by implication, to proclaim). This becomes a pattern for the many other plagues to come.

- Blood (7:14) – no entreaty
- Frogs (8:12) – entreaty
- Lice (8:16-19) – no entreaty, but the lice set God apart from the phony magicians and they recognize the "finger of God" in it and they are not removed
- Stinging flies (8:25-32) – entreaty, but the flies set apart the Jewish people from the Egyptians, and God removed every fly
- Death of cattle (9:1-7) – no entreaty, but Israel's cattle didn't die

- Boils on their bodies (9:8-12) – no entreaty
- Hail and fire (9:13-35) – entreaty
- Locusts (10:1-20) – entreaty
- Darkness (10:21-29) – no entreaty, but there was light in the Jewish homes in Goshen
- Death of the first born (11:1-10 & 12:1-36) – entreaty. God set His people apart so Pharaoh would know that He is God, the only God in in the midst of the land of Egypt.

When Pharaoh says, "You can sacrifice in the land, then you can go to the wilderness, but not too far, now entreat for me," Moses does, and not one fly remains -- **not one fly**! The power of God in prayer is amazing; **first** not one fly flew into Goshen (Ex. 8:22); and **second**, not one fly remained (Ex. 8:31). Do you pray specifically or in generalities? If you pray in generalities, your answers will come in generalities. Prayer is the "pilgrim's greatest tool."

In Ex. 9:22, *"...the LORD said unto Moses, "Stretch forth thine hand toward heaven."* In v.23, Moses stretched out his rod and the LORD sent thunder, hail and fire. In v.27-28, Pharaoh says, *"I have sinned this time... intreat the LORD...(for it is enough)..."* Verse 29 says, *"As soon as I am gone out of the city, I will spread abroad my hands to the LORD,"* and it ceased. Each time Moses prayed he went out from Pharaoh's presence, (8:12, 8:30, 9:33, and 10:18). What are the implications of this principle of prayer with unsaved pagans?

God told Moses to stretch out his hands toward Heaven and God wrought miracles. It is almost as though God is limited by our prayers (I say this with all reverence). He could have sent the hail without Moses and He could have stopped it without Moses, but He didn't! The "power of God" is manifested in the "power of prayer!" Creation, healing, judgment, deliverance, forgiveness, salvation -- why? Ex. 9:16 -- to show in you His power and to declare in you His name throughout the land! Prayer is the all powerful, omnipotent tool of the pilgrim. "Entreat the LORD!" Egypt is destroyed. He spread out his hands and it ceased! *Yeshua/Jesus* did the same thing on the Sea of Galilee in the midst of a storm. We too have the same power available to us, if we will just reach out and grasp it. *"LORD teach us to use this tool to plow the fallow soil and plant and harvest for Your glory."*

Ex. 10:12, what the hail and fire left the locusts would devour. *"And the LORD said unto Moses, Stretch out thine hand over the land of Egypt for the locusts..."* (v.14) The locusts rested on all the territory and they were very severe. (v.15) They covered the face of the whole Earth so that it was darkened. They ate every green thing; nothing remained, nothing!

When God performs a miracle, He leaves no question in your mind, none! The end of every miracle is as miraculous as the beginning. Note v.19 -- there remained not one locust in Egypt, no not one! Why? Moses prayed (v.18) after leaving Pharaoh! Pharaoh had enough (v.16) and admitted his sin against God, Moses and Aaron.

Isn't it amazing how God continues to call upon man to call upon Him? God tells Moses to stretch out his hands in v.12 to Him in prayer. He doesn't need him but He chooses to use him and us in His divine, providential plans. Could He have started or removed certain plagues without Moses' prayers? He certainly could have; He is omnipotent! But the question is not one of **could** but **would**. It is interesting to note that <u>Aaron started the first three plagues</u>, <u>God started the second three plagues</u> and <u>Moses started third three plagues</u>. Then <u>God brought the grand finale, death of the first born</u>. Jer. 15:1 says that Moses was an intercessor before God and recognized as such. Question: would God call on you or me personally to begin a revival, judgment, pestilence, sin, etc.? The question is not one of **could** but **would**? Why, or why not? May we be like Moses and Aaron, and continually stretch out our hands toward heaven!

*(**Prayer** - "LORD, use us to bring about Your divine, providential plans. Stretch our hands, our faith, our gifts, our lives, our ministries for Your glory. In Jesus' name we pray. Amen!")*

Principles for Prayer:

- The power of God is manifested in the power of prayer!

- Prayer is the all-powerful, omnipotent tool of the pilgrim, "Entreat the Lord!"
- God doesn't need Moses or us, but He chooses to use us in His providential plans by prayer.

"Whether we like it or not, asking is the rule of the Kingdom. If you may have everything by asking in His name, and nothing without asking, I beg you to see how absolutely vital prayer is."

C.H. Spurgeon

"The Rod in Prayer" #8
Exodus 12-17

In Ex. 12:27, the people bowed their heads and worshiped after they received all the instruction concerning the Passover: <u>the lamb, the sacrifice, the blood, the leaven, the bitter herbs, the meal, the death of the first born, etc.</u> In v.28, *"The children of Israel went away, and did as the LORD had commanded Moses and Aaron, so did they."* But first, v.27, *"...the people bowed the head and worshiped."* They did this when they first heard from God's deliverer, Moses, in Ex. 4:31. The word "bow" means to shrivel up, to stoop down, to bend over. To worship means to depress, to lay prostrate, to fall down flat in homage to God; and they worshiped prostrate on the ground. In I Chron. 29:20 the people at Solomon's coronation bowed and worshiped, prostrate on the ground. In II Chron. 29:29-30, when Hezekiah's temple was restored, the people fell down and worshiped prostrate on the ground. In Job 1:20, Job bowed and fell to the ground and worshiped.

What does all this say about the way we worship today? When was the last time you bowed, got on your knees, laid prostrate, or wept before the LORD in church publically? "Oh," you say, "that would be embarrassing." So would being nailed to a cross, stark naked, on a hill outside of the city gate in Jerusalem, but He did that for you! Phil. 2:9-11 says that "every knee will bow, and every tongue will confess that Jesus Christ is Lord, to the glory of God the Father." Do you think that will be done in your prayer closet or publically? <u>It might be a good idea to start practicing proper worship before we meet Him. Amen?</u>

Exodus 14:10 says, "...and the children of Israel cried out unto the LORD." Pharaoh and his army are marching after Israel and they see them coming and they cry out to God. This word means to shriek or proclaim in terror. <u>They are scared to death</u>. So they blame the leadership (what else is new?). Why is it we pray so hard when we are in a crisis and we expect an immediate response, when we haven't talked to God for days or weeks or maybe months?

They cried in their crisis, do you cry out in your crisis situations? I love Moses' response in v.13, *"Fear ye not,"* (they are scared to death) *"stand still,"* (they are running like chicks from a fox) *"and see the salvation of the LORD which He will shew to you to day;"* v.14, *"The LORD will fight for you and ye shall hold your peace."* The battle is really His, not yours; and He is quite capable for the task. In v.15, God asks Moses why he is crying to Him, and tells Moses to instruct the children of Israel to go forward! Don't you love it!? "<u>Stop your whimpering and whining and go forward</u>!" Will we never learn from our past? V.16, *"Lift thou up thy rod,* [Moses]*, and stretch out thine hand over the sea, and divide it: and the children of Israel shall go on dry ground through the midst of the sea."*

Lift up your rod! Prayer, intercessory prayer, someone to stand in the gap, someone to make up the hedge, someone to bridge the breach! Where are God's gap men and gap women today?

"But LORD, the water is deep."

"Lift up your rod!"

"But LORD, his army is strong."

"Lift up your rod!"

"But LORD, what about the enemy?"

"Lift up your rod and go forward!"

God destroys your enemies by the same way He saves His children (v.26-28). "Stretch out your hand Moses! **Pray**!" God's work and God's will depend on it. Question: can He depend on you? *"O LORD, may we be gap men and gap women so You can count on us. Forgive us, cleanse us, and teach us to hold our* *hands high in a crisis that we may cry out to You and move forward. Amen."*

Exodus 15:1-19 is a song or a prayer of praise, "The Song of The Redeemed." They were in the desert for three days without water so they murmured against God's servant (here we go again). So he cries out to the LORD, he prays in desperation. They come to *Marah*, but the water is bitter, so God shows Moses a tree in v.25, and he throws it into the water and the waters become sweet. This was a test from God, the tree was the cross of Christ. When the Tree of Calvary is cast into our bitter waters (our *Marahs*) they become sweet. What a picture or type of our life today if we will but accept it.

How is your test today? Many times as a servant or leader for God, His people will not understand and they will murmur against the leadership when life seems a little bitter. We must remember to throw the Tree of Calvary into the arena of life, whether sacred, secular or social. The Tree of Calvary makes all things sweeter.

Then in v.27 they came to *Elim* (the place of 12 wells and 70 palm trees) and they camped by the waters. Remember the refreshing water is just around the bend, just over the hill top. It's always darkest just before the dawn; get up and watch a few sunrises and check it out. Whenever you are caught up in life's struggles and turmoil always remember to pray, to cry out to God. Today the Red Sea, the miraculous; but tomorrow *Marah*, the bitter waters. Every day is a new challenge, a new test. Remember to pray, to cry out to God, to lift your rod high, and He will show you the way. He will show you the tree to throw into your *Marah*, your bitter pond.

In Ex. 16 they complain about food and God sends them *manna* (what is it?), and quail. Then in Ex. 17 they move out and they are out of water. They blame Moses again and strive with him and put the LORD to the test (v. 2). Moses cries unto the LORD, "What shall I do with this people? They are almost ready to stone me." (Ex. 17:4.) *"And the LORD said unto Moses, Go on before the people, and take with thee of the elders of Israel; and thy rod ..., and go!"* (v. 5.) *"Behold, I will stand before thee there upon the rock in* Horeb: *and thou shalt smite the rock, and there shall come water out of it, that the people may drink."* (v. 6.) Moses called the place, *Massah* and *Meribah* because of the striving of Israel and because they tested the LORD there saying, *"Is the LORD among us or not?"* (v. 7.)

It's no different today either, when the sheep murmur against the pastors and want to stone them because they are hungry or thirsty. Pastors need to take the rod in their hand, gather the leaders, cry out to God for wisdom and "go on," because God goes before them. We need to seek God's face and His wisdom in times like that. Instead we often run or strike back.

It wasn't the sheep Moses struck with the rod, it was the rock. *LORD, help us to realize that when the sheep murmur and are contentious to cry out to You, and don't ever let us abandon the ship or the sheep but have the grit to, "go on," because You will always stand before us. You did it for me on several occasions and in several ministries, and never forsook me. Never!*

And He will continue to do it for you and for me. We have His Word on it, and He holds His Word higher than His name (Ps. 138:2). He has never failed to meet me in the hour of my need in over 50 years of walking with Him and serving Him, NEVER! He said to me one morning at the break of day after praying all night, "You go and I will meet all your needs!" He certainly has done that and more than this book can hold!

(**Prayer** - *"LORD, we lift up our rod, we uplift our hands, we cry out to You, hear us O LORD. Lead us and guide us, go before us and watch over us, and lead us in the way everlasting, we ask in Yeshua's name. Amen!"*)

Principles for Prayer:

- What we need today are "gap men & women" to grab a censer and stand between the pestilence and God!
- After every victory Moses faced another challenge, but God always answered his prayers. Always!
- Prayer is not just a good idea; it is God's divine plan and purpose for getting His job done!

"It has always seemed to me that James 5:16 is one of the strongest texts in the New Testament for prayer. I know of no more emphatic statement regarding prayer. Prayer that is led in earnest avails much; prayer that is offered when you forget to eat or sleep avails much; prayer that is offered with an all consuming passion avails much; prayer that is offered with tears in your eyes and a pain in your gut avails much."

J. Wilbur Chapman

"The Prayer of Distress" #9
Exodus 17:4-7

In Exodus 12 the children of Israel celebrated Passover; in chapter 14 they crossed the Red Sea on dry ground; in chapter 16 they got manna and quail; but in chapter 17 they ran out of water and blamed their leader (Moses) and put their LORD to the test. Therefore, *"Moses cried, (sa-aq) unto the LORD saying, "What shall I do unto this people? They are almost ready to stone me."* The LORD told him to take his rod and the elders and go before the people. When it seems like everyone and everything is against you and they are ready to stone you, "PRAY!" Take the "Rod of God," His Book, and His leaders and just stand before His people and watch Him do His work! Then go forward for Him!

Exodus 17:6 says, *"Behold,* [*Hinneh* – particle of interjection] *I* [Jehovah] *will stand before thee there upon the rock in Horeb; and thou shalt smite the rock, and there shall come water out of it, that the people may drink. And Moses did so in the sight of the elders of Israel."* The rock was a type of life through the Holy Spirit by grace; Christ is the "Rock" or "Stone" smitten, that the Spirit of life might flow from Him to all who would freely drink (v.6); I Cor. 10:1-4, esp. v.4 which says, *"And did all drink the same spiritual drink: for they drank of that spiritual Rock that followed them: and that Rock was Christ."*

The children of Israel were totally unworthy (v.2), for they strove with Moses and put the LORD God to the test. In fact, Moses named the place, **"Massah Meribah"** (Trials and Contentions) (v.7), because of the striving and the testing of the LORD. They even said, *"Is the LORD among us or not?"* (v. 7.) But you and I have never said or felt like that, right? The characteristics of grace are seen in this passage and are: that it is free (Eph. 2:8); abundant (Rom. 5:20 & Ps. 105:41); near (Rom. 10:8). All the people had to do was to take and drink of it freely (Isa. 55:1), *"Ho, every one that thirsteth, come ye to the waters, and he that hath no money; come ye, buy and eat; yea, come, buy wine and milk without money and without* *price."* (Free is always better than cheap, Amen?) No cheap grace with God!

Whenever you are confronted by a crowd, by a congregation, by a board or by any group and they are striving with you and putting the LORD to the test, the first thing you need to do is **PRAY**, to cry out to God for help! The word Moses used was *(sa-aq)* to shout, to call out, to call for help, to muster or summon, a cry of desperation or distress, or to raise a cry of wailing. I get the idea that Moses was **DESPERATE**! Do you get that feeling too? This is probably from v.4 where he tells God, "They are almost ready to stone me!" That meant they were already picking up some rocks, Amen? So, *(sa-aq)* is a cry or prayer of desperation or distress, an "**S-O-S**" kind of prayer. This is when you need to pray for wisdom, direction, guidance, and protection! You need to take the "rod of God" in your hand and your godly leaders by the hand and stand before the people on the Rock, Jesus Christ and allow Him to lead you and speak through you.

There is a time to talk and there is a time to walk! I am speaking from many years of experience. There is also a time to smite the rock as Moses did here in Exodus 17:6 in *Horeb* at the beginning of his ministry and there is a time to speak to the rock as he did in Num. 20:11 at *Meribah-Kadesh* near the end of his ministry just before Miriam died. However, in his anger, he struck the rock again "**twice**" and lost his chance to enter the "Promised Land." So, be careful and choose wisely and pick your battles carefully. Remember, Marines and police officers run towards gunfire, not away from it! Pastors, not so much; they bruise easily!

A lot happened in Numbers chapter 20 at *Kadesh-Barnea*. Miriam dies, and there is no water so the people complain again (so, what else is new?). It is after 38 years of wandering through the desert wilderness, and most of the original group is dead and only their children are alive now. Moses and Aaron fall on their faces before the Tabernacle of God. The glory of the LORD appears in v.6 and the LORD tells them to take the rod, gather the assembly and speak to the rock before their eyes this time, and it will give forth water for the people and their beasts, v.8. However, Moses takes credit for this miracle, v.10, *"Must **we** fetch you water out of this rock?"* Then he strikes the rock **twice**, instead of speaking to it in v.11. He also called the people "rebels" in v.10. Furthermore, he did not believe in or trust in the power of God (v.12), *"because you believed Me not, to sanctify Me in the eyes of the children of Israel."* He also failed to glorify God before the nation of Israel and he rebelled against God (v.24), and for all this Aaron also died (v.26).

You see the problem with the prayer of distress is, if you are not careful after your Tsunami, you seem to get a big head and think you can do it all by yourself next time. You forget that God shares His glory with no one! Not with Moses, David, Paul, Daniel, Aaron, and especially not with you and me!

Exodus 34:14 says, *"For thou shalt worship no other god: for the LORD, whose name is Jealous, is a jealous God."* In fact, Isa. 48:11 says, *"…and I will not give my glory unto another."* Use, the prayer of distress, but don't abuse it; and what ever you do, don't let it go to your head. Remember, Ps.65:2 says, *"O Thou that hearest prayer, unto thee shall all flesh come."* God is a prayer-hearing, prayer-answering, prayer-caring, prayer-listening GOD!

In fact Jesus, God the Son, the second person of the Tri-Unity, ever lives to make intercession for us right now (Heb. 7:25). And the Spirit Himself (the Holy Spirit) makes intercession for us with groanings which cannot be uttered. (Rom. 8:26). And He is the second person of the Tri-Unity! There is a lot of prayer going up before God's throne for us constantly. Not to mention the saints who are praying for each other daily. (I Tim. 2:1).

Prayer is the most powerful force in the church and yet the most neglected by His people. Why is that? Because Satan fears it more than any other ministry in the church today and he knows it is the last days of his time on Earth, but it is the force least used by Christians.

(**Prayer** – "Father, when we get into distress (and it will come as sure as sparks fly upward), don't allow us to abuse it or take advantage of it and rob You of Your glory. You are Almighty God, and in control of Your creation, and You share Your glory with **no one**. So, keep us humble, Lord, even in distress. In Jesus' name, Amen!')

Principles for Prayer:

- Whenever you are confronted by a crowd, board, congregation, group, PRAY for God's guidance & help!
- Make sure when God speaks you listen and follow His instructions, no matter where they lead you.
- The prayer of distress can lead to a big head, so be careful after the storm passes that God gets the glory!

"I don't know who said this, but it is true: 'If the LORD has a gigantic task to perform, faith gets the contract.' So pray, 'Lord, give to me more faith. Lord increase my faith, and Lord grow my faith every day!' Great Prayer Warriors have great faith and do great things for God! Romans 10:17 – 'So then faith comes by hearing; hearing the Word of God.' Faith is a conviction based upon hearing. Want to build your faith? Get into His WORD!"

R.T.B

"The Value of Prayer Partners" #10
Exodus 17:8-16

Ex. 17:8-16, *"Then came Amalek, and fought with Israel in Rephidim."* Amalek means "warlike or a dweller in the valley." He is the son of *Eliaphaz* and the grandson of *Esau* and the founder of the tribe of the *Amalekites* (Gen, 36:12, 16; I Chron. 1:36). He appears to have separated from his brethren and became the head of a warlike tribe. *Balaam* describes them as, *"the first of the nations,"* in Num. 24:20; (first to have attacked Israel, that is). How? From behind, <u>like terrorists, attacking the women, children, sick and feeble</u> (Deut. 25:17-19).

These weren't warriors looking for a fight, they were nomads looking to pillage, rape and plunder. So, Moses tells Joshua to <u>choose some men and go out and fight</u> *Amalek* and he will stand on the hill with Aaron and Hur and <u>with the rod of God in his hand and pray</u> (v.10). While Moses held his <u>hands up in prayer Joshua prevailed</u> and when he got tired and let his hands down *Amalek* prevailed (v.11). So, they set Moses on a stone and Aaron and Hur stood on each side of him and held his hands up with the rod of God until the sun went down, and *Amalek* was defeated that day.

<u>There is a principle for prayer here</u> that is so vital to us and our lives and ministries. We also need **"prayer-partners"** to hold us up before the throne of grace as we do battle with the enemies of God as we reach out to the "apple of God's eye," the Jewish People. We are in spiritual warfare and it cannot be won on our own. We have **"rope-handlers,"** those who sacrificially give financially to our ministry so we can go with the gospel and minister to God's chosen people.

Sometimes they are the same people but not always. Both are extremely important; they are like two oars in a row-boat. If you only have one oar you just go around in circles and never really get anywhere. Without prayer on the hill, Joshua was vanquished in the valley. Never forget that or underestimate the power of prayer. **NEVER!** If I had to choose between a church giving us $10,000.00 every month for support or 10,000 "prayer warriors" to pray for us daily, I would choose the "prayer warriors" every time! Of course both would be nice, but the "prayer warriors" would be more important (and, of course, my first choice)!

The LORD told Moses to write this for a memorial in a book or scroll and rehearse it in the ears of Joshua (v.14)! It is good for us to read it over and over and to rehearse it too. The LORD says, "[He] *will utterly put out the remembrance of Amalek from under heaven,"* (v.14). But He has also sworn in v.16 that, *"...the LORD will have war with Amalek from generation to generation."* So, I guess He is not going to wipe them out until He sets up His Kingdom or the new Heaven and new Earth.

So, who are the *Amalakites* today that are warring against Israel and attacking them from the rear killing their women, children, the infirm, feeble, faint and weary, and never really sending their army of men to do battle with the army of Israel? Just shooting missiles at them, blowing up their buses, and killing their babies and children in their beds, and they have no fear of God? I think you can answer that today very easily!

Moses builds an altar in *Rephidim* (the resting place) and called the name of it *"Jehovah-nissi"* (the LORD is my banner). Usually a banner or flag represented conquest or victory. After defeating your enemy, you raised your flag or banner on the highest hill to proclaim your victory. (Like "Iwo Jima" when five Marines and one Navy Corpsman raised our flag on Mt. Suribachi on Feb. 23, 1945. I was born nine days later!) However, here Moses builds an altar on the top of this hill, an altar which consists of prayer, worship, and sacrifice. In the Septuagint, "The LORD is my Refuge;" in the Vulgate, "The LORD is my Exaltation;" in our modern translations, "The LORD is my Banner." Matthew Henry says, "The rod of God was the banner in this action under which they rallied together. It represented the presence and power of God. Therefore they erected an altar and named it, *Jehovah-Nissi.*"

What banner do you rally under when in conflict with your spiritual enemies? How many "prayer warriors" do you have on your team, interceding for you and your family? We could not go forward one day without our team, not one day! Right now my wife is fighting a battle with cancer, it doesn't seem bad at the moment, but no one but God can see inside her body. I am fighting an evil, hateful, invisible enemy of the Jewish people, but what else is new? So we need our "prayer warriors" to hold their hands high, to raise their banners on the top of the hill, to hold that rod up where we can see it as well as the presence and power of our God.

Amalek is alive and well today. He knows his time is short; he is about to be put out of remembrance, but right now he is still at war with the LORD and with His people and we better never forget that. He will sneak up from behind and attack you in your most weak, feeble, vulnerable spot when you are not looking -- **probably your prayer life**. He fears that weapon the most. That's what defeated him in *Rephidim*, the resting place. Listen to me, there is no time to rest right now, the enemy is preparing for war! He is gathering his forces; he is stock piling ammunition; he is drawing his battle plans and we sit around with our heads in the sand.

The only thing that gave Joshua victory over *Amalek* was the prayer on the hilltop. We need to pray. Better yet we all need to find "TWO" prayer partners to pray with and to be accountable to on a regular basis (an Aaron and a Hur), and the sooner the better. By the way, Joshua or *Yahoshua* in Hebrew means, *"Yahweh is salvation,"* and the English form of the Greek transliteration of *Yahoshua* via Latin is *Jesus/Yeshua*. Incidentally, Joshua never grew weary on the battle field with the Amalakites, but Moses could not keep his hands up in prayer; and when they fell the Israelites were over-run. So, he needed two men to hold his hands up to God. The more spiritual the battle, the sooner we run out of strength. So, "prayer partners" are the key to spiritual warfare!

*(**Prayer** - "LORD, help us to build our own "Jehovah-Nissi" and find an Aaron and a Hur to be our prayer partners in this battle with Your*

enemy and ours. It isn't enough to just pray, we need to be accountable, we need prayer partners, we need someone to hold our hands high and we need You to help us to do this. In Yeshua's name. Amen!")

Priorities of Prayer:

- Prayer-Partners are a vital, crucial part of a missionary's field team. They fail without them every time!
- We all need to find an Aaron and a Hur to be our prayer partners and raise our "banners" to God!
- Brethren, the time is short. The little hand is on the 12 and the big hand left the 11. We need to pray and we need prayer partners!

"For real business at the 'Mercy Seat' give me a homemade prayer, a prayer that comes out of the depths of your heart, not because you invented it, but because the Holy Guest put it there and gave it such a living force that you could not help letting it out. Though your words are broken and your sentences disconnected, if your desires are earnest, if they are like coals of juniper, burning with vehement, hot, glowing, passionate flames, God will not mind how they find expression. If you have no words, perhaps you will pray better without them than with them. There are prayers that break the backs of words: they are just too heavy for any human language to carry anyway."

C.H. Supurgeon

"How to Prevent Burn-Out" #11
Exodus 18:18

In Exodus 17 Moses is praying and fighting an external, physical enemy; and prayer is the remedy. However, in Exodus 18 it is an internal, spiritual enemy that he is battling (his ego), and he takes his father-in-law's advice for a remedy: ***"share the load."*** Jethro, the priest of Midian (which was in north/west Arabia), brought Zipporah (Moses' wife) and his two sons Gershom and Eliezer to him, since she turned back at the inn in Exodus 4:24-26. Jethro watched Moses judging the people alone in Ex. 18:13-18 and said, *"The thing that thou doest is not good. Thou wilt surely wear away, both thou and this people that is with thee: for this thing is too heavy for thee; thou art not able to perform it thyself alone."*

Then he gives him some good advice for a heathen (but was he a heathen?): "Stand before God for the people, so that you may bring the difficulties to God." Exodus 18:18 tells us how to avoid burn-out in God's service -- ***share the load!*** As under-shepherds we are to stand before God for the people, His flock. We are to stand in the gap; we are to be intercessors for God, counselors for His sheep. In order to do that we can't be over loaded, because as Jethro said, "You will surely wear yourself out and the people that are with you." So, let's stand before God for the people and <u>let's not burn out, bail out, rust out or run out of gas</u>! Amen? (That was weak!)

Jethro goes on to say that, if we do the first thing, **pray**, then we can do the next thing (v.20), **teach** <u>them the Word</u>. Then we can **show** <u>them the way</u>, and then we can **lead** <u>them in the work</u>. Good advice from a non-believer, especially your father-in-law. We need to learn from this <u>principle of burn-out – ***share the load.***</u>

Then in v.21 he gives Moses some qualifications for choosing leaders to help him. Find able men, who fear/reverence God (men of truth, who hate evil), and make them rulers of 1,000, 100, 50 and 10. You will find this principle laid out in Num.

11:16-25 when Moses is ready to give up and God tells him to choose 70 elders to serve with him, the principle for building a Sanhedrin. It is also in Deut. 1:15, where Moses is repeating the law for the younger generation about to go into the Promised Land. Interesting, because in the Newer Testament when they appointed deacons in Acts 6, it was so the apostles could give themselves to two things continually, "<u>to prayer and to the ministry of the Word</u>."

<u>So, our pastors and spiritual leaders are to give themselves to **Prayer** and to the ministry of the **Word**</u>. Then they are to show us the way in which we are to walk by example, and then <u>lead us in the work</u> of the ministry by <u>equipping us for the work</u> (Eph. 4:11-12). As leaders we must have the mindset to stand before God for the people; <u>to pray first, to pray foremost, to pray always, to pray unceasingly, to pray fervently, and to pray steadfastly</u>! **Keys for Ministry!**

This was preparing Moses for the next event, which was his ascent up the mountain to meet God face-to-face. Exodus 19:3-8, *"Moses went up unto God* [Elohim] *and the LORD* [Yehovah] *called unto him out of the mountain..."* God has led them out on eagle's wings and they are camped out in the Sinai desert, about 2.5 to 3 million of them, and Moses goes up on the mountain of God, it's "<u>communion time</u>!" Moses' greatest attribute was his intercessory power with God, v.8. The people said, *"<u>All that the LORD hath spoken we will do</u>."* And Moses goes back up the mountain to bring God their words again (v.9). The law was not imposed until it was proposed and voluntarily accepted first.

The LORD came to Moses in a thick cloud in Exodus 24:15-18, *"And Moses went up into the mount, and a cloud covered the mount... and Moses went into the midst of the cloud."* Here, I believe the same thing is happening. Moses enters into the cloud, where the presence of God is abiding, the "Shekinah Glory" of God's presence. In Hebrew, the word **"Shekinah" means, to settle, inhabit or dwell**. However, in Exodus 40:35, Moses could not enter into the Tabernacle because the "Shekinah Glory" abode in it, *"And Moses was not able to* *enter into the tent of the congregation, because the cloud abode thereon, and the glory of the LORD filled the tabernacle."*

So there were times when Moses could enter the cloud and times when he could not enter it. It was entirely up to the LORD, not Moses. What made the criteria different, I don't know. I'll ask Moses when I see him. According to ancient Jewish tradition the "Shekinah Glory" appears **1)** in the midst of a *minyan of ten* worshipers when they pray in a congregation; **2)** when two or more Jewish people engage in Torah study; **3)** when a man recites the Shema; **4)** on a husband and wife who live in peace and harmony; and **5)** it rests on the chaste, the benevolent and the hospitable. The ancient sages said it was like a brilliant light and radiance, and before it approached it was preceded by the tinkling sound of an ethereal bell. One interesting ancient Jewish legend even described the dying of Moses as being lovingly enfolded in the "wings" of the Shekinah Glory. It is said that, "Wherever the Jewish people go, the 'Shekinah Glory' follows."

Hebrews 4:16 says, *"Let us therefore come boldly unto the throne of grace, that we may obtain mercy, and find grace to help in time of need."* Then in Hebrews 10:19 it says, *"Having therefore, brethren, boldness to enter into the holiest by the blood of Jesus..."* Therefore, based on the blood atonement of Jesus, the Christ, we have the same privilege to enter into the Holy of Holies and intercede for His people, the Bride of Christ. Because of the blood of Christ we can enjoy the same intimacy Moses enjoyed. **Amen and Amen!**

*(**Prayer** - "Lord, may we enter into that sweet communion, into that cloud as Moses did, and enter into intercessory prayer for Your people. May we, too, stand before You, and for Your people, and bring their petitions, their problems big and small before Your throne. In Jesus' name. Amen!")*

Principles for Prayer:

- Stand before God for the people, so you may bring their difficulties to God in prayer!
- The key principle against burn-out is to share the load with the leaders & pray!
- Our leaders should pray first, foremost, fervently, steadfastly, always and unceasingly

"Pray for 'all men! We usually pray more for things than we do for men. Our prayers should be thrown across their pathway as they rush in their downward course to a lost eternity."

E.M. Bounds

"Prayer for Widows & Orphans" #12
Exodus 22:22-24

"Ye shall not afflict any widow, or fatherless child. If you afflict them in any wise, and they cry (pray) at all unto me, I will surely hear their cry; And my wrath shall wax hot [burn], *and I will kill you with the sword; and your wives shall be widows, and your children fatherless,"* (Exodus 22:22-24). Wow! God is the Father to the fatherless and a Husband to the husbandless. He is their advocate, their protector, their defense, their shield and security, their aegis (shield). *"If they cry (pray) at all unto me (God) I will surely hear."* God stands ready to hear the cries of all who call on Him, especially the defenseless widows and orphans who have no male protector to intercede on their behalf.

The father had a three-fold job: basically to **protect** the family from internal and external enemies; to **provide** the family with all of its needs physically and spiritually; to **prepare** the family to defend itself, to provide for itself, and to go out into the world and **propagate** its own family. Ex. 22:24, goes on to say that His (God's) wrath will wax hot! However, before God will intervene, or stand in the gap for them, they must cry out to Him for His help. <u>After all He is only a prayer away</u>! Let me add another **"P"** to that list, <u>to **PRAY** for them without ceasing</u>, even after they leave the nest. Roots & wings -- that's what you give them, and **pray** they are grounded and ready to fly. <u>It takes patience and **prayer**, love and **prayer**, aspirin and **prayer**, and God and **prayer**... and **more prayer**</u>!!!

The same is true of the poor or your brother who is in need. When you lend them money, you are not to charge them interest. If they cry unto God, He will hear them, too. In fact, Psalm 65:2 says, *"O thou that hearest **prayer**, unto thee shall all flesh come."* Our God is a prayer-hearing, prayer-answering God! **"All flesh,"** especially the afflicted or needy and <u>especially the **fatherless** and the **widows**</u>.

If our human courts and systems fail to administer justice, God doesn't fail to do it, neither does His heavenly court. He promises to avenge His creation, especially those who cry to Him day and night. Jer. 49:11 says, *"Leave thy <u>fatherless</u> children, I will preserve them alive; and let thy widows trust in me."* A Father to the <u>fatherless</u> and a Husband to the <u>husbandless</u>, what a promise! But it is conditional to a degree. I knew it -- there is always a catch, right? The condition? "<u>If they call</u> – at all on Me!" So they must call on God!

<u>What has happened to our ministry to the widows and the fatherless in our churches today</u>? Have we left it up to the system, social services, welfare, big brother and sister? **Shame on us**! If you read Acts 6 the reason for appointing deacons was to care for the <u>Hellenistic widows</u> in the church. How many of those do you have in your church today? How many of you know who they were and why they needed special attention over the <u>Hebraic widows</u>?

It must break our Heavenly Father's heart to see His <u>widows</u> go home on Sunday and eat dinner <u>alone</u> when you have extra chairs and food. Or they have cardboard over a broken window, or a door they can't lock, or a dripping faucet, or maybe there are some <u>bulbs they can't reach</u>. Tea and cookies would be nice, or a shopping trip or a card that says you care! How about that boy or girl without a father? <u>Now you can go fishing or you can take them fishing but you can't do both</u> (but I know which one will please God the most). Take them to a ball game or to a <u>tea-room with a friend</u>. Be <u>a father to the fatherless</u> and co-partner with God to meet the needs of the hurting in your church.

I have met several young adults trying to raise children who have told me they had no male role model in their lives growing up to guide them or look up to. Or even more important to look back to for examples on how to raise their children. They need that guidance in their lives. They are crying out to God and He is looking for some men and women to stand in the gap and make up the hedge, and build a ministry called, *"Tikkun Olam"* (heal or repair the world) one life at a time.

Where is He right now, in His holy habitation, Psalm 68:5, *"<u>A father of the fatherless</u>, and <u>a judge to the widows</u>, is God in His holy habitation."* First Timothy talks a lot about the ministry **of** and **to** widows. In fact, chapter 5 verse 3 says, *"<u>Honour widows that are widows indeed</u>."* However, I think the capstone for this is James 1:27, which says it all, and I will end with it from two different versions and let you wrestle with God on this matter. *"Pure religion and undefiled before God and the Father is this, <u>To visit the fatherless and widows in their affliction, and to keep himself unspotted from the world</u>."* That's the KJV. Now for the Amplified Version, *"<u>Pure and unblemished religion</u> [as it is expressed in outward acts] <u>in the sight of our God and Father is this: to visit</u> and <u>look after the fatherless and the widows in their distress, and to keep oneself uncontaminated by the [secular] world</u>."*

Choose either one and you are without excuse.

*(**Prayer** - "Abba, Father, help us as we <u>co-partner with You in being a surrogate parent to the orphans in need in our churches and a helper to the widows, too</u>. As we reach out in various ways to "Tikkun Olam," repair the broken pieces of Your creation, one piece at a time for Your glory and honor. May they receive our help, through Your hands, with Christ's love. In Yeshua's name we pray. Amen!")*

Principles for Prayer:

- God hears the prayers of all mankind, especially the prayers of <u>widows and orphans</u>; does He hear your prayers for them?
- <u>God is a Father to the fatherless and a Husband to the husbandless</u>. That should be a major prayer concern of ours!
- Nothing quenches divine influence more than this mud puddle we live in, so pray much about your part in their lives!

"You can never be effective for God until you are in communion with God. His order is communion <u>first</u>, prayer and intercession <u>second</u>! There may be moments when God places burdens on your heart and you go instantly into prayer or intercessory warfare, but that is based upon a life of daily close communion with the LORD."

Wesley Duewel

"The Blood Covenant Prayer" #13
Exodus 24

The LORD *Yehovah* tells Moses to come up to Him with Aaron, Nadab, Abihu and the seventy Elders of Israel and worship Him afar off; and Moses alone shall come near the LORD but they shall not approach the LORD, neither shall the people. Moses tells all the people about this and writes it all in a book, the Torah, and they respond (v.3), *"All the words which the LORD hath said we will do."*

Then Moses rose early in the morning and built an altar for prayer, sacrifice and worship and twelve pillars (which you can't find at Mt. Sinai anywhere but you can find them at *Mt. Jabal al Lawz* in Arabia -- we'll save that for another time). Moses then had young Jewish men, probably Levites, sacrifice burnt offerings and peace offerings to the LORD and put the blood in basins. And Moses sprinkled half the blood on the altar. Then in Ex. 24:7, Moses, *"...took the book of the covenant, and read in the audience* [hearing] *of the people: and they said* [again] *"All that the LORD hath said will we do, and be obedient."* They added something this time to their promise -- obedience. Then in v.8, *"And Moses took the blood, and sprinkled it on the people, and said, Behold the blood of the covenant, which the LORD hath made with you concerning all these words."*

Ex. 24:10 says, *"And they saw the God of Israel:"* We know that no man has ever seen God in His spiritual being or essence and lived to tell about it. Ex. 33:20 says, *"Thou canst not see my face: for there shall no man see me, and live."* However, in God's Older Testament, appearances (and especially in Jesus Christ's incarnate appearances), God had been seen by men. What they saw were "Theophanies" or pre-incarnate appearances of God the Son, either in angelic or human form in manifested glory or in a manner not described. (Gen. 32:30; Ex. 33:20; Jud. 6:22; 13:22) Who is the "Angel of Jehovah" in the Older Testament and why don't you ever see him in the Newer Testament? Under His feet was a sapphire stone as clear as Heaven, and they ate and drank with Him. They had communion and fellowship with Him based on the shed blood of the covenant. Half of the blood was sprinkled on the altar and half of the blood was sprinkled on the people. <u>But unless the sacrifice was made and the blood was applied there was no atonement, no fellowship, no communion, no worship, no spiritual *yada*, no intimacy in prayer, no broken bread, no poured out wine -- just cold, dead orthodoxy! Just like today's cold, dead churches.</u>

In Ex. 24:12 the LORD tells Moses to come up on the Mountain and He will give him the tablets of stone. So, he takes Joshua and leaves the rest behind and goes up and a cloud covered the mountain. *"And the glory [kavod – honor, splendor, glory] of the LORD abode upon Mount Sinai, and the cloud covered it six days: and the seventh day He called unto Moses out of the midst of the cloud. And the sight of the glory of the LORD was like devouring fire on the top of the mount… and Moses was in the mount forty days and forty nights,"* (vss.15-18).

The cloud covers Moses and he waits six days before God speaks. How long would you wait on God for Him to speak to you? Five minutes, 30 minutes, an hour, would you wait for a day in a cabin alone in silence? How about two days or three days? Would you wait on God for four days with no food, no water, and no voice from God? How long would you wait to hear from Him? Most of us can't wait five minutes. When was the last time you took a Bible, a canteen, a blanket and a concordance, found a cabin, and got alone with God for three or four days and waited on Him to speak to you? When was it? Can you remember? Have you ever done it?

Moses went into the cloud (into the *kavod*) and spoke to God. There is much more than prayer going on here, wouldn't you agree? Luke 9:34 says, *"While He thus spake, there came a cloud, and overshadowed them: and they feared as they entered into the cloud. And there came a voice out of the cloud saying, This is my beloved Son: hear him."* <u>This is intimate intercourse with the Creator of the universe, and it doesn't get</u>

any more intimate than this! Moses not only saw a pre-incarnate theophany of God, he entered into the very presence of that "Shekinah Glory," that *kavod abode* for forty days and forty nights. Now there is a prayer meeting to write home about! Amen?

You want to talk about "sweet intercession, sweet communion, sweet intercourse" with The Almighty, there it is. We also can have this same sweet fellowship with the Almighty and enter into the holiest of the holies (Hebrews 10:19) through the blood of *Yeshua/Jesus*. *"Having therefore, brethren boldness to enter into the holiest by the blood of Jesus..."* This is the blood of the New Covenant spoken of by *Yeshua/Jesus* in Matt. 26:28, *"For this is my blood of the new testament* [covenant], *which is shed for many for the remission of sins."* Jer. 31:31 speaks of this new covenant, *"Behold, the days come, saith the LORD, that I will make a new covenant with the house of Israel, and with the house of Judah:"* The new covenant accomplished what the Old one could only point to, a child of God living in a manner consistent with the character of God.

In the Newer Testament the word "propitiation" (satisfying sacrifice), appears twice as the means of propitiation (***hilasmos***), in I John 2:2 and in I John 4:10. The means of propitiation is Jesus Christ. It also appears twice as the place of propitiation, "satisfying sacrifice" (***hilasterion***), in Heb. 9:5 and Rom. 3:25. So, by allowing scripture to interpret scripture the word "hilasterion" is translated, "mercy seat" in Heb. 9:5 the place where the blood was sprinkled to make expiation or atonement once a year. Then in Rom. 3:25 we have the word "hilasterion" translated propitiation, and as Jesus Christ hung on the cross of Calvary and the blood from the whip, nails, thorns, buffeting and spear sprinkled down on His body and was poured out at the base of the cross, His body literally became our "mercy seat," and it made expiation or propitiation for our sin, giving us immediate access into the "Holy of Holies" and into the presence of Almighty God. This made intercessory intercession, communion, fellowship, worship, and prayer possible.

Now you can enter into that cloud, so get your Bible, a canteen, a blanket; go find a cabin and wait on God and He will show up. He has never failed to show up for me, so why would He fail to show up for you? Prayer is based on the shed blood of the New Covenant -- Christ's Covenant. Don't ever forget that!

Prayer – *"Abba, Father, can we even begin to comprehend what happened on Calvary? It's far above our pay grade! But we can read it, heed it, and believe it, because we need it. Thank You, Abba, for sending Your Son to die in our place to give us life. In ha shem Yahsua, we pray. Amen!"*

Principles for Prayer:

- Prayer is based on the shed blood of the New Covenant -- Christ's Covenant. Don't ever forget that!
- How long would you wait in a cabin alone for God to come and speak to you: 3 days, 5 days, 10 days?
- Have you ever entered that "kavod" and waited for God to speak? He will show up, and He will speak!

"Your part in intercessory prayer is not to enter into the agony of intercession, but to utilize the common sense circumstances God puts you in, and the common sense people He puts you amongst by His providence, to bring them before God's throne and give the Spirit in you a chance to pray/intercede for them. In this way God is going to sweep the whole world with His saints."

Oswald Chambers

"Prayer Principles for Pastors" #14
Exodus 26:6-38

Exodus 28:12 says, *"And thou shalt put the two stones upon the shoulders of the ephod for stones of memorial unto the children of Israel: and Aaron shall bear their names before the LORD **upon his two shoulders** for a memorial."* He shall bear them up, hold them up, lift them up and carry them up before the LORD on his shoulders in prayer, the place of strength continually.

Listen, we need to "bear up the sheep" God has given us in our ministries -- to protect, feed, nurture, guide and admonish; not just put up with them, but "bear them up" before the Lord! Let them roll their burdens on us, so we can roll them on the Lord. Be a burden bearer, become a wheelbarrow, not a borrowed wheel! In Isa. 9:6 it tells us the One who is coming, the Messiah, will bear the *misra,* dominion, rule, government, kingdom on His shoulders. In Luke 15:5 we have the parable of the shepherd who had 100 sheep, lost one, and left the 99 and went and found that one. *"And when he hath found it, he layeth it on his shoulders, rejoicing."* His shoulders, the place of strength, comfort, safety and rest. Don't you remember when you were a child sitting on your father's shoulders, high above the crowd, you felt like a king or royalty. That's what we are to do with those whom God has placed in our ministries, "bear them up" before the LORD, in prayer continually. Note v.10 of Exodus 26 -- there were six names on each stone according to their birth order and they were evenly distributed, no favorites, all equally brought before the throne, all equally in need of spiritual attention, all equally in danger of attack by the enemy from without and within. Oh my friend, if there ever was a need or a time for prayer, it is now. The hour is late, the archangel is wetting his lips, the little hand is on the 12 and the big hand left the 11 some time ago. We are not in the last days any more, we are in the last seconds of the last minutes! We need to pray like it's up to God and work like it's up to us; we are out of time! "Bear up" the sheep God has given you to minister to on your shoulders in prayer continually, rejoicing before it's too late!

Ex. 28:29 says, *"And Aaron shall bear the names of the children of Israel in the breastplate of judgment **upon his heart**, when he goeth in unto the holy place, for a memorial before the LORD continually."* His shoulders were the place of strength but his heart was the place of passion, affection, love, devotion and compassion. Why? Because he is wearing the breastplate of judgment as he goes into the holy place before the LORD for the children of Israel. We need to be careful we are not to hasty in our judgment of fellow believers in the body of Christ ("but by the grace of God there go I"). Aaron bore their names close to his heart as he went before the LORD. When I was a pastor I kept a small note-book in my shirt pocket and in it was a list of all my people and their prayer needs -- right over my heart, all the time, except when I went to bed. Today you might keep a list in your cell-phone, but where do you keep it, in your back pocket, close to your _____? Never mind.

We, as leaders, will bear the judgment of those whom Christ has placed under us in our ministries. Those under our ministries must be careful how they, in turn, respond to our leadership and how they treat their leaders. Heb. 13:7 & 17 say, *"Remember them which have the rule over you, who have spoken unto you the Word of God: whose faith follow, considering the end of their conversation."* & *"Obey them that have the rule over you, and submit yourselves: for they watch for your souls, as they that must give an account, that they may do it with joy, and not with grief: for that is unprofitable for you."* So, we too, need to continually "bear up" God's children on our shoulders to assure them of His strength and comfort; and on our hearts to assure them of His love and compassion, as well as ours. Ex. 28:30 also tells us that Aaron was to place the *"Urim and Thummim"* in the breast plate of judgment over his heart when he went in before the LORD. **Urim** means lights, and **thummim** means innocent; and these have been translated "lights and perfections." Or in some translations they appear as "revelation and truth or doctrine and truth." You should be aware that *"Thummim"* is pronounced *"Tumim"* in modern Hebrew. Also, although they appear to be in the plural tense with the *"im"* Hebrew ending, they are singular words. The plural ending enhances their apparent majesty. But there was only one *"ur"* and one *"tumm"* in the pocket behind the breast plate of the high priest. Many scholars believe that they are connected to the Babylonian terms of *"urtu"* and *"tamitu,"* (meaning oracle and command, respectively), and that the *"Urim and Thummim"* were used to answer the question, <u>innocent or guilty</u> by reaching into the pouch of the breast plate (Lev. 8:8) and<u> taking out one stone, gem, lot, article or whatever they were. They would have been identical and impossible to tell apart by feel only by color (such as, one black and one white)</u>. There is so little known about these objects I would be in trouble if I went any further.

Then in Ex. 28:38 it says, *"And it shall be upon Aaron's forehead, that Aaron may bear the iniquity of the holy things, which the children of Israel shall hallow in all their holy gifts; and it shall be always upon his forehead, that they may be accepted before the LORD."* This speaks of the "<u>Holy Crown</u>" – **"Holiness to the LORD"** on Aaron's forehead to bear the iniquity of the holy things (that is, be responsible for every neglect or offense respecting the holy things.)

We as leaders, pastors, teachers, deacons, parents, and students need to do more than put up with His sheep. We need to "<u>bear them up</u>" on our shoulders and shoulder their burdens. **Second**, we need to hold them and their problems close to our hearts with compassion and love like Christ did. **Third**, we need to keep them and their needs on our minds and in our prayers unceasingly. What did Paul tell us in I Thess. 5:17? *"<u>Pray without ceasing</u>."* It is actually two words in the Greek, "Unceasingly Pray!" We are also clothed with an *Ephod* just like Aaron when we enter into the "Holy of Holies" for His children, the righteousness of Jesus, the Christ (II Cor. 5:21).

The *"Ephod"* was an article of clothing, an object of worship in ancient Israelite culture, and was closely associated with oracles or prophetic practices. The Jews were the guardians of "the oracles of God" (Rom. 3:2). The term "oracle" is used specifically in the context of Christianity for the concept of "divine revelation;" in Judaism for the *"Urim and Thummim"* in the breastplate; in general for any utterance considered prophetic. Aaron had to come to God through the blood of a **dead animal**, but we can come to God through the blood of a **living Savior**, His only begotten Son, *Yeshua ha Mashiach!* I Sam. 12:23, should be our plea, our pledge, our promise; *"Moreover as for me, God forbid that I should sin against the LORD in ceasing to pray for you..."*

*(**Prayer** - "LORD, help me to bear Your children up before You continually, to shoulder their burdens, to have a compassionate heart for their sins, and to pray for their needs without ceasing; and forgive me my sin of, NOT!" In Jesus' name, Amen!")*

Principles for Prayer:

- Make it your chief business to be more holy every day, and pray for it without ceasing!
- The cares and cookies of this world will choke the word so it will be unfruitful, so pray, pray, pray!
- Keep a sheep list of prayer needs over your heart for times of prayer throughout the day or night.

"Importunity never lets go! Never! It prays through until daylight! To God's answer – till the check is in the mailbox. To press on with troublesome persistence – to request or beg for urgently! To solicit persistently! To be a real pain in the _____!"

Daniel Webster

"Preparation for Prayer" #15
Exodus 29:1-9

The word "priest" can bring many images to your mind, but the one most intriguing is, "Bridge-Builder." *"And this is the thing that you shalt do unto them to hallow them, to minister unto me in the priest's office [kahan]:"* (Ex. 29:1).

The priests (*kohen*) not only conducted religious duties, but also examined people and things to make a medical diagnosis, policed the unruly and taught the Word of God. The word "pontifex" is the Latin word for a member of the counsel of priests in Rome. "Pons" is the word for bridge and "tifex" or "facere" means to fix or make. So, together it means to fix or make a bridge. So, in Latin the word for "priest" means, "Bridge-Builder." This is a beautiful definition for the word, because as believer priests we have a ministry before God to the Bride of Christ, a gift which He gave to His Son.

I Peter 2:5 says, *"Ye also, as lively* [living] *stones, are built up a spiritual house, an holy priesthood, to offer up spiritual sacrifices, acceptable to God by Jesus Christ."* I Peter 2:9 says, *"But ye are a chosen generation, a royal priesthood, an holy nation, a peculiar people* [of His own], *that you should shew forth the praises of him who hath called you out of darkness into his marvelous light."* We are a "holy priesthood," called to offer up spiritual sacrifices, a "royal priesthood" to the praises of Him! That's us, born-again believers in Christ, bridge-builders. Building a cause-way from man to God, standing in the gap, making up the hedge; but there are some things that need to be done first, just like Moses had to do to Aaron and his sons to prepare them for their ministry. We, too, need some preparations to enter into the "Holy of Holies" with God.

First they needed to be **cleansed** -- washed with water (v.4), bathed or "regenerated." Before you can enter into intercessory prayer or any part of the priestly work, you must be born-again (*ano-then* born from above). Titus 3:5, *"Not by works of righteousness which we have done, but according to his mercy* *he saved us, by the washing of regeneration, and renewing of the Holy Ghost."* Lev. 8:6, *"And Moses brought Aaron and his sons, and washed them with water."* Heb. 10:22 -- This washing needs to be distinguished from the daily cleansing in the "Laver." Ex. 30:18-21 -- This washing typifies regeneration. Titus 3:5 -- the laver, daily cleansing. I John 1:9 -- both of them are in view in the upper-room in John 13:10 with Peter.

Second they needed to be "**clothed**" v.5 with the coat, the robe, the ephod, the girdle, and the breast plate, garments specially prepared by the Israelites for their priests to wear in their service for God and for them. We, too, must "put on" the Lord Jesus Christ when we go in to serve Him for His people (Rom. 13:14), *"But put ye on the Lord Jesus Christ, and make not provision for the flesh, to fulfill the lusts thereof."*

When we put on Christ, there is no provision for the flesh! II Cor. 5:21 says, *"For He hath made Him to be sin for us, who knew no sin; that we might be made the righteousness of God in Him."* He took our hell that we might take His heaven! He went to the cross, not because it was fun, but because it had to be done!

How, then, can you make provision for the flesh, in light of the cross? Rev. 19:8 says, *"And to her* (the Church) *was granted that she should be arrayed in fine linen, clean and white: for the fine linen is the righteousness's of saints."* Without Christ's garments of righteousness you cannot intercede on behalf of others. Lev. 8:7-8 -- *"And he put upon him the coat, and girded him with the girdle, and clothed him with the robe, and put the ephod on him, and he girded him with the curious* [beautifully woven] *girdle of the ephod, and bound it unto him therewith. And he put the breast plate upon him: also he put in the breastplate the Urim and the Thummim."*

Third, they needed to be "**crowned**" Ex.29:6, *"And thou shalt put the miter upon his head, and put the holy crown upon the miter."* Ex. 28:36, *"And thou shalt make a plate of pure gold,* *and* [engrave] *grave upon it, like the engravings of a signet, HOLINESS TO THE LORD."* The Bible speaks a lot about crowns. **There** is the "Crown of Righteousness" (II Tim. 4:8), *"Henceforth there is laid up for me a crown of righteousness, which the Lord, the righteous judge, shall give me at that day: and not to me only, but unto all them also that love His appearing."* There is a "Crown of Life" (James 1:12),*"Blessed is the man that endureth temptation: for when he is tried, he shall receive the crown of life, which the Lord hath promised to them that love Him."* There is the "Crown of Rejoicing" (I Thess. 2:19), *"For what is our hope, or joy, or crown of rejoicing? Are not even ye in the presence of our Lord Jesus Christ at His coming?"* There is the "Crown of Glory" (I Peter 5:4), *"And when the chief Shepherd shall appear, ye shall receive a crown of glory that fadeth not away."* Then above all else there is the "Crown of Thorns" (Matt. 27:29), *"And when they had platted a crown of thorns, they put it upon His head, and a reed in His right hand: and they bowed the knee before Him, and mocked Him, saying, Hail, King of the Jews!"* There are many other crowns too numerous to mention here, but it would be a great study, and we all look forward to the day when we can cast our crowns at His feet.

Fourth they needed to be "**consecrated**" (v.9) set apart unto God for His Holy service. Lev. 8:12, *"And he poured of the anointing oil upon Aaron's head, and anointed him, to sanctify him."* I love Ps. 133:1-2, *"...Behold, how good and how pleasant it is for brethren to dwell together in unity! It is like the precious ointment upon the head, that ran down upon the beard, even Aaron's beard: that went down to the skirts of his garments,"* What a beautiful picture of this consecration, this anointing before God. However, in order to be used of God in His work, we need this anointing of the Holy Spirit in our lives and ministries. I John 2:20 & 27 -- *"But ye have an unction from the Holy One and ye know all things." "But the anointing which ye have received of Him abideth in you, and ye need not that any man teach you: but as the same anointing teacheth you of all things, and is truth and is no lie, and even as it hath taught you, ye shall abide in Him."*

In order to function we need Holy Spirit unction! Power from on high! Remember He (the Holy Spirit) intercedes for us (Rom. 8:26-27) as well as the Son of God (Rom. 8:34; Heb. 7:25, 9:24). To be a member of God's holy priesthood you need all four of these: you need to be cleansed – born from above; you need to be clothed in Christ's righteous garments and make no provision for the flesh; you need to be crowned with His holiness as only He can do; and you need to be anointed with unction from above. These are essential for the ministry of intercession, for building a bridge from man to God.

Until the Law was given, the head of each family was the family priest and offered the family sacrifices like Job and Abraham (Gen. 8:20; 26:25; 31:54; Job 1:5). When the Law was proposed, the promise to perfect obedience was that Israel should be unto God a "kingdom of priests" (Ex. 19:6). However, Israel violated the Law, and God had to place the priestly office with Aaron's family. He appointed the tribe of Levi to minister to Israel, thereby constituting the typical priesthood (Ex. 28:1). In the "Church Age" all Christians are unconditionally constituted a "kingdom of priests" (I Peter 2:9; Rev. 1:6); a distinction which Israel failed to achieve by works. The priesthood of the Christian is therefore a birthright; just as every descendant of Aaron was born into the priesthood (Heb. 5:1).

The chief privilege of a priest is access to God. Under the Law, the High Priest only could enter "The Holy of Holies" once a year (Heb. 9:7); but when Christ died, the veil (a type of Christ's human body - Heb. 10:20) was rent from top to bottom, so that now believer-priests, equally with Christ the High Priest, have access to God in the Holiest of all by His blood (Heb. 10:19-22). The High Priest is corporeally there (Heb. 4:14-16; 9:24; 10:19-22).

In the exercise of his office the New Testament believer-priest is a sacrificer who offers a four-fold sacrifice: **1** – His own living body, (Rom. 12:1, Phil. 2:17; II Tim. 4:6; Jam. 1:27; I

Jn. 3:16); **2** – Praise to God, *"the fruit of our lips giving thanks to his name"* to be offered continually (Heb. 13:15); Ex. 25:22, *"...I will commune with thee from above the mercy seat;"* **3** – His substance, (Rom. 12:13; Gal. 6:6; 10; Tit. 3:14; Heb. 13:2, 16; III Jn. 5-8); **4** – His service, "to do good" (Heb. 13:16). The New Testament believer-priest is also an intercessor. Col. 4:12 is a touching illustration of priestly service through prayer, *"Epaphras, who is one of you, a servant of Christ, salutes you, always laboring fervently for you in prayers, that you may stand perfect and complete in all the will of God."* (C.I. Scofield) Wow! What a privilege!

(**Prayer** – *"Father, thank You for all You have done in the lives of the people in my church. You have given them faith and love and strength. Help their testimony to persevere and to grow through trials. I pray that you will fill my church with the knowledge of Your will in all wisdom and spiritual understanding. Give us eyes to see that Jesus Christ is preeminent and that He is all we need to live a life that is fully pleasing to You. Father, may You be glorified in all we say and do! Amen!"*)

Principles for Prayer:

- The Latin word for priest "*Pontifix*" means "Bridge-Builder."
- The chief privilege of a priest is access to God.
- Our job is to build a holy cause-way from man to God, to show them the way.

> ***"'Continuing constant in prayer,' Romans 12:12. The Greek is a metaphor taken from hunting dogs that never give up on their game until they have their prey."***
>
> ***Thomas Brooks***

"Incense Altar – Heavenly Prayers"
#16
Exodus 32:11-14

The incense altar was a beautiful type of Christ our Intercessor (John 17; Heb. 7:25; 9:24; Rom. 8:34) through whom our prayers ascend to God the Father. Prayer was to be a central part of the Tabernacle service. The "Incense Altar" was to be placed right in front of the veil of the "Holy of Holies," where the Ark of the Covenant was placed (v.6). The "Mercy Seat," which was over "The Testimony," covered the law of the tablets and God met His people on the "Mercy Seat."

God meets us on the basis of mercy, too; never on the basis of the law, NEVER! Never pray for God's justice; only His mercy (Heb. 4:16). *"Let us therefore come boldly unto the throne of grace, that we may obtain mercy, and find grace to help in time of need."* Justice is getting what we deserve. Grace is getting what we don't deserve. Mercy is not getting what we do deserve!

The incense of this prayer wafted its way up before the nostrils of Almighty God, hovering over the "Mercy Seat" above the Testimony, behind the veil. Today the same thing is happening in Heaven before God as He sits on His throne and the angels bring the golden censers before Him and ignite them (Rev. 8:3-4). *"And another angel came and stood at the altar, having a golden censer; and there was given unto him much incense, that he should offer it with the prayers of all the saints upon the golden altar which was before the throne. And the smoke of the incense, which came from the prayers of the saints, ascended up before God out of the angel's hand."*

Question: how is your bowl today, full of prayer, ready to be ignited or empty? If the angels called for your bowl to fill the censer for God, what kind of an aroma would it emit, a sweet smell or a stench? Rev. 5:8, speaks of golden bowls full of incense, which are the prayers of saints. I can't help but wonder just how full my bowl is. How is yours? Aaron and the priests were to offer the incense (or prayer) morning and evening (Ex. 30:7-8) for a, *"perpetual incense before the LORD throughout their generations."* Sounds like 1 Thess. 5:17, *"Pray without ceasing."* Or cease without praying! What a beautiful picture of what we are to be doing today, right now! Continually praying for mercy (not justice) before the throne of God. And if the Church dies and falls apart, whose fault is that going to be?

A special incense was to be made for meeting with God, made of stacte (*natap*) gum of the storax tree, a sweet spice; onycha (*sehelet*) the lid of a mollusk shell which gave forth a perfume when it was burned; galbanum (*helbena*) gum from the milky sap of the Syrian fennel, a fragrant spice; and frankincense (not to be confused with incense -- although it might be added to incense it could be used on its own). Interestingly, we are never told in Scripture what frankincense was composed of. The word in Hebrew is *"Iebona,"* and just means Frankincense. There is a city named *Lebonah* in Judges 21:19, I wonder if that is where it came from. We know it was very expensive and presented to our Lord at His birth by the Maggi. Incense is such a beautiful picture of prayer. Its sweet gentle fragrance fills the room; it is quickly noticed by everyone; it has a lingering effect; it penetrates barriers, curtains and walls; it rises heavenward; it soothes, satisfies, and satiates. A child, an invalid, a dying man, or a warrior can ignite it. He waits for the aroma! Psalm 141:2 says, "Let my prayer be set forth before Thee as **incense**; and the lifting up of my hands as the evening sacrifice."

Morning and evening, 9:00 a.m. and 3:00 p.m. every day, was the time of the daily sacrifice and the trimming of the lamps. King David said, "Seven times a day do I praise Thee," every two hours from 6:00 am to 6:00 pm. Man was never to make any incense like this for his own enjoyment or he would be cut-off (***karath***) -- the most feared punishment of the Jewish people -- eliminated not exterminated, banished to hell forever with no hope of an after life, just for offering strange incense or strange fire. What is condemned here is making worship the mere pleasure of the natural man, "will-worship" or "religion" like Cain or maybe Nadab and Abihu, after their own will.

The Samaritan woman asked Jesus an interesting question and He answered her in John 4:23-24 and said, *"...the hour cometh, and now is, when the true worshippers shall worship the Father in spirit and truth: for the Father seeketh such to worship Him. God is Spirit: and they that worship Him must worship Him in spirit and in truth."*

Moses intercedes for God's people in Ex. 32:11-14, after their sin with the golden calf, before he descends down the mountain. God is angry and is about to wipe them all out (vv. 7-9) and make a new nation out of Moses. However, Moses reminds God of the previous promises He made. Have you ever done that, prayed God's Word back to Him or reminded Him of His promises? Many of the great saints of the past have in their prayers. "You said ..., God!" Or, "You declared ... in Your Word, LORD!" Hold Him to His word; He dares you to. But you will have to know it well enough to do that and be ready to uphold your end of the bargain, too! He said He would supply all your needs, if you would go into all the world and preach the gospel. He said He would heal that disease, if you would go to His people and tell them about theirs.

Moses is on his way down the mountain to let the people have it, and stops first to intercede for them, a good principle to keep in mind. Yes, he is going to burn the calf, stomp it, grind it to powder, scatter it on the brook, and make them drink it, and kill 3,000 for refusing (Ex. 32:20-30; Deut. 9:21) *"And I took your sin, the calf which ye had made, and burnt it with fire, and stamped it, and ground it very small, even until it was as small as dust: and I cast the dust thereof into the brook that descended out of the mount."* (Show me one of those on Mt. Sinai or its remains!) Ex. 32:20 -- *"And he took the calf which they had made, and burnt it in the fire, and ground it to powder, and strawed* [scattered] *it upon the water, and made the children of Israel drink of it."* (A dried river bed on Mt. Sinai – good luck finding one!)

In Ex. 32:30, Moses again intercedes for Israel the next day, and goes back up the mountain to make atonement for the people. Many believe he brought with him some of the "colloidal water" from the brook, which was blood-red (Google colloidal-gold), as a type of the blood of Christ to atone for the sin of Israel. It appeases God temporarily, but it is just bloody water and He plagues the people because of the calf and says, *"Whosoever hath sinned against me, him will I blot out of my book."*

From this point on, the LORD had to send His angel to go before them. He had to stay outside the camp; otherwise He would consume them because they were a stiff-necked people (Ex. 33:3). When the people heard this, they mourned and took off their ornaments, but it was too late. They had made their golden calf, and the tablets had been broken. Then Moses took the Tabernacle and pitched it outside the camp, afar off from the congregation, and anybody who sought the LORD went outside the camp to do it.

Does your church provide the right atmosphere and climate for you to get intimate with God, or is it too boisterous, too noisy? Maybe you too, need to go outside the congregation to find God! When Moses went into that Tabernacle, the cloudy pillar descended on it, *"And the LORD spake unto Moses face-to-face, as a man speaketh unto his friend."* (Ex. 33:11).

Isn't it wonderful knowing that because of Calvary and all Jesus did for us, we can have that same intimacy and fellowship with the Father and the Son today? We can have, spiritual "YADA," intimate intercourse with the Tri-Unity of the God-head any time and any where we want it. Why? Because we have a personal relationship with the Son of God. Not because of some "colloidal-water" from a brook, but because of the blood and water which flowed from His side on

Golgotha when He was pierced with a spear for sin and paid the penalty, once for all, and cried, "FINISHED!" *(Tetelestai)*

*(**Prayer** – "Father God, thank You, Lord, that You always meet us on the basis of mercy and not judgment, and may our prayers to You be like frankincense from the City of Lebonah. May their fragrance waft its way up to Your tabernacle daily and be well pleasing to You! In Jesus' name, Amen!")*

Principles for Prayer:

- Never pray for God's justice; only His mercy. Justice is getting what we deserve. Grace is getting what we don't deserve. Mercy is **not** getting what we do deserve!!
- Have you ever reminded God of His promises or prayed His Word back to Him? Try it some time!
- Because of Calvary we can have intimate fellowship in our prayer closet with the Tri-Unity!

"Prayer is the key to unlock Heaven's door, but the Holy Spirit helps faith turn that key!"

T. Watson

"Practicing God's Presence" #17
Exodus 33:14

"...My presence shall go with thee, and I will give thee rest." Ex. 33:14. The children of Israel had just committed the most heinous of sins, the golden calf, and Moses made atonement for them after 3,000 were slain and the LORD told them to depart (Ex. 33:1). He told them He would send an angel (Isa. 63:9) to go before them and lead them, because if He went in the midst of them He would consume all of them (v.3). They had committed a grievous sin against God and He was angry (Ex. 32:10), but Moses interceded for them and God repented (recalled, turned) (v.14) from the evil He was going to do to Israel because of the covenant He had made with Abraham, Isaac and Jacob.

Sometimes after we have really blown it, we feel like Job in chapter 29 or David in Psalm 42, like His rich, full, abiding presence and love is not there, but it is! The fellowship may not be the same (it may be damaged), but confession will remedy that, Amen? The relationship never changes; you will always be His child and He your Father. "Once saved, always saved!" (Heb. 13:8). However, in Moses' day, the *Ruach ha Kodesh* (the Holy Ghost) came upon them and departed from them (Ps. 51:11). He did not indwell them permanently like He does believers today (Jn. 14:16, Eph. 4:30).

The LORD doesn't withdraw His full blessing and presence from His children arbitrarily; it is due to forgetfulness, unbelief or sin on their part. Our sin creates an impassable gulf between us and God, and the gloom of the night overtakes our souls. Thus, we seek an intercessor: the Son (Rom. 8:34), the Spirit (Rom. 8:26), or a saint (I Tim. 2:1). The people mourned (Heb. *bawl*, to cry out loudly) and laid aside their ornaments, their beautiful jewelry. In losing God they lost their glory, their treasure and their joy.

Isn't that true of us today? Without God's glory shining on us, there is no joy, no treasure, no happiness -- nothing! So, they built a Tabernacle outside the camp where Moses and Joshua could meet God face-to-face, *"and the LORD (YeHoVaH) talked with Moses."* (Ex 33:9). Praise God, they had their intercessor! Do you have yours, Son, Spirit or Saint? Then the people saw the *"Shekinah Glory"* standing at the Tabernacle door and the LORD spoke with Moses face-to-face as a man speaks to his friend. Have you ever had this kind of a relationship with God? If not, why not? I can't even fathom this experience, can you?

Then Moses pleaded with God to make His will and way known to him and God said, *"I know thee by name and thou hast also found grace in my sight."* (v.12).

"Yeah but..." (don't you just love the "yeah buts" in the Bible?) "You have not told me who will go with me!" (Yet Joshua has been with him since he left Egypt -- through the desert, through the Red Sea, fighting the Amalekites in Ex. 17, on the Mount in Ex. 24 & 32, in the Tabernacle Ex. 33:11. But Moses had not yet laid hands on him and imparted the Spirit to him [Num. 27:18]. He needed a partner to go with him, to train and to take over for Him. Moses is no spring chicken by this time.

God has also called us His friends, and sons, and His people, so it is not for us to walk in darkness, either. We need to know His way and will too. After all, Psalm 25:14 says, *"The secret of the LORD is with them that fear* [reverence] *Him; and He will shew them His covenant."* Therefore, none of God's people should be satisfied to live in a state of confusion, misery and darkness.

Then comes one of the most beautiful promises in the Older Testament, one that should be written on the mantles of our hearts, **"My presence shall go with thee, and I will give thee rest."** The realization of God's favor, God's presence, will give rest to your soul: rest from your doubts, rest from your struggles, rest from your quest! *"...If God be for us, **who** can be against us?"* (Rom. 8:31). In fact **what** can separate us from the love of God, which is in Christ Jesus our Lord? *"....shall tribulation, or distress, or persecution, or famine, or nakedness, or peril, or sword?"* (Rom. 8:35) *NO!* The apostle Paul wrote in Rom. 8:37, *"In all these things we are more than conquerors through Him that loved us."*

There is nothing that can separate us from the love of God which is in Christ Jesus, NOTHING!!! Read Rom. 8:28-39 over and over until it sinks in and you get it! "My presence, My (*Pan-im*, My face, Me Myself) will go with you, and I will give you rest (*nuah*, settle you, establish you)." That is one vowel point different from the word, "Noah." Rest from anxieties about the way; rest from misgivings about the future.

We may not know what the future holds but we sure know the One Who holds the future, Amen? (Are you paying attention?) When you have a personal relationship with *Yehovah* and with His Son *Yeshua* and His Spirit the *Ruach ha Kodesh* indwells you, then you know His truth, His love, His power, His promise, His presence; and your soul realizes the peace that passes all understanding (Phil. 4:7). That manifested presence is the believer's joy and glory. It's what we live for, serve for, give for, long for, and die for. *Oh Lord, fill us with Thy presence, until we overflow with Your glory!*

If God's *Shekinah Glory* did not go with them, if His abiding presence did not go forth with them, then they did not wish to go forward, not one foot! How about you? Can you serve, give, live, sacrifice, go without the abiding presence of the Almighty? What good is a land flowing with milk and honey without God? It's a mere desert!

He bids us in Matt. 6:6 to enter into our closets (our pantries), and when we have shut the door, to pray to our Father in secret who is already in there waiting for us. He tells us in Ps. 46:10 to, *"Be still and know (yada) that I am God [the LORD]."* That same word appears in Gen. 4:1 when Adam (*yada*) "knew" Eve and she conceived. This word speaks of intimacy, oneness, a closeness too close for words. That's the kind of relationship God desires in your prayer life, <u>intimate intercourse; conversation so close that words are not necessary. Your thoughts are one with His thoughts (*yada*) because you practice the presence of God</u>.

Joshua did not leave the Tabernacle in Ex. 33:11; **he wanted more**. Neither did Isaac in Gen. 22; he stayed on Mt. Moriah. Only Abraham came down in v.19. Have you ever been visited in your closet, or at a prayer meeting or at your study and you had to ask Him to, "**stay His hand**?" And you didn't want to leave? Hopefully you took Him with you and practiced the presence of God throughout the day. You see, it's not Brother Andrew's secret. He didn't invent it or find it. It's God's, and He desires all of us to have it. "<u>My presence, My face, My *Shekinah, My* Majesty, Me, Myself, and I will go with you, and I will give you rest</u>, I will settle you, I will establish you, I will plant your feet on the Rock. <u>Just keep My face ever before you</u>!"

Nicolas Herman joined a Carmelite order in Paris, France at the age of 24 and received the name, "<u>Lawrence of the Resurrection</u>." We know him as "Brother Lawrence." A book was compiled by Joseph de Beaufort of his letters and conversations on the subject of <u>the presence of God</u>. It is a small book, worthy of your reading entitled "The Practice of The Presence of God" by Brother Lawrence. A poem in the book says,

> Lord of all pots and pans and things
> Make me a saint by getting meals
> And washing all the plates!

The key to the book is in the first letter. Brother Lawrence had searched many books to find out how to go to God, but came to the conclusion that, <u>in order to be **holy**, he had to be **wholly**</u> God's all the time. So, he resolved **to give his all for**

His all, all the time. "I made this my business as much all the day long as at the appointed times of prayer; for at all times, every hour, every minute, even in the height of business, I drove away from my mind everything that was capable of interrupting my thought of God."

Brother Lawrence may not be the author of "Practicing the Presence of God," but he sure is known for it (Ex. 33:14-15). Read his book. You'll be really glad you did!

*(**Prayer** – "Father, we seek Your presence, not your presents. We desire to feel Your breath on the back of our necks as we pray, to feel Your garment pass by us as we intercede, to know Your glory is in this room with us as we make our supplication for others. LORD, let us feel Your hand pressing down on ours as we lay our list before Your throne. Hear us, O God, as we step before Your throne. In Jesus' name. Amen!")*

Principles for Prayer:

- "My presence shall go with thee, and I shall give thee rest!"
- Intimate intercourse, conversation so close with God that words are not even necessary.
- Practice the presence of God, and you will pray all day long.

"The man who could get believers to praying would, under God, usher in the greatest revival that the world has ever known."

L. Ravenhill

"Show Me Thy Glory" #18
Exodus 33:18-23

"And he [Moses] said, I beseech Thee, shew me thy glory!" Ex. 33:18. Moses is seeking a new vision for a new task. Have you ever done that? Sure you have, I know I have! The LORD, Jehovah tells him in v.19 that He will let His "goodness pass before him;" He will proclaim the name of the LORD, the LORD God before him; He will be gracious to whom He will be gracious and merciful to whom He will be merciful and all this takes place in Ex. 33:19. But, v.20 says, *"Thou canst not see my face: for there shall no man see me, and live."* Why? Just step outside on a bright, sunny day and stare up at the sun for 30 seconds and you will go blind. So, imagine looking at God's magnificent glory for just one second, and you would be blind forever! Men have seen Theophanies and Christophanies and angelic forms, but no man has ever seen God in His spiritual Being or Essence. The closest man ever came to seeing Him was Jesus Christ (John 1:18; II Cor. 4:6; Heb. 1:3), the visible manifestation, of the invisible glory of God's imminent eminence!

The "Glory of God" was related to the "Face of God" because in response to Moses' request to see God's glory, the LORD responds in v.20, ***"Thou canst not see my face,"*** using face as a synonym for glory. Moses desired to see the full nature of God, to see His glory, the burning presence of God. That's what all of us truly seek in our prayer closets, God's burning presence or a touch of the Master's hand. To see someone's face is to see their whole person, this was very common in the Hebrew Scriptures to describe meetings of men like Jacob and Esau in Gen. 32:20, "and afterwards I shall see his face."

What we need today to revitalize our prayer lives is a fresh look into the face of Jesus. To see Him afresh, to touch those nail prints again, to feel the Spirit's breath brush across the back of our necks letting us know, "this is the way, walk ye in it." To hear that still small voice again, to smell the lily of the valley, to feel the warmth of the "Son of God" on our cheeks, to sense His presence in the room as we pray in His name, to feel our cheeks wet with tears after we have prayed not even knowing that we have cried, to watch with Him all night in prayer until the cock crows, but it seemed like only an hour or two.

The LORD does reveal Himself to Moses, to Israel and to us in a variety of ways: His goodness that passes before us, the revelation of His name suggesting His innermost secrets; His grace (getting what we don't deserve) and His mercy (not getting what we do deserve); His "Divine Presence" in the person of "His Son" and the indwelling "Holy Spirit" who intercedes for us with groaning's which cannot be uttered. He is everywhere, He knows everything, and He can do anything. That's my God, the ***"YHVH"*** the *"Great I AM"* (*Ehyeh Asher Ehyeh*) the One who causes to be, to exist, to breathe, to live and He is your God too, if you will just let your heart become the Bethlehem of God!

Moses wanted to behold Him face-to-face, to know Him absolutely, and to exhaust His depth of being, to remove His last footprint or His mystery of being God. Be careful here -- to try and embrace the full nature of God is to forget that there is a concealed nature of God, and if we ignore it, we do so at our own risk.

Too often we try to fit God into our theological, eschatological, soteriological, ecclesiastical, **box.** Don't do that. He doesn't come in a 42-regular, or a 44-extra large! However, the LORD, Jehovah proposed a solution to Moses' desire to know Him fully. Rather than discourage him, this omnipotent, omnipresent, omniscient, omnificent God, is a fountainhead of hope for all those willing to stand upon the **ROCK** and follow newer and fuller visions, content for now anyway, to behold only His back, never realizing the unfinished quest of seeing Him "face-to-face" at least for now can wait. Whatever we may know or experience about God, there is always more to be experienced, more to know, more to learn, always! For this reason the glory of the LORD remains a hidden glory and for the same reason man's pursuit remains an unending quest!

However, for now as we enter into our prayer closets, our prayer gardens, our prayer chambers, and the LORD covers us with His hand, may we enter into His presence as He passes by and communes with us as He did with Moses on the back side of that desert. May He take away His hand for a moment and may we too see the backside of His glory and be drawn into His presence in prayer as we get to (*yada*) know Him in a more intimate and personal way. You can't leave this section without bringing to mind that old familiar hymn by Augustus Toplady, "Rock of Ages," written in March of 1776, which had four stanzas and has been changed many times:

> Rock of ages, cleft for me
> Let me hide myself in Thee
> Let the water and the blood
> From Thy riven side which flowed
> Be of sin the double cure
> Cleanse me from its guilt and power.

It was the words from a sermon Toplady heard from Dr. Daniel Brevint that moved him after a storm to write this hymn: "Let not my heart burn with less zeal to follow and serve Thee now when this bread is broken at this table, than did the hearts of Thy disciples when Thou didst break it at Emmaus, O Rock of Israel, Rock of Salvation, Rock struck and cleft for me. Let those two streams of blood and water which once gushed out of Thy side…let not my soul less thirst after them at this distance, than if I stood upon Horeb whence sprang this water and never the very cleft of rock, and the very wounds of my Savior whence gushed out this sacred blood."

According to his own testimony, Toplady was so stirred by these word pictures he could not shake them from his memory. Can you? God put Moses in the cleft of a rock and covered him with His hand while He passed by, so he could see His back.

"Glory be to God!" Take that thought with you to your prayer closet and shut the door (Matt. 6:6), and bolt it so the enemy can't slither in and invade your thoughts and prayer time with your heavenly Father. He has been patiently waiting there for you.

*(**Prayer** – "Now unto the King eternal, immortal, invisible, the only wise God, be honor and glory forever and ever. You are the only King, enthroned in joyous praise; You are infinite, immutable, invincible, indivisible, incomprehensible, and impeccable. You are sovereign, supreme, supernatural, transcendent, eternal, glorious, merciful and wonderful. Oh, God I wish I could describe You, there just are not enough words to do it. You are the Great I Am! Praise Your Holy Name!"*

Principles for Prayer:

- What we need today to revitalize our prayer lives is a fresh look into the face of Jesus!
- Show me Thy glory, LORD, just a glimpse, just the backside LORD, just a passing shadow will do!
- Rock of Ages cleft for me, let me hide myself in Thee! Let the water and the blood… Pray it brother (and sister)!

"Importunate prayer is not an incident, but the main thing: not a performance, but a passion: not a need but a necessity."

E.M. Bounds

In these 213 Principles for Prayer there may be some repetition, but a famous author once said, "Repetition is the mother of all learning." So read them, heed them, and if you need them, use them for God's great glory. More will be included with each volume.

- Prayer is simply the desire, opportunity, or privilege of talking to God. Don't make this difficult; God didn't!
- Sometimes prayer to God can become defiant and almost irreverent, so be careful in your approach to God!
- Only man has been afforded this privilege, not animals, angels or demons. What a precious privilege mankind has been given by God!
- God is the first to pray by blessing His creation.
- To bless God is an act of adoration.
- To bless man is an act of benevolence.
- God sought for Adam and God spoke first and He still does.
- Form, posture, language is unimportant to God, just talk to Him.
- You can exchange intimate feelings and thoughts without speaking. Did you know that?
- We need to hear the voice of God and be in tune to it.
- You will never be more filled with the Spirit than you are filled with His Word.
- The lost art in the ministry of prayer is listening.
- God will meet you in a specific place for prayer; Adam had a garden.
- God will meet you at a specific time: morning, noon, evening, night, anytime.
- Just make sure you close the gate or the door and turn off your phone.
- We must come before God naked and unashamed; confession first, petitions last.
- Satan will do anything to destroy your prayer life, prayer time, or prayer meeting. Remember that!

- The sequence of backsliding is run, hide, lie -- in that order.
- Without Christ as our substitute and sacrifice, there is no approach to God.
- One of the greatest sins in a Christian's life today is the sin of prayerlessness.
- The dynamic for prayer is the power of His presence and the presence of His power.
- I believe the mark of Cain was the ancient Paleo-Hebrew (tav) resembling a cross.
- Appropriation and application are needed for salvation; both the shedding and sprinkling of blood are needed.
- Prayer is one of the most common forms of devotion and yet it's the one that is the least understood.
- Man was created by God for sweet, intimate communion and fellowship.
- Abel was the first martyr; the word in Acts 1:8 for "witnesses" is (*martus*) for martyr.
- Prayer is the highway to the throne of God, and so few Christians ever get on it.
- Prayer has to be from your heart, genuine acts of contrition, adoration, confession, thanksgiving, supplication;
- Sacrifice has to be from the heart, the very best you have, perfect, spotless, prime, the first born, no blemishes;
- Worship has to be from the heart, genuine, real, authentic, true praise and adoration, accompanied with tears
- The only place you can find intimacy with the entire Tri-Unity is in <u>prayer</u>.
- Biblical names are very important; so don't skip over their meanings.
- We need to "practice the presence of Christ" like Brother Andrew suggests, especially in <u>prayer</u>.
- To walk (*eth*) with God is to enjoy uninterrupted, conscious intimate fellowship.
- To walk with God means you have been conformed to His image, not He to yours.

- Without faith it is impossible to please God, but without risk, faith is impossible.
- True Faith is believing that God **will** do it; not that God **can** do it.
- If you live in the inner presence of God, He'll reveal His innermost secrets.
- The only time shamelessness is used in the Bible is in reference to praying for a friend.
- May we, like this <u>prayer warrior</u>, be just, lawful, righteous a (*tsadik*).
- May we, like this <u>prayer champion,</u> be complete, without spot or blemish, full of truth and integrity.
- May we, like this <u>prayer guardian,</u> walk with You and go on habitually (*yalak*) to live.
- Our highest form of service is the ministry of intercession, the ministry of the interior.
- Just like Noah, the LORD is inviting you into your closet, Matt. 6:6. He's already in there waiting.
- Just like Jer. 33 tells us, our part is to call/pray; His part is to answer – and He will!
- Not only do we need to pray, talk to God, we need to sacrifice, worship, and walk with God.
- When was the last time you offered a sacrifice of praise to God, the fruit of your lips?
- Our prayers should emit a sweet smelling aroma, not the odor of a decaying corpse.
- What a privilege to bless not only the creation but the Creator as well.
- Lack of faith in the integrity of His Word is a chief cause of prayerlessness.
- Prayer is undoubtedly man's greatest obligation and yet it's the one most neglected.
- Noah found **grace** and Noah was **just**: two very important principles for our prayer lives.
- Divine approval on God's part does not imply perfection on man's part.
- Integrity in prayer means "what is complete, entirely in accord with truth and fact."

- Without faith we are absolutely powerless to please God and pray to Him.
- The key to Effectual Fervent Prayer is to be a God pleaser, not a man pleaser.
- Matthew Henry said of Abraham, "Wherever he had a tent, God had an altar sanctified by prayer."
- Why is it that when we fall or backslide, we forsake our prayer-life? Why, God, why?
- Prayer is simply an address or petition to God by word, note or thought!
- Remember: don't wait for trouble to build your altar; the cement won't have time to dry!
- How we need the Amen of faith today in prayer. As Martin Luther said, "Make it strong!"
- Man's blessings are dependent on prayers, and God is limited by them many times.
- A Gentile has been used many times in history to rescue God's chosen people. Eliezer is one example.
- Pray, give, go, teach, serve, but leave God "elbow room" to work in lives.
- God said in Gen. 12 that He would bless those who bless Israel. Can God lie?
- He also said He will call evil down on those who lightly esteem the "Jewish people."
- It was God who drew Abraham back to Bethel, and God had Pharaoh throw him out of Egypt, to restore him.
- In the O.T. God spoke more to men than they spoke to Him. Why? They listened more, and we don't know how!
- Prayer is a two-way street, not a turnpike, or an expressway. You speak/God listens, God speaks/you listen! Got it?
- Oh, the promises and fellowship you can experience at your altar with God, but are you?
- Blessing man is simply invoking God's riches and grace on them.
- To pray for God or to bless God is a radical, startling thought, is it not?

- When you pray, if you hold back nothing from God, He will hold back nothing from you!
- Like Abraham with Ishmael's banishment and Isaac's sacrifice, his prayers were too deep to utter!
- Only effectual, fervent prayer opens our eyes to God's blessings and provision.
- Listen, only a true friend can ask a true friend to sacrifice something!
- Listen, there is nothing happening in your life right now that God is not aware of and in total control of!
- The Chinese word for **crisis** is made up of two words: danger & opportunity. How is yours spelled?
- What God wanted on Mt. Moriah was a living sacrifice, not a dead one; this was Abraham's test!
- The **real** test of **real** faith is in its willingness and readiness to abandon all and devote all to God. ALL!
- If you are truly saved, there are two words you can never say in the same sentence, "No, Lord!"
- Prayer opens our eyes so we can see God's provision and His answers.
- The test of faith is total surrender, but the fruit of faith is total obedience!
- Prayer – the test: trust Him implicitly. The fruit: obey Him explicitly!
- The Angel of the Lord comes searching for us <u>to pray and to seek God's face.</u>
- You can't run from an <u>omnipresent God</u> because, every direction you run, He is there!
- Abraham's prayer life influenced Ishmael's life, **for life**; it had to. The Angel heard the **lad's** cry, not Hagar's!
- Confession is good for the soul, gives glory to God, is part of the restoration process, and is the heart of <u>prayer</u>!
- Remember, we confess our sins to God and our faults to mankind, not the other way around!
- God knows where we are, who we are, why we are there, and what we will become. So talk to Him; He knows!

- In prayer, our extremities become God's opportunities.
- Cry out in your affliction. God will hear, God will see, and God really cares. That is such a comfort!
- Prayer's most effective language is a cry, a groan, a moan, a sigh; don't worry, the Holy Spirit will translate.
- Prayer is a two-way street; we need to listen twice as much as we talk in prayer.
- God reveals His will and plans to man so he can intercede and pray for them.
- Ishmael loved, honored, obeyed, trusted and worshiped his father. Do that with God and He'll answer your prayers!
- <u>If you stop breathing, you will die physically; if stop praying, you will die spiritually</u>.
- Man gave Hagar a bottle of water; God gave her a well of water. Prayer showed her where to fill it!
- It's a shame we wander in the desert dying of thirst when water is just a prayer away!
- What changed Moses from a stuttering coward into a startling leader? One word: **prayer**!
- **Prayer** removes Satan's scales from our eyes so we can see what God's plans are and what He wants us to do.
- If you can't see clearly, ask God to open your eyes. If He did it for Balaam's donkey, He can do it for you!
- In prayer we need to meet God face-to-face and take Him at His Word literally!
- God will do what He has promised in His own time frame, but He will do it!
- What we need today is the <u>"Amen" of faith in our prayers</u>, like Abraham had.
- God has revealed His will and His intents in His Word so we can pray for them <u>with Him</u>.
- Sometimes God meets with you because He has something special for you to <u>pray about</u>.
- Remember, it's the <u>omnipotent, omniscient, omnificent</u> God who meets with you for prayer.
- We need to be open, honest and humble when we pray. Humility and Honesty are key in prayer!

- God doesn't answer <u>prayer</u>! He answers desperate, determined, destitute <u>prayer</u>. <u>Prayer</u> that sweats, bleeds and cries!
- The key to <u>prayer</u> is "don't stop short - don't hang up - don't quit" and <u>pray</u> through, until you get an answer from God!
- <u>Does intercessory prayer work</u>? Ask Lot when you see him or Abimeleh, or Isaac, etc.
- Memorize Isaiah 45:11, *"and concerning the work of my hands, command ye me."*
- The costliest service and the most fruitful a Christian can enter is, <u>intercessory prayer</u>.
- Know how to commune with God; meditate on God and entreat God.
- A person's prayer life should encompass more than their prayer list.
- Always remember to take time to commune alone with God; Jesus did, and He **was** God!
- "Occupy till I come." This is the Greek word (*pragma*) which means, put feet on your prayers – *practicology*!
- Spiritual intimacy means having some one-on-one time with God. A time out with Jehovah!
- Is there room in the Bethlehem of your heart for Jesus to be born afresh today?
- Have you shown up for the work party today to <u>party</u> or to <u>PRAY</u>?
- Have you sold your birthright or blessing for some beans and an old goat's opinion on <u>prayer</u>?
- To commune is to have in common in thought, word and deed; in giving and in receiving.
- Biblical prayer is spontaneous, personal, motivated by need and unconditioned by time and place.
- The Lord can be approached anytime, anywhere, for anything, in a sinner's simple childlike manner.
- Prayer should be like a child talking to their father or mother and asking for something they need.
- When was the last time, Dads, you laid your hands on your children/grandchildren and prayed a blessing over them?

- Pastors, when was the last time you prayed a blessing over your congregation at the close of a service? A blessing!
- Husbands, when was the last time you laid your hands on your wife and prayed a blessing over her?
- Availability is more important to God in our prayer lives than ability!
- Are you in the way **for** the Lord like Eliezer, or are you in the way **of** the Lord like Judas?
- Spend 60 seconds in your prayer time just adoring God, for His attributes. Nothing else, just adoration!
- One of the major keys to answered prayer is obedience, and God can't stress it enough.
- God never leads His children astray, He leads them in the way of truth.
- The servant had a specific answer to a specific prayer to indicate God's specific presence.
- Don't make deals with God; lay hold of His promises, and then hang on with both hands and pray!
- They built altars in the "Holy Land;" outside of it they planted trees, poured oil on a stone, or piled up rocks.
- You can't reverse God's blessings; What's done is done! Just accept it and deal with it.
- God's plans are always accomplished in spite of our sneaky schemes.
- Is your womb barren for spiritual children? Then you need to pray to *El Shaddai* for souls!
- Leah was in prayer to *El Shaddai*, the One who enriches and makes fruitful!
- May those three words become a part of our "Prayer Life"– "**For You said!**"
- Do you pray to "God the person" or do you pray to the "Person of God?" It makes a big difference!
- God is not just the "God of the Word;" He is the "God of His Word." He wrote it, He signed it, He believes it, so Pray it!
- Many times our prayers do more to soften an offended heart than a large gift, though the gift still helps.

- Prayer does not always remove our fears; it gives us strength to face them, head on, with God by our side.
- Persistence in prayer, importunity, persevering until we get an answer – that is what is vital!
- Gen. 35, the first recorded revival in the Bible, began with <u>prayer</u> at an altar in Bethel, "The House of God." ***Oi Vey!***
- Jacob knew how to wrestle with man, but he needed to learn how to <u>wrestle with God in prayer</u>, and not let go!
- What has happened to <u>tenacity in our prayer lives</u>? Why don't we <u>pray through</u> any more? We quit too early!
- Your walk talks and your talk talks, but your walk talks louder than your talk talks.
- Maybe we talk too much and walk too little. Jesus said, "Sell it all, and follow Me!" That's pretty simple!
- The power of prayer linked with the promises of God is a force to be reckoned with!
- God is waiting for a man/woman to pray back His promises and hold Him to His word! Are you that person?
- Pray that you will be faithful right to your very last breath, like many of the faithful patriarchs.
- If God can change a supplanter into a supplicater – imagine what He can do with you, if you let Him!
- Jacob/Israel, with his last dying breath, worshiped, praised and prayed to God. How about you?
- The power of blessings is something we seriously need to consider in our prayer life.
- There is no genuine repentance apart from a bitter sense of sorrow over one's own sin against God.
- Jacob's prayer blessing on Joseph's sons was the transferring of his own name and promises unto them.
- God hears, God remembers, God sees, and God knows your problem!
- God sees, God hears, God knows, and God delivers His people!
- Groanings which cannot be uttered are <u>prayers</u>, which cannot be denied!

- Know before Whom you stand before you begin to pray!
- Holiness leads to Godliness and opens the door into God's presence!
- *"Dah Lifnay Me Attah Omed"* "Know Before Whom You Stand!"
- Listening is the lost art in the science of prayer.
- It takes far more patience to listen in prayer than to speak.
- The words "silent" and "listen" have the exact same letters.
- True prayer does not change God's will; it conforms us to His will.
- Remember, "Why" is the first step to disobedience, and rebellion is the final step!
- The key to "being in the way" for the LORD is **availability**, not **ability**!
- Groaning in the Spirit, in prayer, is a depth few of us know anything about!
- Spurgeon said, "Groaning which cannot be uttered is prayer which cannot be refused!"
- M'Cheyne said, "The most spiritual prayer is a, "groan that cannot be uttered."
- Prayer should be a two-way conversation with God. If it is not, fix it immediately!
- Prayer is a direct address to God, an approach to the living God, on an intimate level.
- We need personal intimacy with God (*yada*) for an effective prayer life, we need to (know) Him!
- The power of God is manifested in the power of prayer!
- Prayer is the all-powerful, omnipotent tool of the pilgrim, "Entreat the Lord!"
- God doesn't need Moses or us, but He chooses to use us in His providential plans by prayer.
- What we need today are "gap men & women" to grab a censer and stand between the pestilence and God!
- After every victory Moses faced another challenge, but God always answered his prayers. Always!

- Prayer is not just a good idea; it is God's divine plan and purpose for getting His job done!
- Whenever you are confronted by a crowd, board, congregation, group, PRAY for God's guidance & help!
- Make sure when God speaks you listen and follow His instructions, no matter where they lead you.
- The prayer of distress can lead to a big head, so be careful after the storm passes that God gets the glory!
- Prayer-Partners are a vital, crucial part of a missionary's field team. They fail without them every time!
- We all need to find an Aaron and a Hur to be our prayer partners and raise our "banners" to God!
- Brethren, the time is short. The little hand is on the 12 and the big hand left the 11. We need to pray and we need prayer partners!
- Stand before God for the people, so you may bring their difficulties to God in prayer!
- The key principle against burn-out is to share the load with the leaders & pray!
- Our leaders should pray first, foremost, fervently, steadfastly, always and unceasingly
- God hears the prayers of all mankind, especially the prayers of <u>widows and orphans</u>; does He hear your prayers for them?
- <u>God is a Father to the fatherless and a Husband to the husbandless</u>. That should be a major prayer concern of ours!
- Nothing quenches divine influence more than this mud puddle we live in, so pray much about your part in their lives!
- Prayer is based on the shed blood of the New Covenant -- Christ's Covenant. Don't ever forget that!
- How long would you wait in a cabin alone for God to come and speak to you: 3 days, 5 days, 10 days?
- Have you ever entered that "kavod" and waited for God to speak? He will show up, and He will speak!

- Make it your chief business to be more holy every day, and pray for it without ceasing!
- The cares and cookies of this world will choke the word so it will be unfruitful, so pray, pray, pray!
- Keep a sheep list of prayer needs over your heart for times of prayer throughout the day or night.
- The Latin word for priest "*Pontifix*" means "<u>Bridge-Builder</u>."
- The chief privilege of a priest is <u>access to God</u>.
- Our job is to build a holy cause-way from man to God, to show them the way.
- Never pray for God's justice; only His mercy. Justice is getting what we deserve. Grace is getting what we don't deserve. Mercy is **not** getting what we do deserve!!
- Have you ever reminded God of His promises or prayed His Word back to Him? Try it some time!
- Because of Calvary we can have intimate fellowship in our prayer closet with the Tri-Unity!
- "My presence shall go with thee, and I shall give thee rest!"
- Intimate intercourse, conversation so close with God that words are not even necessary.
- Practice the presence of God, and you will pray all day long.
- What we need today to revitalize our prayer lives is a fresh look into the face of Jesus!
- Show me Thy glory, LORD, just a glimpse, just the backside LORD, just a passing shadow will do!
- Rock of Ages cleft for me, let me hide myself in Thee! Let the water and the blood… Pray it brother (and sister)!

www.ingramcontent.com/pod-product-compliance
Lightning Source LLC
Chambersburg PA
CBHW030511080526
44586CB00011B/146